BELICHICK AND BRADY

Two Men, the Patriots, and How They Revolutionized Football

MICHAEL HOLLEY

hachette
BOOKS

NEW YORK   BOSTON

Hachette Books
Hachette Book Group
1290 Avenue of the Americas
New York, NY 10104
hachettebookgroup.com
twitter.com/hachettebooks

First Edition: October 2016

Hachette Books is a division of Hachette Book Group, Inc.
The Hachette Books name and logo are trademarks of Hachette Book Group, Inc.

The publisher is not responsible for websites (or their content) that are not owned by the publisher.

The Hachette Speakers Bureau provides a wide range of authors for speaking events. To find out more, go to www.hachettespeakersbureau.com or call (866) 376-6591.

Library of Congress Control Number: 2016945321

ISBNs: 978-0-316-26691-8 (hardcover), 978-0-316-26689-5 (ebook)

Printed in the United States of America

RRD-C

10 9 8 7 6 5 4 3 2 1

For Oni, Robinson, Beckham, and Ava
Because of you all, every prayer I have is one of thanksgiving
Deut. 6:5–9

CONTENTS

Contents

Chapter One

BEATING THE SYSTEM

The system is one of trapdoors and tricks, meticulously rigged at its core. The appeal for its thirty-two participants is that all of them have an equal chance of winning; the trick is that it is the same game for all of them until one of them actually wins. Then the system warps, resets, and becomes half mathematical formula and half social science. So the losers gain and the winner is squeezed and told to get lost. It is a system corporately sponsored by Give Someone Else a Chance. The worse you are, the easier the course. The better you are, the more mazes you have to master. It is intentional mediocrity: identify a shining star and then bring it back to the middle.

In a sense, the National Football League has a multi-billion-dollar system built on a participation trophy premise.

Each September, at the beginning of the sixteen-game NFL season, the previous year's champion feels the systematic drag. The reward for conquering the hill is to be stranded there. The first-place team is given the most difficult schedule in the league, assigned the college draft's worst slots (where, theoretically, the least-desired young players are), and forced to balance the most challenging budgets as a result of winning. The league is so awash in cash now, so Ivy League and MBA, so public-relations spin and appropriate business etiquette, that it can't plainly announce what it truly wants: No repeat winners. Please. Return to the end of the line.

There are success penalties at each step, some as obvious as daylight and some hiding in crevices. The league's computerized scheduling system doesn't like you when you win, but the league's human beings do. There is usually a lucrative landing spot for a good free agent player on a great team. His connection to greatness gives him a favorable profile in the market, and now he is too expensive for his old team to keep and too intriguing for someone else to pass up. The market is abuzz with conversations about winners, especially those who have escaped the system's engineering and discovered how to win consistently. There is always a knock at the door from an opponent, seeking permission to talk to, hire, and sometimes triple the annual salaries of top assistant coaches, administrators, and scouts. They want a piece of something, even if it's a piece of the vision, because the code-crackers don't come along very often, and they want to be sure they're not missing the next one.

This system was born twenty-two years ago. It's when the NFL introduced two things: true player free agency and team salary caps, which it never previously had. Since that moment, participants in the game have wrestled with the same questions:

How do you create separation from someone who, initially, was designed to be just like you? Same money. Same rules. Drawing from the same talent pool. How do you get away?

How do you become a standout in an atmosphere that gives no air to sustained excellence?

How do you outrun a twin?

The NFL's owners all take their portion, nearly 53 percent, from a stunning $13.3 billion revenue pool. Whether the owner is in New York City, Chicago, or Jacksonville, the national revenue portion is the same for all of them, $215 million apiece. That figure mostly comes from smart television deals and, based on America's passion for pro football, that number will be rising, sharply, each year. With a salary cap of $155 million per team, it is possible for every franchise to easily make payroll and the bulk of expenses before it sells a single game ticket, hot dog, parking space, or jersey in its gift shop.

To turn a profit in the NFL, all an owner needs to do is be still. The league is a jungle of muscle and money, where hundred-dollar bills descend from advertising trees and into choice accounts and funds. Just as the NFL began to relent to free agency and put on its cap, Robert Kraft, a lifelong Boston fan and businessman, bought the New England Patriots for $172 million. In 1994, it was a record amount paid for a football team; that record has been broken thirteen times since. Today, the Patriots are one of the richest sports franchises in the world, worth $3.2 billion. Going into his twenty-third season of ownership in 2016, Kraft has seen his team's value increase $144 million per year. The story is similar for all of Kraft's colleagues. There is no such thing as overpaying for a team. If you can't make a profit in *this* business, you can't make a profit anywhere.

Kraft was making money, but he wasn't happy in January 2000. He was fifty-eight years old then, older than the pro football team that he owned. He needed to figure out a way to rescue that team, which had begun an undeniable slide from very good in 1996, to good in 1997, to above average in 1998, to the muck of the middle in 1999.

Even if Kraft had been content with that production in early 2000, the people in his hometown would have rebelled against it. They had the same calloused sports outlook that he did. They were raised in a city that was long known for American history and had gained a reputation for sports heartbreak. They took the essence of the two, history and heartbreak, and made a necklace to be worn at all times, whether at the stadium, Symphony Hall, or the halls of Harvard. That was being a sports fan in Boston in a nutshell. They didn't follow the local teams as much as they possessed them. The teams and their moves and their histories were a part of life, part of their identity, and it could become personal very quickly if there was a sense that their team's owner or head coach or star player didn't feel the same way.

Kraft understood that it was time for one of those press conferences that New England sports fans had gotten too used to hearing and mocking over the years. How many hearts had been hardened by the Red Sox across the generations, with eighty-two years of teases and promises of a championship next year? The Bruins, in a twenty-eight-year Stanley Cup drought, always seemed to be a dollar short. The Celtics, eight years since Larry Bird retired and fourteen years since the last title, were earthbound, constantly looking up at a laundry line of Boston Garden stars and championship banners. And then there were the Patriots, who had never won anything and, for that reason and more, were in the worst shape of all.

They were millions of dollars over the projected salary cap. They finished last in their division, five games worse than the Indianapolis Colts and star quarterback Peyton Manning. They were awarded extra draft picks from the New York Jets, as compensation for former coach Bill Parcells going there, but even that felt like a wasted opportunity. They used the picks because they had them, but the selections were random and lacked vision. Most of the kids they drafted couldn't play, and a couple of young veterans that they liked, Tedy Bruschi, twenty-six, and Troy Brown, twenty-eight, were free agents. There wasn't a lot for a new head coach to look forward to.

Kraft would deal with that later. Three days into the twenty-first century, when the owner fired coach Pete Carroll, he gave a brief statement that looked and sounded like dozens of others delivered by some of his disillusioned colleagues.

"This is a business of accountability and two years ago we won the division," he said that day. "Last year we barely made the play-offs, and this year we were 8-8. We need a momentum change."

The change happened three weeks later when Kraft hired Bill Belichick, who had spent the previous four seasons as an assistant coach to Parcells. It was a momentum change for Belichick, too, who had worked for Parcells a total of twelve seasons. That was exactly half of his NFL existence. He had his own ideas and personality, but they were often muted by the policy and personality of Parcells. But Kraft's move, which required the Patriots to relinquish their first-round draft pick in 2000, wasn't just about momentum. It was the beginning of a partnership that forever changed the Patriots, New England, and all of football. It would lead to coverage, both fawning and withering, unlike anything in the history of professional sports. No, it wasn't a momentum change. It was a generational shift.

Four years before being hired by the Patriots, Bill Belichick was one of the undervalued gems on the shores of Lake Erie. The coach had been replaced by the Browns, on Valentine's Day no less, and even the breakup was a struggle. The worst season in Browns' history, a season that ended with no play-offs and a franchise move to Baltimore, concluded on Christmas Eve. Yet, for seven weeks, there was no announcement on the status of the head coach. When it was finally time for the Browns to speak, Belichick didn't appreciate the way they tried to do it. The coach and representatives of owner Art Modell spent hours arguing back and forth over the wording of the press release because, essentially, it seemed as if the organization wanted him to absorb the blame for everything. They still owed him $1.6 million, and they were going to get their money's worth. They timed his official firing with the formality of their address change, letting him share, one more time, the brunt of rage from their abandoned fan base.

It certainly wasn't his idea to relocate the team his own father had cheered for and admired. In 1991, when Belichick took the job, he approached it as if he would have it for a lifetime. He went heavy on infrastructure, light on cosmetics. He overhauled the scouting system, knowing that it would be years before there would be the perfect marriage of the older scouts accepting the new and the younger scouts understanding it. He was a football historian and he knew that the godfather of the Browns, Hall of Fame coach Paul Brown, had modernized the NFL with his teaching and classroom work. Belichick wanted to do the same thing. He emphasized note-taking and attention to detail for his players, sometimes to the point of micromanagement.

"As soon as I got there from Atlanta, I felt I had gone from kindergarten to graduate school in a day," recalls Louis Riddick, a former Browns safety. "Belichick and [assistant coach] Nick Saban were smart as shit. You never relaxed. Never. You'd get quizzes in the middle of team meetings. You had to take a written test every week. You were always on your toes."

Belichick was thirty-eight, the youngest coach in the league. His plan was to search for the brightest and hungriest football souls, many of them in their early twenties, and teach, train, and promote the hell out of them. He reasoned that they would weed themselves out by embracing his demanding tasks or backing down. At the menial level, the only motivator was football adoration because the money was better in several other places, including burger joints.

He loved students. Students of football, students of people, students of things. It often threw folks off. They couldn't read his expressions amid his silence, although all he was doing was listening and thinking about how something worked. Or how it could work better.

One thing the coach didn't do was dwell in the past. Even if the "past" was thirty-five minutes ago. Riddick was one of the defensive standouts in Belichick's lone play-off win with the Browns, a victory over the Patriots. The safety had an interception and several timely tackles. He was given a game ball. As he was walking out the door, all the head coach wanted to know was if he could do it again the next week. "He was all about sustaining it," Riddick says. "He couldn't stand the inconsistency, the players who were up and down."

In his first year with the Browns, Belichick interviewed Lionel Vital, a former running back who wanted to become an NFL scout. At one point the two men began watching college football game film, and Belichick asked a question about a player. Vital didn't know the answer and admitted as much in front of the head coach. He left the interview, convinced that he had blown it with that foolish *I don't know*. Three days later he got a call back and a job offer. He was ecstatic and confused. Why had they hired him?

"One of the most impressive things you said in that interview," Belichick told him, "was 'I don't know.'"

The coach brought a new wrinkle to the job each year. He knew what he didn't know, and he had begun to correct the deficiencies.

He was his father's son when it came to money, or any type of capital, and that meant he didn't believe in spending without regard for tomorrow. He'd officially earned an economics degree at Wesleyan University in Connecticut, but anyone who knew his parents realized that the unofficial degree was in Belichick Family Business.

They were an efficient trio, free of excess. Dad didn't believe in buying what one couldn't afford, and therefore was against credit cards. Mom so loved language that she taught it in school and, as a devoted reader of the *New Yorker* magazine, preserved the best of it in her basement. Belichick had never subscribed to financial waste; a lot of people in the league, including Modell, were the opposite. It was the by-product of a lot of things: lack of financial discipline, impatience, and an overreliance on what was being said in the media. By the time Belichick reached his final season in Cleveland, he had evolved enough to view draft choices as one of the foundations of organizational wealth. You could trade that draft capital and invest for the future, or you could maximize that singular capital by trading it for more, albeit less glamorous, pieces.

By the time he had reached that level of understanding in 1996, it was too late. There was no desire or need to dig for the real Bill Belichick. Since he was part of the NFL's dominant Sunday afternoon and evening programming, he had become a TV character just like everyone else in the league. He didn't win enough, nor did he carry on and smile for the cameras, so he was easily typecast. Coach Hard-Ass. His dismissal was seen as another dysfunctional transaction between a franchise and head coach, neither worthy of serious analysis.

But the league didn't know Belichick or itself. He was a football and economics savant, and that's what the game was all about now. It had changed with the smack of a federal court judge's gavel, granting true free agency to the players. It changed when the TV networks kept demanding more of and paying more for the NFL. Modell, of all people, should have seen that one coming. He had made his money in advertising. He was on the league's TV committee, for goodness' sake. More available money, more available players, and more cameras to capture it all. You had to be quick and decisive in this game. The skill wasn't just in acquiring good players anymore. It was an athlete/asset puzzle now. You had to know the players, know their market value, and know precisely when to either commit big dollars or say good-bye for better, and cheaper, options.

The Browns didn't see it that way, and neither did anyone else. Clevelanders were convinced that their head coach didn't know a thing about offensive football, especially quarterbacks.

As Belichick packed his bags for a long drive east to once again assist Parcells, this time for one season in New England, a story that would eventually affect him was developing on the Michigan side of Lake Erie. There, a two-hour drive from Cleveland, an eighteen-year-old college quarterback named Tom Brady was the subject of a magic trick. He had been recruited by one of the best-known programs in the country, yet he was an unknown. And not just by the public. Those who saw him daily at the University of Michigan had no idea that he thought about the game as deeply as he did, and that in his mind, the matchup of Football versus Almost Anything would result in a victory for Football. He loved preparing for practices, being better than yesterday, and bonding with his teammates.

He was a California kid, six feet four inches tall, and handsome, and it was as if there was disbelief that he actually chose to be there rather than somewhere on the West Coast. Michigan football made you grow up fast. More was expected of college kids than the pros in Detroit. At least the Lions played inside, protected from the too-cold-to-think midwestern winters. Michigan football was big, straightforward, and all outdoors, with "down south" being Indiana, Illinois, and, of course, the hated Ohioans.

How was the California kid going to deal with that?

He was low on the quarterbacks' depth chart, way down in the nether regions of legacy athletes (yep, the coach's son was there) and walk-ons. In his freshman year, the starting quarterback, Scott Dreisbach, got hurt and had to miss a game. That meant Dreisbach's backup, Brian Griese, would start. And when Griese, the son of Hall of Fame quarterback Bob Griese, got hurt, next in line was the coach's kid, Jason Carr. Had anything happened to Carr, then and only then would number 10, Brady, get a chance to play.

Sure, this was a teenager's typical introduction to life on a big-time football campus. Brady didn't think like that. Underneath the sunny disposition was the sun itself. The kid would be hot if someone picked off a pass in practice. It would stick with him for far too long, hours after his teammates and coaches had found another distraction, and he'd be back in the dorms in tears. Anyone who competed with him in video games or cards could see it. It was another magic trick. The movie-star smile was flashed, and then, in an instant, flash point. He didn't just expect to win. He had already planned for it, envisioned it, and collected it. Not winning, frankly, was a surprise.

At his core, there was an intersection of things that had been argued about for years. Nature versus nurture. The idea of the debate was that you had to pick a side. The problem with Tom Brady was that he was both, a real-life example of what happens when those disparate worlds collide. Yes, he was a natural athlete, considered to be one of the best football and baseball players in the country. His three older sisters were all exceptional athletes, too. He saw excellence in the house as well as when he left it. His family had San Francisco 49ers season tickets, and no sports fan his age could have asked for a better deal. From preschool to senior year, Brady watched his Niners go to five Super Bowls and win them all. The team had two quarterbacks in that span, Joe Montana and Steve Young, both worthy of the Hall of Fame. The architect of the teams, Bill Walsh, was nicknamed "The Genius." Many suggested that the top receiver, Jerry Rice, was the greatest player in NFL history. Even one of San Francisco's down years, at 10-6, was good for one of the best records in the league.

How could you have those talents and watch those talents and not be affected?

He briefly thought of leaving Michigan and transferring to Cal, the school most people expected him to attend after high school. But the challenge, or the need, of getting to the top of that depth chart was far greater than the urge to go back home and play. People were too caught up in appearances. They didn't understand that this place, the anti-California, was home now. He was going to play at Michigan. It was another competition, climbing that chart, and thus another opportunity for him to get a win. All he had to do was make everyone see it and get it.

Michigan coaches and others saw some of it when they recruited him, but not as much as they should have. On national signing day, when the country's championship contenders beam over their rising stars, the Wolverines got credit for securing four players among the nation's top 100. Brady was obviously good, just not mentioned with those four: Daydrion Taylor, Josh Williams, and two athletes who could seemingly play any sport in the world, Tai Streets and Charles Woodson. Streets once long-jumped twenty-three feet and seven inches in high school. Woodson was a record-setting running back, Mr. Ohio from nearby Fremont, who had it all. But he wanted to be something new in college, so he decided to be a defensive back. Just like that. And he was immediately an impact player. It's supposed to be a hard game, but those guys and their supreme adaptability made you wonder. Brady's athleticism seemed quiet next to those outsized two, and so it went for the rest of his time in Ann Arbor.

With all the things happening on campus, it would have been intolerable for Brady if he lacked a sense of humor. He enjoyed pranks as much as anyone, even though if you traced the anatomy of his jokes, there seemed to be a lesson for the good of the group. He and buddy Aaron Shea once got hours of entertainment at the expense of brash teammate David Terrell. They called the receiver, pretending to be reporters from a fictitious Michigan paper, the *Brighton Bee*. In the course of their mock interview, they managed to be put on hold several times by the player and they also got Terrell to quickly acknowledge that one of his big goals at school was to win the Heisman. The kicker: It was just his first week on campus. The message, if they had chosen to share it with the rest of the team, was to stay humble. But they laughed so hard at the outrageousness of the interview that they couldn't share its contents with anyone but themselves.

At quarterback, Michigan always seemed to be looking for something else. Even when Brady took over the job and won his teammates' trust by being named a captain, head coach Lloyd Carr and his staff had roving eyes. Brady was a winner and a good athlete. The coaches seemed to view "winner" all wrong, as if it were a pejorative linked to "limited" or "unathletic." There was a sense that good athletes weren't enough; they wanted athletes who wouldn't be out of place in the Olympics. That's how Brady, despite a 20-5 record as a starter, wound up sharing time with a highly recruited Michigan native named Drew Henson. Henson was viewed as a serious two-sport threat, football and baseball, while Brady, who had technically come to Michigan with the same credentials, was... well, all Brady had done was win.

If the presence of Henson didn't undermine Brady as a captain, it crushed his stature in the job market at the end of his Michigan career. He played his final college game two days before Pete Carroll was fired by the Patriots, and it was one of his best. He passed for 369 yards and four touchdowns, and he helped his team overcome two 14-point deficits on the way to an Orange Bowl win over Alabama.

There were some commonsense hints in that game and others that, at the very least, suggested that Brady wouldn't embarrass himself in the NFL. His teams won in college, and he was a respected leader on those winning teams. The scouts said he was skinny, which was true. He was twenty-two years old and college skinny, a condition that could be cured easily with consistent meals, training, and rest. He was smart and composed in any situation, whether it was taking a sack or an unspoken slight from the coaching staff. His hands were unusually large, and fitting for a former baseball catcher, he was adept at securing the ball when it was anywhere near him. This was not going to be a high-turnover quarterback in the pros. Finally, there was the weather. He had passed the weekly tests of playing in some bad-weather towns, from Hoosier country in Bloomington, Indiana, to Happy Valley in State College, Pennsylvania. He wasn't a polished pro yet, but all the elements were in place for exactly that, which made him a prospect in whom a team would be wise to invest.

Shortly before the 2000 NFL draft, he temporarily moved to Metairie, a New Orleans suburb, so he could work on his body and impress the experts. As it was, they were more impressed with some of his roommates and training partners. Corey Simon, Adrian Klemm, and Tee Martin were all there with him, with the pull of the French Quarter testing their collective self-restraint. Simon, from Florida State, was being discussed as a top 10 selection. Klemm, a Los Angeles native who ambitiously went to the University of Hawaii, was optimistic about being called late in the first round or early in the second. Martin, a Tennessee quarterback, had a higher ceiling than Brady, and therefore was targeted between rounds three and four.

The best news for Brady actually happened 1,500 miles away in Massachusetts, and it was described in a brief *Boston Herald* article. Belichick had hired a new quarterbacks coach for the Patriots and, as the story highlighted, the coach had picked "a veteran NFL assistant who's never before coached quarterbacks." The coach's name was Dick Rehbein. He had played some college ball himself, at center. While he didn't have the perspective of someone who had played quarterback, he was often the quarterback of the offensive line. Even better, he was an informed outsider. He had coached for fifteen years, but analyzing quarterbacks was new to him. He'd bring fresh eyes to the job. He was hired eight weeks before the draft, and there was plenty of work to do. One of his assignments from Belichick was to study college quarterbacks and find one who could potentially back up Patriots starter Drew Bledsoe.

On April 16, 2000, the second day of the draft (as well as Belichick's forty-eighth birthday), many selections had unfolded as planned. Simon went sixth overall to the Eagles. Klemm, the kid whose wardrobe had consisted of flip-flops and surfer shorts in Honolulu, was going to need some winter boots and a parka now. The Patriots called his name in the second round. Martin, who followed Peyton Manning at Tennessee and won a national championship, was expected to go shortly after Klemm. But the next quarterback taken, Gio Carmazzi, was the embodiment of the road less traveled. As in, the Long Island Expressway and Hofstra. That was a long way from Martin's prestigious Southeastern Conference, but the draft could be funny that way. He slid all the way to the fifth round and went to the Steelers.

Brady was watching it all in California with his parents. Once again, there was a sizable gap between the way Brady viewed himself and the way professional evaluators like Belichick viewed him. The same thing happened to Joe Montana. Well, almost. He was also a great college player who had to wait for someone to verbalize what he already knew: He could play. But Montana had gone in the third round. The Bradys had watched the third round pass hours ago. They got some joy in the fourth round when a couple of Michigan guys, Shea and Josh Williams, one of those top 100 recruits from freshman year, went off the board. In the fifth round, there was a smile for Martin. At the beginning of the sixth round now, two men who had never met, Belichick and Brady, were thousands of miles apart, going through various anxieties.

For Brady, it was a matter of being drafted before all the selections were exhausted. He hadn't made the top 100 players as he entered college; it was officially worse on the exit because the arrow was on pick 167 and his phone still hadn't rung. For Belichick, now three months into the job, the reality was sinking in. His new team stunk. It was the unfortunate kind, too, when the public thinks you're a couple of players away from being good and the truth is that most of the roster needs to be on a curbside.

Belichick had managed to re-sign those talented veterans, Troy Brown and Tedy Bruschi, but the team needed much more than that. It needed everything except a quarterback. Bledsoe was twenty-eight and had already been to three Pro Bowls. The general sense in New England was that he needed help, not competition for his job.

At pick 177, Dhani Jones, another Michigan player, was drafted by the Giants. Those player reunions in Ann Arbor were going to be something. All of Brady's old teammates could talk about the NFL and Brady could ask them about their insurance. The thought had crossed his mind. He was a college graduate, and he was going to need a job. If not football, premiums. Luckily for Brady, the new quarterbacks coach in New England, Rehbein, had a few things going for him. He was wildly respected by his boss; he had been remarkably thorough in his first quarterbacks analysis; and he loved what he saw from Tom Brady. As a result, Brady's name and draft grade practically shouted from the whiteboard in the Patriots' war room. He was clearly the best remaining talent.

The economist, Belichick, weighed the team's needs and resources. He was trying to extract the team from financial mismanagement, and the Patriots needed cheap talent to fill out roster spots. He reluctantly passed on Brady at 187, instead taking Antwan Harris, a defensive back from Virginia with sprinter's speed.

Just to add more intrigue to Brady's already dramatic Sunday, the two picks before him weren't players he played with. This time they were opponents, from Michigan State and Iowa. In this prank, God was on the phone and Brady played the role of the unsuspecting David Terrell. Come on, now. Who else was going to have his name called before the starting quarterback of the fifth-best team in the country heard his?

There was an uproar on the West Coast, similar to a Montana-to-Rice celebration, when Brady was drafted by the Patriots at pick 199. It was the perfect Brady pick because no one could quite explain it. It was a compensatory selection that the Patriots had received as a result of NFL math, in which the league distributes bonus choices based on a value formula of players who left via free agency. Someone's New England departure created a slot for Brady, but no one is sure whose. That didn't dampen the celebration in the Bay Area, and it didn't cause much of a reaction in the quiet New England war room.

Belichick hadn't run his own draft in five years, and he was much more focused now than he was then. He had a vision for what his team in New England was going to be, and he had talked about it so passionately with his staff that the conversations flipped the calendar. A Saturday night could easily become a Sunday morning, with the main topic being organizational dreams. The new quarterback, Brady, could have added valuable insight to their conversations because his favorite childhood team is who the Patriots wanted to be. Belichick and his staff loved the rhythmic drumbeat of the 49ers, winning year after year. Some years they were the favorite to win it all, some years there were a few teams better, but in all years they were championship threats. Always. It was that way for nearly two decades. It was exactly the idea Belichick had for himself and everyone who played and worked for him.

They would be that one day, Belichick thought. The modern-day 49ers. They were a long way from that when they called Brady's name at 199. At number 201, the Patriots selected a defensive end who would become one of Brady's roommates. Soon after that, the team signed a local free agent, a tight end, who would also live with Brady. The quarterback had gotten a step closer to the pros, and he and his new housemates would have plenty to discuss at dinner. They had barely entered the league, through the back door. They weren't expected to stay for long.

Chapter Two

A NEW WAY OF DOING BUSINESS

As Bill Belichick prepared for work on April 17, 2000, one day after directing his first draft in five years, he was aware of something that ran counter to everything he believed in as a coach. He was rushing.

Here he was, nearly five months into the year, and he still hadn't taken the necessary deep dive into the Patriots, piece by piece. He was normally the guy who loved homework, so much so that when he finished, he'd find even more to devour. But not now. There wasn't enough time.

He had spent most of January trying to free himself from his contract with the New York Jets. He had tried to do it first through a subversive press conference, in which he was supposed to be accepting the head coaching job but instead scrawled a desperate note of resignation/escape. "I resign as HC of the NYJ" was how he coded it. Next he threw himself at the mercy of the commissioner, and then the courts, failing both times until he finally landed in New England when his old boss came to a token truce with his new one. Bill Parcells agreed to trade Belichick to the Patriots as long as Robert Kraft included a first-round pick in the 2000 draft. February felt like a month of errands and catch-up. Hire new coaches. Hire new scouts. Re-sign players. Go to the scouting combine, heavily rely-ing on information from scouts you don't know and haven't trained.

March was a monthlong cram for the test. By draft day, nor-mally, he'd have had a handle on everyone's story.

On April 17, when everyone took an early assessment of how great their draft weekends had gone, there were a couple of truths that football insiders didn't even try to debate. One was that the Patriots had done an okay job on their draft homework. The other was that the Jets had gotten straight A's. The Patriots' closest and most hated rival entered the draft with four first-round picks, which was the most first-round capital in league history. They selected two defensive ends, a tight end, and, all the experts agreed, the draft's best available quarterback in Chad Pennington from Mar-shall University.

Will McDonough, the legendary *Boston Globe* columnist and close friend of Parcells's, captured the spirit of the day in a column entitled MASTER STROKES FROM GROH AND THE JETS. Parcells was still the Jets' general manager, and he had turned to longtime assis-tant Al Groh to coach the team when Belichick very publicly dis-played his defiance. Groh recapped the Jets' plum draft choice with McDonough.

"At the start of the day we didn't figure on taking Pennington," Groh said. "On our board we had him going to Pittsburgh in the eight spot, which would let Plaxico Burress [Michigan State wide receiver] drop to us. But they took Burress, and when Pennington was still on the board at eighteen, his value was just too great to let go. Teams try for five or six years to get a quarterback this highly regarded, so we took him for the future."

In yet another *Globe* article on the same day, New Englanders were told exactly what they didn't want to hear: The New Yorkers, under the leadership of sure Hall of Famer Parcells, had done well. Parts of the article by football columnist Ron Borges downright taunted. "Sorry, Patriots fans," it read, "the Jets did some damage." There was another reference to Pennington and how his selection gave the Jets "possession of the only signal-caller who should have been in the first round this year." Locally and nationally, the mentions of Tom Brady were dismissive. Borges's and the *Globe*'s competition, Kevin Mannix at the crosstown *Herald*, found the selection of Brady incomprehensible: "With one of their three picks in the sixth round, the Patriots took Michigan quarterback Tom Brady. So what's with that? Why another quarterback? The Patriots already have their franchise starter in Drew Bledsoe, a proven veteran backup in John Friesz, and a young developmental player in Michael Bishop."

This wasn't Michigan, just the professional version of it in Massachusetts. He was once again Tommy Anonymous.

Pennington was being lauded as a smart quarterback who didn't have superior arm strength. The same label had been attached to Brady. Pennington's passing statistics were gaudier, and his team had finished undefeated. But he was reading the defenses of Northern Illinois and Liberty and Western Michigan, earning a destination, the Motor City Bowl, that would get a Michigan coach fired if he wound up there more than once. Brady had just completed a season in which Notre Dame, Ohio State, and Alabama were on the schedule. His team had finished fifth in the country, and there was a sense of disappointment because it wasn't first.

All things considered, he had dominated his opponents equal to the way Pennington had done his. But when it was time to pick... You could spin yourself into a dozen philosophical circles trying to understand the nature of the draft and the visions of the people who conducted it.

If the newest Patriots quarterback had been paying attention to the reports, he would have taken the advice given to many borderline talents, which is to rent and not buy. But what fun was that?

He needed a place to live, and so did Dave Nugent, a Purdue defensive end whom the Patriots drafted two slots after Brady. Chris Eitzmann, an undrafted tight end from Harvard, was also a friend of theirs who needed a better housing situation. Technically, Eitzmann resided in a lovely Canton, Massachusetts, home. The reality was that the home belonged to one of his classmates' parents, and Eitzmann was living in the basement. Luckily for the three rookies, there was a condominium available in Franklin, about twenty minutes from Foxboro.

The place, located at 9 Cherrywood Lane, had been in the Patriots family for several years. It was originally bought by Scott Zolak, Bledsoe's former backup, in 1993. It had over two thousand square feet, a couple of bedrooms, a nice basement, and a shared wall that often led an elderly couple next door to call the police in music-volume disputes with Zolak. Two years after buying the place, Zolak sold it to the team's first-round draft pick, cornerback Ty Law.

Four years later, Law found himself in a different financial world. He signed a $50 million contract with the Patriots, which included a $14.2 million bonus. He wasn't going to stay in the condo for long, and he found the perfect buyer when Brady was drafted. Like Brady, Law went to school at Michigan. He knew how competitive one had to be to thrive in Ann Arbor, so the quarterback from his alma mater got his attention. Law remembered his own fight to play immediately at Michigan. He had asked to go one-on-one with future first-round pick Derrick Alexander in practice. When Alexander caught a short pass, the freshman corner said, "Is that it? You're supposed to catch that. That ain't nothing. Where I come from, it's the best two outta three." He broke up the next pass and intercepted the third. He quickly became a starter.

In the pros, Brady was unlikely to be as bold in his first year as Law was in his. Once, Bill Parcells challenged veteran receiver Vincent Brisby to humble the talkative rookie. Brisby and Law went one-on-one in a drill, a drill that Law dominated. He celebrated by ripping off his Nike cleats and saying to his teammates, "Anybody got any goddamn Reeboks? Because this is my planet." Law was a hard worker, and he respected Brady for always being in the weight room. Plus, he was a Michigan man. He was going to make a special condo sale to Brady.

"I knew he wasn't making any money. I said, 'You know what, I'm going to leave all the furniture for you,'" Law says now. "I left all the furniture, TVs, pool table, everything. I left him everything, move-in ready. I said, 'Just bring your bags, man.' Sold it to him for like a hundred grand less than what I could have gotten. I had just signed this new deal. He was a Michigan guy. And I saw the kind of work that he put in. This dude worked hard. I didn't know if he'd ever get on the damn field. But he worked hard."

This was part of life in the NFL now for Brady, hanging out on Cherrywood Lane and trying to hang on to a roster spot. Brady was the fourth quarterback, Nugent was a long-shot defensive end, and of the six tight ends the Patriots listed on the depth chart, Eitzmann was sixth.

They had fun, though. They'd shoot pool in the basement and have what they would call a house tournament playing an old Nintendo football video game called *Tecmo Bowl*. Nugent and Eitzmann had become wise to one of Brady's signature moves while losing: throwing one of the controllers at a wall to reset the system. He liked to win at pranks as well. One day he and Eitzmann approached a napping Nugent and drew all over his face with Magic Markers.

They then put on boxing gloves and hit the sleeping giant until he came to. The belly laughs came from Nugent's reaction. He immediately got up and decided to go to the grocery store. He casually walked the aisles there with his face covered in elaborate markings, wondering why he was getting so many odd looks.

When they all went out together, Eitzmann would get the superstar treatment. He had gone to school locally, after all, and he had been the subject of several articles in training camp. Brady would watch at restaurants and gas stations when fans would approach and ask for his roommate's autograph.

In a way, Brady and his friends were actually going back to school in the NFL. Anyone who was going to play for Bill Belichick had to be willing to engage in detailed study. He had to know his own playbook and the tendencies of his opponent's, too. Despite what the public thought of it, Belichick knew that the team wasn't a few complementary pieces away from a championship. This was a top-to-bottom renovation job, and it needed to happen physically and psychologically.

The first thing everyone had to realize was that Belichick's perspective of what made a team good was different from theirs. He didn't see the game the same way as his players, his bosses, or even Patriots fans and media. One side, either his or theirs, had to change because the only common ground they had was the will to win. The disagreements would eventually come in the How To.

"It's hard to fool the players; you just know good coaching when you see it," says Damien Woody, who was a second-year Patriots center in 2000. "Bill came into that first training camp and you could see his plan being executed. He was on top of everyone. It didn't matter who you were, he was coaching you up hard. I had played the year before, but I felt like I was seeing a different NFL. I knew it was going to be tough. He was clearly weeding some guys out."

He liked and appreciated the transcendent abilities of stars, but he did not have a star system. He didn't promote players simply because they were first-round picks or even *his* picks. He didn't hold on to players just because they had the reputation of being good. It's one of the qualities he had in Cleveland, and it was a clear-eyed way of looking at team-building, a method eloquently and emphatically endorsed by Bill Walsh, the man who built the 49ers.

"I have seen coaches who are simply too sentimental, who allow themselves to be too maudlin about 'breaking up the old family,'" Walsh told the *Harvard Business Review* in 1993. "They are going to lose sight of the bottom line. And there is another kind who are severe, tough, and hard-hitting. But they sacrifice the loyalty of the people around them. In that situation, people are always afraid that they are going to be the next to go. These coaches rarely have sustained success.

"Somewhere in the middle are the coaches who know that the job is to win, who know that they must be decisive, that they must phase people through their organizations, and at the same time they are sensitive to the feelings, loyalties, and emotions that people have toward one another. If you don't have these feelings, I do not know how you can lead anyone."

Walsh made those comments in the first days of the salary cap and free agency era, so the essence of them was true, although Belichick understood that he would have to tweak some methods to fit the modern NFL. He believed in seeing and building football teams in equally solid thirds. Financially, it meant that the Patriots would never have a top-heavy salary cap at the expense of the bottom half of the roster. On the field, it meant that the fans would be deeply dissatisfied if they expected him to pluck fleet receivers in the first round to help out Bledsoe. He thought a quarterback's more important weapons were dependable offensive linemen, intelligent play designs, and solid receivers who could get open, catch, and stick their noses into blocks every now and then.

A former special-teams coach, he was a passionate advocate for the men who held the job he used to have and was compelled to have his best players be involved on "teams." He was probably the only guy who, when speaking of former New York Giants great Lawrence Taylor, emphasized how dominant LT had been in "the kicking game." His Patriots would never view being on teams as a demotion or an afterthought again. They would learn to see the creativity and game-changing potential in them like he did.

This was still a business, and a deep-pocketed one at that, so some of the things Belichick stood for were going to require significant trust from his players, and a relatively quick payout of wins. For example, he wasn't concerned with the statistics that often launched defensive ends and linebackers into the Pro Bowl, although, for a player, those stats could be valuable leverage for a new contract. His position was that he valued winning, and the team, over everything else. Winning, the team, and the present.

"I think I understood him very early," says former Patriots linebacker Tedy Bruschi. "It was short-term focus. It wasn't new to me, but it was new to a lot of people. We had a lot of players who were thinking, 'I want to win a bunch of Super Bowls.' He wasn't talking that way. I said, 'I get this guy.' I get it. I don't think I'll be going out to eat with him or anything like that, but from a very early point I understood it. I just need you to show me how to win. I mean, I've got a wife at home; I'll be good. I don't need you to love me. If it happens, that's great."

Belichick didn't want his organization to be the first to run to free agency and set the market; rather, he spoke a new language, referring to players who had "good value" and "position versatility." He emphasized conditioning and doing it together in Foxboro. He brought a boat anchor into the locker room to illustrate just how much extra weight the team was carrying. At a certain point daily, he was a media coach; he reminded his players to know what was important to the media (inside information and tension), to know what was important to the team (winning and inside information), and to know when to end conversations with the dead end of clichés.

Of course, there would be homework.

One of the frequent visitors to Cherrywood Lane, a linebacker named Matt Chatham, created a niche by studying and figuring out ways he and his teammates could apply what was learned. It began simply enough when Chatham and others, under the direction of assistant coach Pepper Johnson, were part of a subset they called the Ghetto Dogs. They were members of the scout team, and it was their responsibility to simulate the upcoming opponent.

"We would have to watch double the amount of film as everyone else," Chatham recalls. "We would have to emulate different players and teams. They'd say, 'This week you're James Farrior.' You'd have a list of notes of things that the player did and they'd want you to do it that way in practice. So they'd say, 'He's a guy who bites really hard on play-action, so every time you see this play, do it that way. You want to give the quarterback a good look. You're not reading it as you, you're reading it as them. Play how they play and not how you play.' Now, you've got to learn all your stuff, too, because you want to be on the team. So you're watching film of you being him and you being you."

There were oral presentations from the Ghetto Dogs as well. They were expected to document their film study and then share all relevant information with the team. Imagine transitioning from college stardom to giving book reports in the pros. They were a helmeted research department. At times, the thought would sneak up on Chatham: *Does this even matter? Are they really paying attention to this stuff?* The question was answered over a sequence of film sessions when Chatham noticed that a Buffalo Bills player was doing the same thing each time there was a running play. One hundred percent of the time, it was the same. "This is the most ridiculous tell I've ever seen," Chatham said to himself, and made a note of the detail. He shared the information with Johnson, who in turn had him share it with the defense. Chatham was good at film breakdown, so good that he had just studied himself into a job.

"They became more comfortable with me," he remembers. "Every Friday I would come in and give a presentation to the entire defense, generally on tight ends and tackles. It's something that gave me equity in the room. It kind of became my thing."

For Belichick and Brady, the 2000 season was about training, mental and physical. Belichick had gotten such a late start on the job that his ideas of what his team was going to be didn't match up with the personnel that he had. That was true of his players and his coaches. His offensive coordinator was Charlie Weis, an imaginative and acerbic Jersey guy, who had worked with Belichick in three organizations. Belichick trusted Weis and knew that he could coax the maximum out of what truly was a meager offense.

On defense, he needed someone who could teach what he wanted done, even if all the players weren't capable of performing what they had learned in the classroom. Belichick agreed with Walsh's point that it was important for employees within football operations to be empowered. There were coaches that he liked and hired, such as twenty-nine-year-old Eric Mangini and one of Buddy Ryan's thirty-eight-year-old twin sons, Rob. He also had brought in a twenty-five-year-old coaching assistant, Brian Daboll, who had been recommended by Nick Saban. Belichick envisioned the coaching assistant slot as sort of an immersion program. The position would be held for a year or two, and then there would be a graduation to either coaching, scouting, or, in some cases, both.

"There was a lot on his plate that year," Bruschi recalls. "We'd be on the sideline during the game, and he'd be talking to us on defense. I'd be thinking, 'Bill, you're the head coach, man. Big situation here in the game. You gonna punt that?' In the beginning, it was just base stuff. He wanted to make sure that we got it. I can't tell you how many times I heard him say, 'Set the edge.'"

Brady's progress was measured strictly in-house, and most of his teammates had little reason to pay attention to what he was doing. He still wasn't the backup, nor was he the backup to the backup. It was fair to say, in September and October, that the rookie was effectively experiencing a redshirt year. He was expected to know the playbook and add some muscle to his thin frame. That was about it. Those who were paying attention noticed that he had the same curiosity as Belichick and competitiveness equal to anyone on the team. Members of the defense would taunt him when they intercepted him in practice. He'd talk back and then, after practice, he'd want to know, "What did you see? What did I give away?"

The Patriots had begun the season with four losses, won two consecutive games, and then bookended those with four more defeats in a row. They were just 2-8, once again the worst team in their division, after a November loss in Cleveland.

There was fan frustration with just about everything: the poor record, the dullness of the team, being stepped on by the 6-4 Jets, Bledsoe's interminable patting of the football, and, honestly, the performance of the other Boston sports teams. The Bruins had traded Hall of Fame defenseman Ray Bourque the previous season and, in the fall of 2000, had fired popular coach Pat Burns. The Celtics were learning, painfully, that the energy and charisma of Rick Pitino wasn't enough to revive the franchise, and that the young team actually was regressing under the president-coach with the $50 million contract. The Red Sox' streak of running in place, paternalistically held back by the Yankees, had reached eighty-two years. There was a different twist to the misery every fall, and this year's story was that the Yankees had lost fifteen of their final eighteen games and still finished two games ahead of the Sox to win the division...and yet another World Series title.

What fans started to grumble about was entertainment and hope from the Patriots, especially since Bledsoe had hurt the thumb on his throwing hand. Belichick continued to give Bledsoe starts, although there was a public push for a young backup. No, there weren't any requests for Brady. The exciting name was Michael Bishop, a Heisman Trophy runner-up while in college at Kansas State and an absolute rock-star performer in Patriots preseason games. He was all freestyling dynamic motion in the summer games, outrunning all who chased him and flicking the football, with perfect spirals, farther than any quarterback the Patriots had. The season was already lost, and there was nothing an inert Bledsoe could do to save it, so why not?

It was a popular sentiment, which is why the controversy of undercards going into a game surprised so many people. The constant studying and body sculpting had paid off for Brady, who had moved up in the crowded quarterback rankings. He was now third on the depth chart, still behind Bledsoe and John Friesz, but in front of Bishop for good.

Bishop was furious and wanted to be released. Instead, two weeks later on Thanksgiving, he got a chance to watch Brady play briefly in a blowout loss to the Lions. Brady was back in Michigan, once again trying to scale an intimidating depth chart. But those were the only parallels. As a teen, eighteen and away from home for the first time, his disappointment led him to consider running from the situation. He was mentally and physically stronger now, and maybe even a little outrageous in his ambitions.

Bledsoe wasn't just one of the Patriots' stars; he was one of the most recognizable personalities in New England. He was the highest paid player on the team and had endorsement deals with a local pizza company, a local truck dealer, and a local bank. He was geographically and symbolically a long way from the Chestnut Ridge condos and Cherrywood Lane. He and his wife had just built a nine-thousand-square-foot mansion in Medfield, with a $10 million price tag. Bledsoe was well liked, too. His baritone was the smart and articulate radio voice of the Patriots after wins, and the humble and well-balanced one after losses.

He was a former number one overall pick, just like division rival Peyton Manning, and the obvious truth, so obvious that it didn't have to be spoken, was that New England would collapse without Bledsoe just as Indianapolis would without Manning. But this was just the type of situation of which Bill Walsh had spoken seven years earlier.

"Most people don't realize it, but the players who get all the attention are usually the ones on the downside of their careers," the coach warned. "Ironically, the organization is often paying the most money to the team members who are on the descending curve as players. When players are starting to wind down their careers but are still playing effectively, you have to remind yourself how to use them. You have to gauge how they practice, what you ask them to do on the field, what kinds of situations you use them in, how much playing time they get. These are all factors that ultimately lead to the point where you judge that a younger player could do the job as well. That younger player is on an ascending curve on the arc. That is when you have to make your move."

What Dick Rehbein, the first-year quarterbacks coach, had seen from Brady in February was now apparent to the rest of the coaches in November and December. Brady had something. Maybe it was the element of surprise. He drove a canary-yellow Jeep that he had bought in Brockton, so there were a thousand jokes about the California kid in the sunny Jeep. Yet there was toughness just below the appearances, and an ever-present willingness to compete and win. It could be heard with the thud on the shared condo wall. It could be seen with a broken Ping-Pong paddle after a loss that he thought should have been a win. It could be felt, by a few, with the pursuit of that top job.

He was a climber. Eitzmann, the roommate from Harvard, certainly had seen his share of those in the Ivy League. So when Brady made that subtle move from fourth to third on the depth chart, the ascending player in flight, Eitzmann thought of a conversation they'd had in the summer. They were at a small college in Rhode Island then, staying late after their second practice of the day. Eitzmann was worn out, by the heat and the workload, and Brady continued to push. He asked for one more route. He made the argument for one more drill. One more, one more. Finally, the quarterback who had never played a down in the NFL looked at Eitzmann and told him what was going to happen.

"I'm going to beat out Bledsoe," he said. "You watch."

CHAPTER THREE

NO ONE SAW IT COMING

In the spring of 2001, no one was taking Tom Brady seriously. As usual, he was the king of the shadows. He worked out, quietly and constantly, determined to improve his balance by strengthening spindly legs. He studied the playbook, its language and concepts, because at least he was equal with Drew Bledsoe when it came to offensive philosophy: He and Bledsoe had been with Charlie Weis, the offensive coordinator, the same amount of time. So the advantage would go to the quarterback who could best comprehend, retain, and coolly run the plays amid the motion and violence of the games. Nothing against Bledsoe, but Brady liked his chances.

In every other category, viewed objectively, Brady's quest appeared hopeless. After much media speculation about Bledsoe's contract status with the Patriots, the deal was finalized the first week of March. The numbers said it all: ten years, $103 million. It was the biggest contract in league history. Bledsoe had just turned twenty-nine and was clearly entering the sweet spot of his athletic and business career. Bledsoe was a deal-maker now. He admitted as much during the celebratory press conference, when he mentioned that a couple of one-on-one conversations with owner Robert Kraft made it all come together.

This was gentlemen's agreement territory, with the principals making big deals in private, and then summoning the lawyers much later for the mundane dotting and crossing tasks. This was next level. Bledsoe wasn't just the Patriots quarterback anymore. He was a junior partner in the firm.

Kraft said that Bledsoe could be similar to New England icons Ted Williams, Bill Russell, and Larry Bird, all athletes who played for Boston teams their entire careers. "I remember feeling sad when Bobby Orr left," Kraft said at the Bledsoe announcement. "I saw this as an opportunity to sign one of the great Patriots for the rest of his career." Orr, the most dynamic performer in Boston Bruins history, ended his career in Chicago. Bledsoe was motivated to stay in one place. He said he signed his lengthy contract because he wanted to align his business and sentimental interests.

"I've expressed over and over again my desire to play my entire career with the New England Patriots," he said. "It looks like that is a very real possibility."

The month of March wasn't being very kind to Brady. A couple of weeks after signing Bledsoe, the Patriots spent another $3 million on twenty-seven-year-old quarterback Damon Huard. And just for the purposes of psychologically piling on, the Denver Broncos signed Brian Griese, whom Brady backed up at Michigan, and gave him a $12.6 million signing bonus.

Bill Belichick wasn't going to suddenly overshare and explain why the Patriots invested the way they did, so it seemed fair to draw conclusions by following where the economist put his money. He loaded up at quarterback, which Brady found interesting, since he was the cheapest and, in his mind, best one. Belichick insisted that he believed in competition in its purest form, with draft status and reputation not factoring into the decision. If that were truly the case, Brady was excited about the chance to compete against the two older quarterbacks on the field.

He was never going to be able to out-corporate Bledsoe. No way. Bledsoe could hold court with the owner any time he wanted. They'd talk football, current events, wives, kids. Bledsoe could wink at certain media members and they'd fight his causes for him on the air or in print, keeping him entirely clean. He was a wine expert, a business and family man, as influential and connected as any athlete in town. Fortunately for Brady, the Bledsoe signing was historic for a reason no one could immediately see. One day it would be viewed as the last contract of its kind with the Patriots, a massive deal that was a patchwork of paying for past performance, good public relations, and romanticism.

In fact, there were several acquisitions that more accurately reflected who the Patriots were becoming, but those deals were in the shadows, right there with Brady. All of the signings were similar in that they were either for $477,000, which was the veterans' minimum, or they were relatively cheap deals with modest signing bonuses. Over the course of the offseason, there was a steady beat of these signings, featuring names that led to shrugs and indifference. Mike Vrabel, Larry Izzo, Anthony Pleasant, David Patten, Mike Compton, Antowain Smith…They seemed to arrive daily. They were welcomed the way floorboards are to a house that lacks them; more necessary than exciting.

Excitement for New England fans would have to come in the draft, where the Patriots held the sixth overall selection. Belichick had already made enough dollar-store purchases to last a lifetime of springs. Now it was time for a wide receiver for Bledsoe to throw to or an elite offensive lineman who could protect him.

Typical frustration could be felt in a *Boston Herald* article headlined PATS' PLAN FULL OF HOLES. "So, other than showing fiscal restraint, what's the plan?" football columnist Kevin Mannix mocked. "Don't ask. The only answer involves the meaningless words of 'improving the team every way we can.' That's not a plan, that's a platitude. A plan involves doing what San Diego and both Super Bowl teams did. Get impact players...The Patriots? They've signed Larry Izzo and Mike Vrabel and re-signed Matt Stevens. So far, their chances of turning a 5-11 team into a winner don't look too promising."

The reality was that fans and media weren't the only ones skeptical of what the Patriots were doing. Roman Phifer, a linebacker who had played for Belichick with the Jets, was released by New York in late February. His agent let him know that three teams, Oakland, San Francisco, and New England, had the most serious and consistent inquiries about him. Phifer told his agent to explore Oakland and San Francisco, but he didn't want to go to New England. He had many personal and professional reasons for feeling that way. He was going through a divorce, and he wanted to remain close to his three-year-old son, who was living in Los Angeles. New England didn't work, geographically or competitively. And the latter was really starting to affect Phifer.

He was thirty-three and had never won anything of significance. Ever. There were no state championships in high school. At UCLA, where he went to college, his teams never appeared in the Rose Bowl on New Year's Day. In the pros, in his first eight seasons with the Rams, his teams never had a winning season. And then, as soon as he left for the Jets, his new team was rocked by injuries and his old team won the Super Bowl. He was tired of it. He wanted to win something, and the 2001 Patriots weren't going to give him the opportunity. He told his agent he'd likely sit out a season before signing with them. He was still watching and waiting in April, when it was time for the Patriots to make their draft selections.

There were no surprises in the top five, with a quarterback, Michael Vick, taken first by the Falcons. When it was the Patriots' turn, they had a menu of electric options before them: All of the top receivers were available, in addition to a left tackle projected to go in the top ten. It was fitting, though, that Belichick had his eye on the son of a mason. Richard Seymour was twenty-one, six feet six inches tall, and the namesake of a man who paid his bills by laying bricks. The younger Seymour, a University of Georgia defensive lineman, was exactly the cornerstone Belichick envisioned for his defense. Phifer understood what the presence of Seymour meant for Belichick and for himself. Guys that big who actually played to their size could protect linebackers in Belichick's defensive system. They drew two and sometimes three players to them, allowing linebackers like Phifer to run freely and make unimpeded tackles.

Seymour, who grew up in South Carolina, had hoped to be drafted by a warm-weather team. His family was delighted that a young man who was lightly recruited in high school was even in position to be drafted. Many of them were Raiders fans, and they knew Seymour wasn't going to fall all the way to twenty-eight, where Oakland was picking. But being in the same league that many of them had watched from afar was exciting enough. An elaborate country feast was planned. There were hogs and chickens roasted, cakes and pies baked. The guest list included aunts and uncles, cousins, neighborhood friends, and even Mark Sanford, South Carolina's governor at the time. It was a joyful moment for father and son, who were best friends. Even though the elder Seymour separated from his son's mother when the boy was six, the family bond was strong. As a teenager, Seymour worked in his father's construction business. When Seymour went off to school at Georgia, nearly three hours away from home, father and son continued to spend time together. They would sit in the dorms and watch film of the Bulldogs' games. This day, this opportunity, was validation of all the lessons, football and otherwise, that the elder Richard Seymour had given to the younger one.

According to the immediate draft reviews, Seymour had something in common with New Englanders; many of them wished he had landed elsewhere, too.

The *Boston Globe*'s Ron Borges, a longtime football writer and Hall of Fame voter, immediately panned the selection:

"Seymour has been compared most often to Packers defensive lineman Vonnie Holliday, whom the Patriots should have drafted two years ago; if they had, they wouldn't have had to waste their first-rounder yesterday on a tweener like Seymour, who at 6'6½" and 298 pounds is too long in the leg to play inside in the NFL in the opinion of some league scouts and lacks the quickness to play as a pass-rushing end despite what you'll hear over the next few days.

"However, Seymour's odd build for the position he plays is not the real problem with his selection. The real problem is that Bill Belichick passed on greatness for need, a decision that has blown up in the face of more coaches than anyone can imagine."

Across town, the *Herald* was even more succinct and caustic. Playing off the name of Kenyatta Walker, the talented left tackle passed over by the Patriots, a headline in the tabloid declared, BLEDSOE MAY END UP NEEDING A WALKER.

There was no praise, locally or nationally, for the maneuverings of Belichick. He had been on the job for fifteen months and had cleared a significant amount of refuse in the organization. In theory, it was akin to the approach he had taken with the Browns, but this time he was having more luck and more roster flexibility due to unrestricted free agency, which wasn't available to him his first fifteen months in Cleveland. He and Brady were essentially doing the same thing: making huge strides, backstage.

Belichick was ecstatic with the sudden growth of the Patriots. He had been able to hire Romeo Crennel, a defensive coach he'd known for twenty years, away from the Browns. His first coaching assistant, Brian Daboll, had been a success, so now it was time to promote him and bring in two more low-level employees in their midtwenties, Josh McDaniels and Nick Caserio. Belichick and his top personnel man, Scott Pioli, had been able to rewrite the scouting manual, and they'd had a full year to train the scouts in their football hieroglyphics. The free agency haul, with lots of good players for a reasonable price, had been remarkable. And now the draft had yielded what Belichick believed to be a dominant defensive tackle in Seymour and, through a flurry of trades, a left tackle in Matt Light who could protect the quarterback for the next decade.

The quarterback. Well, if there was something negative to say about the changes in the franchise as spring turned to summer, it started with what was a trace of uncertainty at the position. It was a peculiar space, tucked between pleasant surprise and buyer's remorse. Bledsoe was healthy, strong, and overwhelmingly professional. His name still meant something in the league, as most teams continued to rate him as a top-tier passer. That wasn't the issue. What Belichick talked with his coaches about, in amazement, involved the kid, Brady.

His offseason had been phenomenal. His strength was up and his body fat was down. He challenged himself in the weight room with squats and leg lifts, knowing that his best throws began from the bottom up, with proper footwork and balance, and then on to arm position and follow-through. He was fluent in the offense. And if he had any bitterness about the generous paydays that had happened for other quarterbacks in Foxboro and around the league, he didn't show it. He had natural leadership qualities, and he was rapidly developing a game that was in sync with his intangibles.

Brady was one year ahead of where the Patriots had projected him to be. That much was clear, as was the fact that Dick Rehbein hadn't recommended an ordinary backup. If the push continued at this pace, Brady would move from third quarterback to second by September. Eventually, the progress of Brady would become one of the big stories of training camp. Another summer story had already been established in the spring: More low-priced veterans were on the way.

One of them was the unfiltered Bryan Cox, who had acquired the affectionate nickname "Loud and Wrong" due to his animated, split-second opinions. He signed at the beginning of August and immediately brought familiarity from all angles. He knew the defense intimately, and he often talked about it and other things like an R-rated uncle. Another linebacker, much more reserved than Cox, arrived at the beginning of August as well. His opportunities in the Bay Area had disappeared, and his best chance to play was in New England. So Phifer, who once hosted Willie McGinest on a recruiting trip to UCLA (McGinest went to rival USC instead), was finally teammates with his buddy in New England.

Phifer noticed an authenticity in the group. There was a collective love for football and one another. Phifer told Belichick about the situation with his son, and the coach gave him permission to commute weekly between Foxboro and Los Angeles, as long as he returned in time for practice on Wednesday. It was McGinest who became Phifer's six-foot-five-inch tour guide, driving him around Providence and Boston so he could get a sense of the area. The two had kept in touch long after that recruiting trip in the early 1990s, and it was McGinest who gave him the final push and convinced him that the Patriots represented exactly what he had been searching for in football.

"What really hit me, as soon as I got there, was the blessing that God had for me," Phifer says. "I had resisted it for six months. I had focused on the cold, the crusty locker rooms, the old stadium. I'd convinced myself that it was going to be the same old story. But

I love football, and that's what was so obvious when I got there. Willie, Ty, Tedy, Lawyer, Drew. Those guys were so inviting, so humble. I knew it right then: 'This is where I belong.'"

There was genuine love on the team, and it seemed to go beyond football. It needed to, because the entire team would confront a wide range of issues that had nothing to do with blocking and tackling.

First, in August, there was tragedy. Rehbein had been working out at a local gym, with the younger of his two daughters nearby, when he suddenly lost consciousness on a treadmill. He went to the floor but quickly recovered and was able to stand on his own. Thirteen years earlier he had been diagnosed with a diseased heart muscle, cardiomyopathy, and was taking medication. But his condition had never hindered him in his exercise and, in fact, he ran several times a week. He was alert and communicative when he walked to an ambulance, and he checked himself into Massachusetts General Hospital.

That night, he talked with members of the coaching staff and told them that he would see them the next evening at a meeting. His family spent some time with him as well, and there was a sense that he was going to be just fine. He slept well that night and was given a stress test the next morning. After the test, his heart stopped. He was forty-five years old.

Rehbein was survived by his wife, Pam, and daughters, Betsy and Sarabeth, sixteen and twelve years old, respectively.

All of the Patriots and Giants, who happened to be in town for a joint practice, attended Rehbein's memorial service. The coaches and especially the quarterbacks checked in on Pam and the girls. Someone came up with the idea that all player fines, which could total well over $100,000, would be put into a fund and given to the Rehbeins at the end of the season. And, without question, the team unanimously agreed that the 2001 season would be dedicated to Rehbein.

At the beginning of September, five days before the season opener in Cincinnati, the shadows that Brady operated in began to wane. He had passed Huard, and now the only quarterback separating him from his promise of the previous year, beating out Bledsoe, was Bledsoe. The phenom, Michael Bishop, was gone. John Friesz had been released. Huard had been leapt.

Locally, there still wasn't a complete grasping of who Brady was. It was like that in high school, at Michigan, and now. His ascent was franchise-altering, and the Franchise himself, Bledsoe, didn't sense it.

After all, Bledsoe had missed just six games in his first eight seasons. Bill Parcells was his first coach, and he once let Bledsoe play an entire season with a separated shoulder. When asked why, Parcells seemed insulted by the question and replied, "Players play on Sunday."

That seemed to stick with Bledsoe a few years later when, with his index finger on his throwing hand broken and swollen, he tried to keep playing. He just didn't like coming out of games, and it had nothing to do with insecurity. He'd never had a backup as good as Brady, but he still thought his job would be there. Even with Brady in the same room, the kid already an equal in processing the game, Bledsoe was relaxed. He was confident in himself, his durability, and that contract. What were they going to do, have him hold the clipboard and be one of those visor-wearing backups? Not a chance. Brady, then, was a nice story, even with the backup's prophetic words when he talked about rising to second on the depth chart:

"At some point, they're going to need all three of us, whether it be in practice or on the field. So I think that we've got a good quarterback position."

Nice sentiment, but very few people believed it. On the first series of the season against the Bengals, CBS broadcaster Gus Johnson reminded everyone watching that Bledsoe had "signed a multiyear, multimillion contract that should keep him a Patriot through the end of his career." It's what people said and thought. It was just obvious. So when the Patriots lost that first game to the Bengals and looked bad on offense along the way, there was no suggestion that a change at quarterback needed to be made.

Two days after the game, the team was looking to its quarterback and other team leaders for guidance and structure. There had been a terror attack on American soil, in New York City, and the reality of airplanes being intentionally flown into skyscrapers needed context, discussion, and consolation. One of the Patriots linemen, Joe Andruzzi, had firefighting brothers in New York, and the brothers Andruzzi were fortunate to escape the wreckage of the fallen World Trade Center as they attempted to save lives. The entire team gathered at Bledsoe's house to be together on such an awful day in American history. It was hard to think about football, and no one in the league had to; the games scheduled for September 16 were rescheduled for the twenty-third.

After a pregame display of unity of patriotism on the twenty-third, the Patriots and Jets got back to some degree of normalcy by acting the way they always did at Foxboro Stadium. It was 10–3, Jets, with five minutes to play when Bledsoe began to run toward the right sideline. He was trying to pick up ten yards on third down, and he was doing just fine until he picked up his eighth.

He was met on the sideline by Jets linebacker Mo Lewis, listed at 260 pounds. It was far from Lewis's biggest hit of the day, given that he delivered the brunt of it solely with his right shoulder. But it was a shot to the chest of the quarterback, legal in terms of the game, and it was significant for football reasons and otherwise.

Will McDonough, the *Globe* columnist with a penchant for getting people to talk, was eventually able to unearth the real story. The first several hours after the Lewis hit weren't just confusing; they had been life-threatening.

Bledsoe had gone back into the game after the hit by Lewis, even though, unbeknownst to the quarterback, his blood pressure was falling. Blood was also draining from his chest into his chest cavity. That wasn't known until after the game, when he was taken to Massachusetts General Hospital and diagnosed by a doctor, Daniel Berger, who had been at home watching the Patriots game. Obviously, Brady was going to be the Patriots quarterback for several weeks. But more than that, Berger explained to McDonough, Bledsoe's injury could have led to the second Patriots tragedy in the span of six weeks.

"We were fortunate that the bleeding slowed down, and eventually stopped," the doctor said. "If we had to operate, we would have had to try to check the area around his ribs and lung first to see if we could find the problem and repair the damage. If that didn't work out, we would have had to operate, and make the incision in the middle of his chest, pull the ribs back, and make the repair that way. If that had to happen, then his career would have been in jeopardy."

The Patriots were 0-2, and just 5-13 since Belichick became the head coach. There were lots of questions about Bledsoe's return in 2001, why the quarterback had been allowed to reenter the game, and the readiness of Brady to rescue a team that was unlucky enough to have the high-powered Colts next on the schedule. Perhaps Belichick could sense the skepticism of the media crowd, representing the uneasiness of the region. Or perhaps it was a rare slip, where he uttered in public the same things he had said previously to his staff. Whatever the reason, Belichick gave his most honest Brady response during a particularly intense back-and-forth with the media.

"I don't think we're talking about John Elway here, but I don't know how many of those there are," the annoyed coach said. "He's got a good NFL arm. I really don't think I'm going to be standing here week after week talking about the problems that Tom Brady had. I have confidence in him."

What the coach didn't realize was that his statement had officially begun campaign season, and he had presented the first endorsement. For Brady. It's all people talked about in New England for weeks and weeks. A simple question—Brady or Bledsoe?—would generate hours and days of discussion on sports-talk radio. The arguments never cut conveniently across generational lines. There was never a simplistic conclusion based on the value of experience versus the possibility of the new. The argument never stopped; it would be paused for a while and then resumed. It was on late-night sports shows where, going in, several segments had been planned, yet the participants had gotten stuck on this one. Brady or Bledsoe?

Players were asked about it, and they certainly had opinions, but they were too smart to answer. Belichick, after his initial honesty, was noncommittal. But just like at Michigan, there were hints about what was coming with Brady, some nuanced and some overt. Adrian Klemm, the offensive lineman who lived with him before the draft, noticed a distinct Brady style in the huddle. "There's a certain presence that he has there," Klemm says now. "He's emotional, but he's never out of control. He really has a command of it." It probably was a reflection of what he truly was thinking about, opinions he shared only with those who were closest to him. He was actually the topic when several members of the defense got together shortly after Bledsoe was injured. They talked about picking the kid up, rallying around him, just doing whatever they could to give the team a chance until Bledsoe was ready to return.

Soon after that conversation, there was a fun team dinner during which the players laughed, drank, and teased one another. At one point, Brady and Law began to chat. The quarterback was calm and direct. "Ty," he said, "I'm not giving that job back."

"I was thinking of the business side of things," Law recalls. "I thought, 'Oh, yes you are.' But I didn't say that to him. I actually got a kick out of it. Lawyer was my boy, so I had to tell him. 'Hey, this young dude, he's got some spunk to him. He says he's not giving that job back to Drew.' But I didn't think it would be his choice. There was a man called Mr. Kraft, there was Bill Belichick, and there was that big check that they were writing that all said otherwise. I thought, 'When he gets healthy, he's coming back.'"

Brady, showing his political acumen, played the role of someone who was just happy to be there and help the team. The public bought it. They hadn't seen the real Brady, sweating behind the curtain to get himself ready for this stage. So why did they think they knew him now? The unknown from the discount bins of the previous season's draft, just trying to find his way in the pros.

Cute. And pure fiction. He was smart, athletic, and gifted. Bledsoe or Brady?

Brady.

Of course. His circumstances in high school, college, and now the pros had given him an identity. He had been buried so much on depth charts and draft charts that, just to be noticed, he had been forced to climb. So he'd put that label with the one he already had. Now he was Tom Brady, climber and winner.

Chapter Four

THE GREATEST REALITY
SHOW ON EARTH

Once a week, the five of them met in a tiny Foxboro Stadium room and shared their precocious football thoughts. It was Bill Belichick, Charlie Weis, and the three quarterbacks, in order of the depth chart: Tom Brady, Drew Bledsoe, and Damon Huard. Two of the men, Belichick and Bledsoe, rarely spoke directly to each other, but that didn't seem to matter. The important things were always covered, and that's one of the reasons they could live with the dysfunction without it becoming destructive.

Well, that and the performance of the team. It was late November and a year that seemed to be lost was now being salvaged. The Patriots were actually winning some games, and there was a chance they could make the play-offs. Because of this, a season wasn't the only thing being saved; a city's potential for optimism was. It was hardly news that people in Boston monogrammed their sports teams and consistently made the business of the games personal. That's the way it was, they were used to it, and no seminar on balance and proper perspective was going to change it.

The sports year hadn't been all that encouraging, and the bitterness of it could be heard and felt in the city's casual conversations.

Predictably, Rick Pitino quit the Celtics. The surprise was that he did it after a road game in Miami, with no plan to return to Boston for an explanation. He never produced a winning team in Boston, but he did have a read on the city that wasn't wholly unfair: "All the negativity that's in this town sucks. I've been around when Jim Rice was booed. I've been around when Yastrzemski was booed. And it stinks. It makes the greatest town, greatest city in the world, lousy." Nomar Garciaparra, frustrated with Red Sox personnel decisions, shouted after a loss to the hated Yankees, "That's why no one wants to fucking play here." The comment stung, and it just seemed to be destiny that the New Yorkers would go to the World Series, again, while the Sox would mark eighty-three years without a championship. The Bruins had gone through five goaltenders and two head coaches, on their way to missing the postseason for the second consecutive year. Then there was that ferocious hit on Bledsoe that was scary only well after the fact, when the quarterback realized that it could have killed him.

It turns out that Tom Brady had prophesied more than two months earlier without even knowing it. On the day that he officially became the Patriots' backup, he told reporters that the team would eventually need contributions from all three of its quarterbacks. That's exactly what was happening: Brady was the starter, Bledsoe was his backup, and Damon Huard was on levity/atmospherics duty. The Brady-Bledsoe debate had consumed the region for weeks, and then it had gone national. There were several teams better than the 5-5 Patriots, but none had a more compelling in-house drama.

"Drew was pissed every day coming into work," Ty Law says. "I don't give a damn what he says. He was pissed. He wasn't the same person, because he wanted to get back on the field. He had a bad injury and he got knocked out. He wasn't a happy camper."

The Brady-Bledsoe watch started in earnest with Brady's debut as a starter, on the last day of September. The Patriots had managed just 3 points the week before, but that number ballooned to 44 with an emphatic win over the Colts. It quickly decelerated the next week with a loss to the Dolphins and a lean eighty-six-yard passing day from Brady. "A week later the question isn't whether Brady ought to be starting in place of Bledsoe," George Kimball wrote in the *Boston Herald*, "but whether or not Bill Belichick will pull the trigger and make Damon Huard his quarterback when the Patriots entertain the Chargers."

Belichick stayed with Brady, and it picked up again with a victory that would have looked familiar to anyone who saw Brady at Michigan: The team was down 10 points with four minutes to play and, miraculously, Brady led them to an overtime win and threw for 364 yards. Just as impressive was the next week when, for the second time in less than a month, the Patriots blew out the Colts. Belichick was usually understated after games, especially ones so early in the season, but the 38–17 triumph inspired him to reflect.

"When I think about this game and two of the key players, David Patten and Tom Brady, probably the guy that's most responsible for both those players being here is Dick Rehbein. We tried to sign David as a free agent a year ago, but lost him to Cleveland. When he became available again, Dick said, 'Look, we can't lose this guy.' He vouched for how good a kid he was and what a good playmaker he was.

"The quarterback situation was one where, prior to the 2000 draft, with John Friesz getting up there in age, we felt we wanted to take a quarterback. I sent Dick to see two guys and he liked them both. But when I put his back to the wall he came on strong for Brady and said, 'This is our guy.' It's with a great deal of gratitude that I say thank you to Dick. Even though he's gone, he's not forgotten by any of us."

When Rehbein died in August, Belichick decided not to hire a new quarterbacks coach until after the season. In the meantime, he took on some of Rehbein's responsibilities and met with the quarterbacks to go over coverages and tendencies, and also listened to their feedback and observations. The arrangement worked just fine then, and when Bledsoe got hurt he happily dispensed advice to Brady. He knew that if the kid kept the Patriots afloat, he could then resume his starting position and lead the team into the postseason.

But it sounded like Belichick believed that he had something special in Brady. The coach was usually a postgame minimalist. He wouldn't have been that expansive in Indianapolis if the kid was a fluke, would he? The opinions began to stream in from all angles. Bill Parcells, still a respected voice in New England and now doing a national radio show, went on the air and was prescient prior to the next game, at Denver.

"Someday he is going to be in a game where he and his team take a beating, like 31–10 or something, and he throws four interceptions," Parcells said of Brady. "The other players will be mad at him, the assistant coaches will look sideways at him, and he'll finish the game with a broken nose.

"Now, what he does the next Wednesday, when he practices with the team for the first time, and what he does the week after that, is where he is going to find out what he is made of. It's easy when you have a great start, and you haven't gotten beat up yet. The great ones are the guys that go through the bad times and keep on getting better."

On cue, Brady threw four interceptions in Denver and the Patriots collapsed in the fourth quarter. His nose wasn't broken, but Brady's momentum in the Brady-Bledsoe battle was. It returned the next two weeks with comfortable wins, one on the road against the Falcons and the other at home over the Bills. The team's next game was its only scheduled national TV appearance, and it was against the Rams. They were the best team in the league by far, had won seven of their eight games, and halfway through the season, remarkably, their average win came via doubling the score of their opponents. They gave teams plenty to think about on their own, so any distraction during Rams week was more than an opponent could handle. The same was true of the Patriots. The week of the game, Bledsoe held a press conference at Massachusetts General Hospital with his doctors. He was cleared to play and, naturally, ready for the starting job. He had been away for seven games, and the team had gone 5-2 in his absence.

"I've been the starter on this team for eight years and I want to be the starter again," Bledsoe said as he was flanked by the doctors. "I have to show I'm the guy for the job and the guy who gives us the best chance to win ball games." He later added, "The guys still look to me. I still have a presence in the locker room."

He had been the starter for those eight years, and so it didn't seem fair that the erasure of the culture he'd known had taken place in mere weeks. He still had a presence in the locker room due to who he was as a man. His teammates could still love and respect him yet want Brady to remain the starter.

Besides, the shift at quarterback wasn't the only difference on the team. The Patriots were benefitting from, perhaps, the most successful offseason in modern NFL history. The belittled free agency class, full of the rejected, repurposed, and discounted play-ers, had turned up several productive starters. The first two selec-tions in the draft, Richard Seymour and Matt Light, had become starters also. And the young veterans Belichick had re-signed in 2000, Troy Brown and Tedy Bruschi, made an improbable leap from complementary players to essential members of the core.

The Brady-Bledsoe undercard had already played out on

defense. At the beginning of the season, the starting middle line-backer was the audacious Bryan Cox. He had been released by the Jets in a salary cap move, and had been scooped up by the Patriots on markdown. He was thirty-three, a veteran who was just a step away from retirement. But he knew all the inside tricks, he could work the officials, and, his shocked teammates quickly realized, he could play and speak the position as crudely as the situation called for.

"When Cox came in, he brought a new dimension to the meeting rooms, the locker room, and even a way to behave in front of the coaches," Bruschi recalls. "He cracked us all up. He could be disgusting. He could mention sites that you'd never dream of visiting on the Internet. That's just who he was; he was a hilarious and nasty dude.

"He would have conversations with our positional coaches in ways that were off the wall and aggressive, but still respectful. He would say it in his way if he had a suggestion, and he always found a way to stay within the framework of the team. But that type of communication was so valuable to us. Cox helped us develop that 'F everybody else' attitude. He'd have it with the other team, obviously. But sometimes he'd bring it to us. If the defensive line or someone else didn't like the call from the linebackers, his position was, 'F you. If you've got a problem with it, take it to the coaches.'"

In Brady's first start, the play of the game was made by Cox, not the young quarterback. He crushed a receiver who had the nerve to cross him in the middle of the field. After the game, firmly in character, he gave a profane analysis of life in the NFL. The public-relations staff blushed, and the surprised TV stations that showed it live had to beg the Federal Communications Commission for forgiveness. But the team, which had lacked sufficient talent and aggression in 2000, loved it.

Brady's worst game of the season, the four-interception game in Denver, was also a transitional moment for the defense. Cox absorbed a hit that he and his teammates believed was illegal, and the blow broke his leg. The injury provided an opening for Bruschi at inside linebacker. He was much shorter and lighter than Cox, but he used his quickness and instincts to play the position well enough to satisfy the exacting specifications of Belichick and defensive coordinator Romeo Crennel. When Cox neared a return to the field, he understood what was happening. He was a backup to the younger and now more talented Bruschi. Yet he roamed the locker room looking for media members that he could educate on team dynamics and the Brady-Bledsoe debate.

"Half of you guys have never played organized sports at this level or college, and you don't understand how much damage you can do by just starting a bunch of mess," Cox lectured. "To get caught up in who's the guy, that's taking away from both of those guys. Both of them are very capable, and I won't get into it and I won't take sides. Whoever is the starter, I'll support. Whoever comes off the bench I'll support. I ain't feeding into that foolishness."

Bledsoe prepared to take a good share of practice repetitions before the game against the Rams on November 18. He was disappointed when he didn't get as much time as he'd envisioned. He sounded angry and looked hurt when Belichick told him the plan for the rest of the season shortly after a 24–17 loss to St. Louis: He was the backup. Brady was the starter.

Bledsoe's return, in part, served as a reminder that there was nothing proprietary about player positions in the league. They were all tenants at will, the head coach included, and the comfortable slot could be flipped at any time for any reason. Belichick didn't expect the players to understand it while they were playing; in fact, it was probably better that they didn't think like he did as they pre-

pared for this sport featuring millionaires masquerading as gladi-
ators. Belichick couldn't be inhibited by fear of criticism, public
sentiment, or the uncomfortable moments that hovered during the
weekly quarterback meetings.

Everyone wasn't going to like him. Bledsoe wasn't going to like
him. But he insisted to Bledsoe, the rest of the team, ownership,
and the media that he didn't make this or any other decision simply
for his own enjoyment.

Belichick was definitive, but the debate was an organism unto
itself now. Brady or Bledsoe? You couldn't straddle. You couldn't
take a long time to answer. You had to pick one. The *Herald*'s TV
reporter, Jim Baker, talked with several ex-players and asked them
what they thought.

Troy Aikman: "Right now, it's the right decision to stick with
Brady. Is he a better quarterback than Bledsoe? I don't think so."

Boomer Esiason: "I have a lot of respect for Drew, but frankly
the team was not responding and not playing well under him...in
this situation, the way the team has responded to Brady, I'd leave
him in."

Cris Collinsworth: "Maybe I'm crazy, but I think substitute
quarterbacks can have a run and then scouting reports develop,
teams start to figure them out, and you get game plans against
them. In my heart, Bledsoe will be the guy down the stretch."

The best comment of all, though, came from a general manager
whom the newspaper quoted anonymously: "If they're giving Brady
the job because Bledsoe isn't medically ready to play, it makes sense.
If they think that Brady gives them a better chance of winning than
a healthy Bledsoe, that's another story. If that's the case, they're in
trouble. It will be a while before they'll see the play-offs."

Belichick said he sought definition for one position; what he got
instead was an entire team growing into its personality. Brady was

a fast learner in all quarterbacking matters, and one of the subtle changes he made underlined a message to his teammates. While Bledsoe often drew such a large media crowd that his press conferences were held in a separate room, Brady refused to do it that way. He made a point of standing at his locker, with his peers nearby, to speak with reporters. It wasn't practical, but it was in line with what the rest of the team was doing. He wanted the other players to always be mindful that he was one of them. That mentality encircled the team.

"It's the most fun I ever had playing football," Seymour says now. "We bonded. We joked together, had dinner together, and hung out together. Even the kids of players would hang out together. It was like we were a college team in the NFL. I just felt that on the field or personally, I'd be willing to do anything for those guys."

Seymour wore number 93, and because the lockers were positioned numerically, his neighbor was number 95, Roman Phifer. They had both looked at New England from afar and hoped to be playing football elsewhere. Seymour was a southerner, from a small town in South Carolina, and the idea of the Northeast and its polar conditions didn't appeal to him. Phifer was thirty-three, and he still longed to experience what one of his early pro coaches, Chuck Knox, described as an ideal: "The best combination in football is winning and getting paid."

Phifer was in his eleventh NFL season, so he had gotten paid. His struggle to be a part of a winner, though, had been epic. As the Patriots piled up wins after the Brady announcement, four in a row heading into a late December game with the Dolphins, Phifer teased Seymour about the rookie's instant success. He told him that the league really wasn't like this, and that winning seasons should never be taken for granted. He thought of his time with the Rams and Jets and compared it to what he was experiencing with the

Patriots. He concluded that he was part of the problem with his first two franchises.

"I wasn't a good leader with the Rams," he says. "And when I went to the Jets, I was jumping on the bandwagon. They had lost the year before in the AFC Championship Game, and everyone was saying that they were stacked, that they were a couple of players away from getting to the Super Bowl. But when I got there, I found a lot of guys like me. They weren't bad guys at all, but it was more about individuals than team. I was the same way. I was that way when I tried to avoid New England, because I wasn't thinking from the perspective of team. I wound up there by divine intervention."

Phifer's father, James, was a minister, and he frequently taught from the book of Proverbs. Specifically, the passage that reads, "God opposes the proud, but gives grace to the humble." Phifer had been talking to his father about football for twenty-five years, and this was the first time that he could see his own career within a sermon. Indeed, he had been the proud one for a decade.

He had become a dutiful note-taker, and his notebook pages were filled with painstaking instructions from Belichick. He thought to himself, *This could be an MBA program. It's like I'm going to grad school for football, and Bill is the professor.* He knew that Belichick and the other coaches got to the old stadium long before the players did, and departed who knew when. They had watched more film than the players had, and considered more game possibilities than the players had. Given that, it always amazed Phifer that the professor could stand in front of the group and condense that mass of information into three things. It was always, *Do these three things and we should be in position to win.*

It was genius, and several layers of it: of football, of efficiency, of leadership. James Phifer sure had been onto something when he preached about humility. His son's team was 9-5, getting ready to take on the 9-4 Dolphins, with the winner likely to finish first in the division. That was surprising to most people, but it wasn't even the best part of the story. The stadium, the bland jewel of Route 1 in Foxboro, was coming to a close. A sprawling construction site was next door, preparing the way for a new stadium, opening in 2002, that would bring the organization into the twenty-first century.

The good fortune of the Patriots had extended beyond the drafting and emergence of Brady, the immediate impact of Seymour, and the sparkling success rate of the free agents. The Jets had appeared to be thousands of miles beyond their grasp one year earlier. They had all those draft picks, and they still had Parcells in the front office. But Parcells learned that he wasn't made for the executive life, and he resigned shortly after his coach, Al Groh, left the Jets for the University of Virginia. The Bills had a new coach and general manager and had replaced the Patriots at the bottom of the division; the Colts, young and talented, were moved out of the AFC East due to league expansion; and the Dolphins, who had won six of their previous seven games against the Patriots, were suddenly at eye level.

Maybe they were temporary, but the headlines and the stories beneath them began to change as well. In two games against the Dolphins, Brady hadn't totaled two hundred passing yards. But the Brady-Bledsoe election was over, and the focus had long shifted to overall results. The Patriots beat the Dolphins, 20–13, on a day that was all about smiles and storytelling. At the urging of an enthusiastic Belichick, dozens of Patriots players ran to the packed stands and celebrated with their fans. Former Patriots players and coaches paraded through the stadium, waving and high-fiving in all directions, for what they thought was the final game in the stadium's history. Someone even tracked down Mark Henderson, who in 1982 famously drove a John Deere on the field to clear the snow, making it easier for a Patriots kicker to provide the only points in a 3–0 snowstorm win over the Dolphins.

Even the appearance of Henderson seemed like a Christmas miracle because, for at least ten years, he was reported to be dead. When he was seen driving his John Deere again, he easily qualified as the author of the greatest comeback in stadium history.

It was hard to top Henderson's narrative, but the Patriots tried over the next several weeks. They finished the regular season with an easy win over the Panthers.

With eleven wins, the Patriots had not only reversed their record from 2000; they had captured the division title. As soon as they found out their play-off opponent and the forecast for the game at Foxboro Stadium, they might have been wishing for Henderson again. The Oakland Raiders were coming to town, and so was a blizzard.

Both Belichick and Brady had connections to the franchise, personal and professional alike. Belichick was drawn to the iconoclastic owner of the Raiders, Al Davis. Slicked-back hair, tinted glasses, all-white track suits, and an accent dripping Brooklyn by way of Brockton, Massachusetts, Davis was begging to be caricatured. But that aside, Belichick respected his football savvy and his history of coaching in the American Football League. He often referred to him as "Coach Davis." A few years earlier, the two had discussed the head coaching vacancy with the Raiders. They spent the day talking football and had great, lengthy talks about the game they both loved. Belichick, though, finally mentioned an important point that hadn't been covered.

"Why are you trying to hire me?" the coach asked. "You only hire offensive coaches, because you're the one who wants to run the defense. You've never hired a defensive head coach."

It was true, and Coach Davis knew it. He wouldn't be happy letting someone else set the defensive philosophy for the Raiders, and neither would Belichick. They kept their relationship intact, and Davis hired the offensive-minded Jon Gruden as head coach. A few months later, the first draft choice on Gruden's watch was someone Brady knew very well. His name was Charles Woodson, the superhero from Michigan.

He and Brady were in the same recruiting class in 1995, although Woodson was considered class valedictorian. He never gave anyone time to ponder why. He started as a true freshman, became a defensive standout on a national championship team, and became the first defensive player ever to win the Heisman Trophy. Brady had practiced against him many times, and he knew how lethal Woodson's combination of length, athleticism, and intelligence could be.

The postseason, then, made way for a new campaign. This one was Brady versus Woodson, and it became the story of the night. A national TV audience got a chance to see a New England storm in progress, with the tufts of snow making it appear as if Foxboro Stadium had been staged by overzealous set designers. The field was essentially a snow-covered slick, with the yard lines visible only occasionally.

"Bear with us on the placement of the ball," broadcaster Gil Santos warned his radio audience in his authoritative bass, "because it isn't going to be easy." The Patriots started the game slowly, so slowly that as they ran off the field trailing 7–0 at the half, they were booed. Tough crowd. Many of the same folks, less than a month earlier, had tried to pull players into the seats for hugs and kisses.

The game became more interesting in the second half with the Patriots trailing 13–10 with two minutes remaining. Brady had smartly avoided Woodson for most of the night, knowing that the cornerback thrived on the baiting game. He liked to appear to be distracted, not seeming to be aware of a small passing window. But as soon as a throw went in that direction, he'd quickly seal the space and intercept the ball.

He had a more traditional move with 1:50 remaining: He blitzed. Brady dropped back to pass, and a sprinting Woodson was on his right arm in two seconds. The ball came loose, the Raiders recovered, and the season of surprises appeared to be over. People in Oakland thought it was clearly a fumble; people in New England saw it differently.

"As we looked at it, Brady's arm was coming forward," Santos said as officials reviewed the play.

Santos was making a reference to the Tuck Rule, a phrase that would send the majority of puzzled fans and media scrambling to the NFL rulebook. There, it stated, "When [an offensive] player is holding the ball to pass it forward, any intentional forward movement of his arm starts a forward pass, even if the player loses possession of the ball as he is attempting to tuck it back toward his body."

The broadcaster, who had begun calling Patriots games thirty-six years earlier, had seen his share of bizarre and arcane football business. His instincts were correct in this case. The official ruling was that Brady had been attempting to throw the ball just as Woodson hit him. The game-ending fumble recovery had simply become an incomplete pass that extended the season.

Coach Davis, a longtime NFL critic, believed that this was some league conspiracy to hurt the Raiders and reward the Patriots. (It would be several years before anyone could see the irony in the suggestion that the league would do anything to benefit the Patriots.) Woodson and his teammates were stunned. The Patriots continued their drive until they got themselves in position for kicker Adam Vinatieri. The confident Vinatieri cleared the snow with his shoe and then powered the ball forty-five yards through the wind and snow to send the game into overtime. Once there, as everyone could see coming, he made the winning kick to vault the Patriots into Pittsburgh and the conference championship game.

Beyond the breaks, though, was an identity. The team loved its reputation of being a bunch of starless rejects, knowing full well that the label was inaccurate. They had stars. They just didn't have hyped stars. They loved the concept of crashing the parties of the entitled and becoming uninvited dancers on the red carpet. The very thought became real to them as they prepared to play the Steelers.

There was just one week of prep time between the conference championship games and the Super Bowl, so it would take precise planning from all four participants to transition from their home cities to New Orleans, the site of the game. Three teams planned their contingencies in private. The Steelers went the other way, and even allowed their players to devote an entire day to Super Bowl planning.

"They didn't respect us and we knew it," Damien Woody, the Patriots' center, recalls. "That whole team, that whole city, thought there was no way that we could win the game. You could tell by the way they were talking. Even in our hotel, it seemed like the whole city of Pittsburgh was there. It was like the whole city was there to intimidate us."

The Patriots were convinced that they could expose two things: the Steelers' overconfidence and their poor special teams. Anyone who played in New England understood how obsessive Belichick was about the kicking game. "It didn't matter who you were," Phifer says. "Bill was going to put you on special teams if he thought that you could help. You had no choice."

In that spirit, the Patriots' best receiver, Troy Brown, was a core member on teams. If the Belichick ideal could be distilled into a single player, it would be Brown. He thought the game, long before it was played. He was athletic and versatile, a highly capable football handyman. Like Brady, he had been marginalized by the draft and had to listen to 197 names called before it was his turn. The Patriots, under Parcells, had cut him once and brought him back. He made himself indispensable with all of his skills, and he set a tone in the locker room both with his toughness and his usual combo of few words, bold actions.

He was responsible for the first points of the game, taking a punt in the middle of the field and weaving fifty-five yards for a touchdown. It was a good start, but a snag came late in the second quarter. Brady completed a long pass and was hit low by safety Lee Flowers. He immediately grabbed his left ankle, was attended to by doctors and trainers, and limped off the field. That left an opening for the best backup quarterback in the league, Drew Bledsoe.

The preseason words of Brady resonated again. *They're going to need all three of us.* The biggest conflict of the season had been Brady versus Bledsoe, but now the only path to the Super Bowl was Brady *and* Bledsoe. The older quarterback sprung off the bench and quickly completed a pass. Then he did something that made you wonder if the entire Patriots season was just a satirical reality show. He ran toward the sideline, just like he had against the Jets. And he got hit high by a defender, similar to the blow by Mo Lewis. Fortunately for Bledsoe, he was hit by a cornerback this time, and he bounced up shouting and clapping his hands. The next play was a touchdown in the corner of the end zone to David Patten.

The entire day wasn't perfect for Bledsoe, but it didn't need to be. There was joy in watching yet another special-teams touchdown, this one in the third quarter, that Brown helped create. There was joy in playing and feeling like a playing contributor and not just a meeting-room intellectual. There was joy in winning, 24–17, and putting his hands on that conference championship trophy.

They did things in the game that often went unnoticed, such as having a role player like Adrian Klemm play left and right tackle and left and right guard. This was the Belichick view of team-building as much as a player's height, weight, and speed. This game, won this way, was perfect for a Belichick team: game-changing plays on special teams, a starring role for a backup, and multiple players capable of excelling in multiple positions. The Patriots lingered on the field, wave after wave of them going to Bledsoe and squeezing him for several seconds. They didn't have to say much, and neither did he. They had all added something to this game, from the Rehbein family's presence as honorary captains, to the 14 points off special teams, to the forgotten quarterback on the bench. They'd all been a part of it.

It didn't make sense that Patriots-Rams would be the matchup in New Orleans. One team was known for things that seemed to be euphemisms for a lack of beauty. It was industrious and hardworking, gritty and conscientious. The other team had won it all before, two years earlier, and was even better this time. It was stacked with speed and style, two MVP candidates, and a colorful nickname that belonged, in circus font, on the side of a traveling bus: THE GREATEST SHOW ON TURF.

Not surprisingly, there weren't a variety of perspectives on what the game might become. The Rams had played the Patriots once already, in Foxboro, and won. It was popular and understandable to reason that if the Rams had handled the Patriots in outdoor conditions, which wasn't their preference, they might annihilate them in the comfort of the Superdome.

The problem with that logic is that it works only if teams remain static. The Rams very well could have been a different team, even a better team, than they had been in November. Time in the NFL doesn't function in a normal continuum, so a game three months earlier felt like it was from another generation. The Patriots were also changed, in some ways that could be seen on the field and in others that could be measured only in fraternity and brotherhood.

"We were in that space where we knew we had a good football team and no one else knew how good," Seymour says. "If we were talking boxing, we'd have been the boxer people should have been afraid to fight."

Several hours before the game, Seymour, who was just twenty-two years old, had a moment with Romeo Crennel. The defensive coordinator hadn't looked at and spoken to him like this all season. He gave his youngest defensive starter permission to do as he saw fit on the field. The veterans sometimes did that on their own, changing plans and assignments just before the snap, with no time to run it by the coaches for approval. Rookies rarely got that luxury. But what Crennel was telling Seymour, essentially, was that he was in the club now. He was no longer a rookie. He was valuable and they trusted him.

The relationship had deepened between a coach and player, and that was consistent with what was happening all over the team. Willie McGinest had taken giant steps as a leader, more than the coaches realized. He connected with veterans like Phifer and instructed rookies like Seymour. He was a big brother as well as Big Brother.

"Willie was a man among men," Phifer says. "He got into a couple of scuffles with teammates. They were bigger than him; he got the better of them. But Willie comes in peace. If you wanted to be loud and boisterous, he would let it be known who was in charge. But people had so much respect for Willie that the atmosphere wasn't one of fear; it was about unity. And he was probably the biggest reason of why it was like that."

Before the game, one gesture captured the journey from New

England to New Orleans. One look, and listen, got to the foundation of the Patriots' story. "And now, ladies and gentlemen," the public address announcer began, "choosing to be introduced as a team, the New England Patriots…" And out they ran, a mass of red, white, and blue. It was the first surprise of many more to come.

John Madden, during the Fox telecast, said that he had spoken with Rams coach Mike Martz the day before, and Martz thought the game would be lopsided by halftime. "I think he felt he was going to open up this game the first half and blow the roof off this stadium with this offense," Madden told the largest football audience of the year. But if national football fans hadn't been paying attention to the Patriots since the emergence of Brady, they were now.

In fact, the Rams game was an anthology of the Patriots season, neatly packaged into sixty minutes, no overwhelming backstory required. It started with Belichick, who had deconstructed the Rams offense and then, just as Roman Phifer had grown used to, broken the game plan into three key points. Number one was to stop running back Marshall Faulk. It continued with Brady, who, despite speculation that he might not start the Super Bowl, heavily taped his left ankle and prepared to make his decisive calls in the huddle.

From there, really, the formula was the opposite of touristy New Orleans; it was, in a word, unadorned. While Martz was telling Madden that the game shouldn't be close, Belichick was explaining how the Patriots planned to slow it down. He may have understood complexities, but his appeal to those around him was that he made the complex quite simple.

"He's the smartest guy in football," says Lionel Vital, who scouted for Belichick in Cleveland and New England. "Yet he never flexes the mental muscle over anybody. When he's in Germany, he speaks German. When he's got an audience of sixth-graders, he can speak to them so they understand exactly what he's saying. He's very deep; very discerning."

His idea was for the Patriots to treat Faulk as if he were the quarterback. He wanted to concede shorter passes because he figured the Rams really wanted the deep ones. He wanted a defensive approach just short of bullying, because the Rams were prone to turnovers.

Martz was right in that the game wasn't all that close at half-time. The Patriots, on the strength of two turnovers, including an interception that Ty Law returned for a touchdown, led 14–3. "If I had dropped that, I would have been pretty damn clumsy," Law says. "I would have been a nonathlete because the pass was right in the bread bucket. I mean, it wasn't hard at all." The lead inched to 17–3 at the beginning of the final quarter. That's when the Rams finally played to Martz's expectations and tied the score.

With eighty-one seconds remaining and no timeouts, Brady calmly took the Patriots from their own seventeen-yard line to the St. Louis thirty. In the Super Bowl dream, the starting quarterback drops back and surgically places one into a receiver's hands in the end zone. But this way was better. This involved a drive in which the 199th pick in one draft completed passes to the 198th pick in another; this was a drive that a born-and-raised Bostonian, tight end Jermaine Wiggins, was a part of; this drive was going to give the last word to the special teams, which they all were a part of, and give some glory to the kicker.

It was the least dramatic dramatic kick in team history. It was thumped with force, and it was geometrically perfect. Right down the middle.

"I've only seen my father cry twice," Phifer says. "My grand-mother's funeral and this game."

James Phifer was not alone. There were tears and deep exhales all over the field. Belichick ran to the turf to get a better view of the forty-eight-yard kick, and he was still there when it went through. He was sandwiched in a hug by his daughter, Amanda, and his Pro Bowl safety, Lawyer Milloy. Some players danced, some prayed, some openly wept, and a few of them approached Scott Pioli and simply expressed thank-yous.

"When we won, it really was that feeling of emerging from the dark tunnel and seeing the light," Damien Woody says. "Playing for Coach Belichick, you were on edge every single week. You got comfortable being uncomfortable. It's never easy. He demands a lot, all the time. If you can't get it right, he just gives this cold stare like, 'Are you shitting me right now? How do you not know this?' So to win it, and hold that trophy, it was finally relief."

Brady stood on a podium with both hands on his head, smiling. On the same night, he had become a champion and a victim of his team's accepted script. Since the story was that the Patriots were the recipients of good luck and magic, those qualities were assigned to him as well. He was the game's MVP, although most people still considered the Rams' Kurt Warner the better quarterback.

In fact, the Rams had been so impressive during the regular season that a young woman had bought her boyfriend, a University of Louisville football player, a Rams jersey with his name on the back. The Rams seemed to be in a dynamic offense and a paradise for receivers, so she thought the gift made sense. But Deion Branch's girlfriend, Shola, had the right idea and the wrong team. They watched the Super Bowl together and imagined his future. He'd be there one day, too, with the Patriots.

CHAPTER FIVE

LEAVING THE PACK

They all sensed it as soon as they piled into trucks and rolled through the narrow streets of downtown Boston. It was twenty-eight degrees, and the windchill made it feel like zero. And yet there were two sixteen-year-old boys, bare-chested, with one rib cage painted GO and the other PATS. They should have had shirts and coats on. They should have been in school. There were a lot of should-haves that were being overlooked and, as the Patriots were witnessing, all of it was taking place in the biggest crowd anyone had ever seen.

It was just after noon, and some people had come as early as six a.m. to stake their positions at City Hall Plaza. That's where the trucks were going to stop and spill the Patriots onto a performance stage. But the people swarmed everywhere. On Boylston and Tremont Streets. In Boston Common. On top of buildings, where another shirtless man ran across a roof in boxer shorts and sneakers. On Court and Congress Streets. On shoulders. On trees. Out of windows. City officials knew it would be the party of the year, or more precisely, the after-party of the year. State employees were given the day off, and although most schools were open, thousands of students happened to be missing with mysterious colds and coughs. Ten bus routes were diverted, the subway service on the T was increased, and parking bans were in effect until the celebration ended.

A police spokesman was asked when, exactly, the party would stop. He answered, half-jokingly, March. For the players, most of them born and raised outside of New England, it was shocking that 1.2 million people showed up in the early February cold to celebrate the win over the Rams. But this outpouring is exactly what many of the fans had been trying to express over the years as they discussed their local teams. Yes, they were tougher on their pro teams than most American cities were on theirs. The rationale, though, was often parental: We scold because we love. At the root of the hysteria and overwrought calls to sports-talk radio stations was hunger for a champion who could accurately reflect them. Now they had it.

They had always related to the passionate Lawyer Milloy, and the connection became even deeper when the Patriots safety, snug in a black fur coat, held the Lombardi Trophy to the sky and shouted from the stage, "City of Boston! It's been a long time coming, huh?"

Everyone could sense that Milloy was the perfect personality for the region. He heard everything that was said about his team, and he took it personally. Two days before the Patriots played the Steelers for the conference title, Milloy heard a line of questioning that he felt was insulting to the Patriots. He was in a Pittsburgh hotel ballroom when he heard it, and he frowned and paced. "I feel like Mike Tyson right now," he said with fists clenched. After the win over the Rams, he sat on Fox's on-field studio set and told the nation what the win symbolized.

"Look, we shocked the world. This is not for anybody else but us and our fans, the greatest fans in America. This is what it's all about. Can't nobody take this from us, for life!" He was asked, truly, if he thought the Patriots were capable of shutting down one of the best offenses in NFL history the way that they had. "We believed," he replied before the question was fully complete. "People die for their beliefs, and we believe in our team."

He was that guy. And he was speaking to thousands of people who felt and thought the same way he did. There were several dignitaries on the City Hall stage. The mayor of Boston and governor of Massachusetts both were there, and so was Senator John Kerry. The Patriots were bigger than all of them on this day. Milloy used the stage as a club floor and danced with teammate Ty Law, who reenacted his end zone celebration in New Orleans. Law then made Tom Brady and Bill Belichick dance for the excited crowd. Then the cornerback said, "Hey, Mr. Kraft. Can I get an ownership, I own the team, I pay all y'all fools' money . . . Can I get a little dance?" So Robert Kraft from Brookline, who understood the psychology of the crowd as much as anyone there, danced.

But despite all the smiles, painted faces, pennants, amplified music, a Jumbotron at City Hall Plaza, and, of course, chants of "Yankees suck," all of it was going to end in a few hours. The kids would be back in school and the adults would be back to work. That included the Patriots.

The freezing parade had been fun, and it distracted some people from the notable absences on that stage. Willie McGinest, who cried bittersweet tears after the Super Bowl, was missing. His salary cap number for the upcoming season was a bulging $8.3 million, and he and many of his teammates thought that his last game as a Patriot had taken place in New Orleans. It was also a smart bet because the Patriots had already submitted their names for the expansion draft. McGinest's was on the list. If the Houston Texans wanted him, they could have him.

Also missing from the parade was Drew Bledsoe. Many in the crowd called for him, cheering wildly each time they did it, but

Bledsoe was thousands of miles away at his ranch in Montana. He hadn't even returned to Boston after the Super Bowl. He had flown in a different direction, symbolic of what was going to inevitably happen.

The campaign was long over. Brady-Bledsoe buttons, bumper stickers, and arguments were artifacts. The kid had dramatically taken the job, and it was amazing how quickly the majority of people in the region, fans and media alike, had moved on. No one had expected the Patriots to win the Super Bowl, but if that prediction had been made months earlier, the thought would have been that Bledsoe would be the quarterback dancing near Milloy and Law. Instead it was the twenty-four-year-old Super Bowl MVP, wearing a black trench coat, standing in the background, and listening to squeals from the crowd.

Never again, absolutely never, would he be the anonymous friend when hanging out with his buddies Chris Eitzmann, Matt Chatham, and Dave Nugent. No more wry smiles as they were asked for autographs while he was ignored. No more background duty. His address was going to change; no more neighbors trying to remember the name of the tall, skinny young man in the Chestnut Ridge condos. He got a Cadillac Escalade for being the game's MVP, and he said on national TV that it now belonged to the team. He hadn't allowed himself to think like this, because you never outperform your heroes, but he had become the youngest quarterback to ever win a Super Bowl. Before him, it had been twenty-five-year-old Joe Montana.

It was crazy. Exactly one year earlier, the team had been finalizing Bledsoe's record $103 million deal and providing quarterback insurance by signing Damon Huard as a backup. Now, everyone was familiar with a clause in Bledsoe's contract that had initially been skipped over due to it being so unlikely and insignificant. It stated that trading Bledsoe would result in limited salary cap damage to the Patriots, less than $1 million. In other words, there was no reason *not* to make a trade. The next few months would be devoted to trading Bledsoe, signing free agents, and figuring out the best way to approach the college draft.

It was hard to describe where the franchise was. It was cool and weird. Belichick would never forget the night they won the Super Bowl. He didn't sleep at all, and around two or three a.m., he had been talked out of walking to the French Quarter and Pat O'Brien's for their legendary hurricanes; he settled for conversation and drinks in the team's hotel bar. It had been yet another strategic win for the coach. All of the celebrating and memories didn't stop him from thinking that his winning team now needed to be rebuilt. It was exceptional in some areas, but others were not at a championship standard. People weren't just being rude when they had favored the Steelers and Rams over the Patriots. There was a noticeable talent gap in the overall rosters, and Belichick felt it had to be fixed.

As for fixing it with the right people, that was the weird part. Two years earlier, the coach didn't feel that he'd had sufficient time to do his draft homework because the Patriots' job wasn't officially his until late January. He'd be playing catch-up this time because of winning. Imagine that. Winning on the field automatically meant scrambling to keep up in scouting. There was no way around it. Both things couldn't be done simultaneously, so the field took priority.

The difference between February 2000 and February 2002 was striking in terms of scouting personnel. The room was now populated with a good cross section of smart guys who were trained to find exactly what Belichick was looking for. There were scouts in their twenties like Nick Caserio, Bob Quinn, and Kyle O'Brien; men in their thirties with more responsibilities like Scott Pioli,

Jason Licht, Jon Robinson, Thomas Dimitroff, and Lionel Vital; there was even a consultant in his eighties, Bucko Kilroy, who had either played against or scouted every type of player imaginable over the years. All, with the exception of Kilroy, were on a rising general manager track.

As spring approached, everyone in the organization knew that they were scouting for Brady's offense now. Everyone in the NFL knew it, too. No one wanted to meet the Patriots' hefty price for Bledsoe, a first-round pick, if they didn't have to. It was a harsh business, so teams wanted to see if they could make the Patriots trade from a position of duress. It wasn't possible to keep Brady and Bledsoe on the same roster again. Even the teams who most needed quarterbacks refused to give in and create a bidding war for Bledsoe. But one team, the division rival Bills, seemed to inquire too often in the name of due diligence. The Bills tried to be coy, but Belichick and Pioli knew they had their buyer.

There were weeks of haggling between the franchises, and things got so bizarre that Buffalo general manager Tom Donahoe attempted to "tattle" on Belichick and Pioli by going over their heads to Kraft. Donahoe's strategy seemed to be: *They won't make a reasonable deal with me; maybe you can talk some sense into these two.* The Super Bowl after just two years on the job had given Belichick and Pioli tremendous freedom in the building, so Kraft ignored Donahoe and let his football guys sort things out. Besides, the problem was that Donahoe was insisting on a second-round pick for Bledsoe, and the Patriots were adamant that it had to be a first. They went back and forth, agitated at times, before there was a breakthrough. Finally, in April, the deal was complete. Drew Bledsoe to Buffalo for the Bills' 2003 first-round pick. The initial reviews were that the Bills were big winners.

Locally, in the *Boston Globe*, frequent Belichick critic Ron

Borges warned that the glare of the Lombardi Trophy was blinding fans, and team personnel, to the risks in the trade. Specifically, Borges pointed out, Brady's numbers began to decline as the games became more important and teams familiarized themselves with his weaknesses. The team scored just three offensive touchdowns in the postseason "and one of them was thrown by Bledsoe."

"The moment Belichiek nodded his head in the direction of Scott Pioli and OK'd trading Drew Bledsoe to Buffalo for the Bills' number one draft choice in 2003, he said 'I do' to Tom Brady," Borges wrote. "They're wedded now, the coach from Wesleyan and the quarterback from Michigan. Either they go on to a future of unbridled success in the National Football League or they go together into this good night."

If the Patriots had lost to the Rams in the final seconds, the trade might have unsettled the majority of New Englanders. A loss in that game, after leading by two touchdowns in the fourth quarter, would have strengthened the fear that every big game, and transaction, was somehow going to lead to humiliation. But the win provided an alternative to the shared wall of misery that some Boston fans automatically went to.

There was a change afoot in town, and it was tangible. There was the trophy, of course, which would be the first thing moved into the new home, Gillette Stadium. There was also a new vocabulary for a generation that wasn't used to talking about clutch plays and smart decisions that led to parades in their city. In the spring of 2001, they had been the ones asking for a wide receiver in the first round and looking for something beyond the low-priced free agents that had been signed. In 2002, people took pride in not having to rely on high-maintenance receivers, and they wondered, Belichick-like, if the newest Patriots would submit to the team-first ethic that had been established.

So on his way out of town, Bledsoe was generally applauded for his dignified run with the Patriots. He gained even more respect throughout the region when he paid for local newspaper ads and thanked fans for their support during his career as a Patriot. He was sent off to western New York with blessings and bouquets.

It was a remarkable transition. Bledsoe's job had been taken by Brady, and his stardom had been eclipsed by Belichick. The championship had turned Belichick into the region's biggest nonplaying star since Red Auerbach, the coach and craftsman of the dynastic Celtics. The new era story line from the Super Bowl had naturally focused on Brady because of his age and the position he played. But Belichick had entered a new realm as well, although that point was lost in the rush to compare him to Bill Parcells. It had nothing to do with winning without Parcells. For Belichick, now fifty years old, the title was validation of all the ways he saw himself fitting into a franchise. Public perception had always locked Belichick into one of two circles, neither of which captured him or his passions.

One was a circle of success, ironically, perfectly illustrated on the front page of the *New York Times* fifteen years earlier. There he was at Giants Stadium, moments after winning the conference championship, being carried off the field by his Giants players. He was called a defensive genius, over and over, which in a way is not a bad thing. Who has a problem with being known as a genius? The picture was there, but it was incomplete. He was the genius of defense because that was his assigned area. Before that, he had been the Giants' special-teams coach and had excelled there as well. He was just thirty-four, and he had been in the pros for a dozen years. His was still a young, evolving football mind. He had his own ideas about the business, ideas that went beyond defense, the head coaching methods of Bill Parcells, and the general managing of George Young. He loved everything about football: watching and teaching it, reading about it, thinking of ways to improve it and what he'd like to do if he were given resources and tools in a football organization and told to build it.

The second circle, then, was more complicated. He had become that builder in Cleveland when he was thirty-eight. One of his football gods was Paul Brown, who was also thirty-eight when he began coaching in Cleveland. This seemed destined to work. When the results weren't good enough, one play-off appearance in five seasons, he was dismissed as someone who couldn't shape an entire franchise. He was well rounded only within the dimensions of that first circle. He was trapped in those confines from the day he drove out of Cleveland, in 1996, until the moment the first strand of confetti fell on him in New Orleans.

In April 2002, like Brady, Belichick was just getting started in this new phase of his career. He, too, had been underestimated, and had invested more time in remaking himself than anyone had considered. The remake did not always include smooth public relations with the media or sometimes with his players. He was a good listener and weighed all information before making a decision, but when it was time to declare a direction, he was forceful and left no wiggle room. He asked his scouts to be the same way. Be thorough, be clear, and be decisive. That was his approach to in-house communication; for outsiders, it wasn't as satisfying. Sometimes he played the media game, smiled, and gave them the anecdotal and expansive responses that they craved. At times, mostly on Fridays, he even engaged reporters with playful trivia questions. Usually, though, his comments to them were stick-figure sketches of his true thoughts.

That approach was a virtual guarantee of critical coverage, regardless of the decisions he made as a coach. There was an implied reciprocity that the sports media sought. Full cooperation didn't give a subject full immunity, but it at least ensured a degree of humanity within the reporting. One of Belichick's first hires in New England had been Berj Najarian, who had been an assistant in the Jets' public-relations department. Najarian, from Long Island, was a Boston University graduate and had initially planned to be a sportswriter. He wound up in PR, with the Knicks and Jets on his résumé. Belichick trusted his scouting reports on the media, his intelligence, and his organizational skills, which at least rivaled Belichick's and sometimes exceeded them. Najarian was going to need to stay close by, because there was plenty of controversy on the way.

Some of Belichick's decisions were made by other teams. The new franchise, the Texans, decided not to select linebackers McGinest and Ted Johnson in the expansion draft. The Patriots sliced their salaries and brought them both back. The status of two other linebackers, Bryan Cox and Roman Phifer, was pending. Cox, the fearless mouth of the defense, got tired of waiting and signed with the Saints. He wasn't happy about it, telling the *Globe*'s Will McDonough, "I talked with them after the year to find out my future, and they said they would get back to me. Never did. Never even gave me a phone call…Roman Phifer was the MVP of our defense last year, in my opinion, and they haven't called him either. He doesn't know what is going on."

Phifer did hear back, and he was returning. Jermaine Wiggins, the tight end from East Boston who caught Brady's final pass in the Super Bowl, was not. The collegial atmosphere of the parade had given way to economics. The chief economist planned to upgrade the tight end position through free agency and the draft. He began by targeting thirty-year-old Christian Fauria, who wanted to be anywhere but New England.

Fauria had remembered the intense Belichick from years earlier, when the coach was still in Cleveland and the player was a draft prospect from Colorado. They were at the Shrine Bowl in San Francisco, and Fauria had watched film in Belichick's hotel suite.

"He had a bunch of tapes in his room, all of my tapes from college," Fauria recalls. "It was like Roy Hobbs in *The Natural*: dark room, one light. He said, 'Pick out your best game and your worst game.' I thought it was some type of trick. My worst game, I thought, was Nebraska. We put it on and I was kicking somebody's ass. He said, 'That's your worst game?' He was going over every game, and he knew about everybody on the field. I was thinking, 'Please don't draft me.' He had a reputation as a taskmaster, and I just didn't want to deal with it."

In the spring of 2002, Belichick was asking about Fauria again. Once again, Fauria didn't want to go. He loved football and had gone through some excruciating medical procedures so he could stay on the field. Once, there was pain like he'd never experienced, when he tore every ligament in his right ankle. It had taken a plate, eight screws, and a stabilizing bolt to put him back together again. He'd had three microfracture surgeries. Shattered and dislocated fingers. An old back injury from college that would flare up every now and then. Pulled hamstrings. He played through many of the injuries, convincing himself that he could start caring about his body at the end of the season. His brother, a foot specialist, was one of the many people who told him he was nuts. It didn't matter. He played, with frequent help from Tylenol and Vicodin.

Despite all that, Fauria wanted to play six more years. There's no way he could pull that off with daily gladiator practices. He expressed his concerns to Belichick, and to his surprise, the coach listened and said, "Once training camp starts, we'll take care of you."

Belichick didn't always do what was expected, whether it was a conversation with a player, a signing, a release, or a draft pick.

That, combined with his poker player style with the media, made it impossible to predict what he would do next.

He surprised many in April, including Fauria, when he traded up eleven spots in the first round, from thirty-two to twenty-one, to select Colorado tight end Daniel Graham. At the end of round two, he went for a five-foot-nine-inch receiver from Louisville named Deion Branch. The surprise there had actually happened weeks earlier, when Belichick had gone to the team's war room and stared for a long time at the draft board. He looked at the magnetic strip containing Branch's name and draft grade, and then weighed it versus what he had seen on film and the player's production. In the Patriots' 1 to 9.99 grading system, a system that did not acknowledge perfect 10s, Branch's number fell below the 5.50 minimum to be considered a "Make It," or backup player. He thought Branch was out of position, so he moved the strip from the "back board," where "Free Agents" and "Pats Rejects" reside, to the front board, with the best prospects.

It was clear, in rookie minicamp, that Branch wasn't going to have a problem learning the offense of coordinator Charlie Weis. His understanding of the concepts seemed natural and, physically, he almost always caught what was thrown his way. When the entire team was together, the new additions blended with the holdovers, and it was as if this were the postscript to 2001. Fauria, for example, had no idea what to expect from his new quarterback, the Super Bowl MVP. He was immediately taken by Brady's confidence and his odd sense of humor.

When Fauria introduced himself as "Christian," Brady smiled and started calling him "Motoring." He noticed Fauria's bewildered look and began singing "Sister Christian" by the early 1980s band Night Ranger to explain himself. A lyric about motoring was tucked in there. Random. An instant friendship was born with Fauria. It was much the same with Branch, who was struck by how grounded and competitive his quarterback was. The season hadn't started yet, and already Ping-Pong paddles had been broken after Brady challenged Branch and lost to him.

Weis watched it all and was pleased. He was looking forward to the season where, theoretically, this team would have more offensive talent than the Super Bowl winners. That was his professional outlook. Personally, he planned to have routine gastric bypass surgery before the season opener in September.

In the summer, he entered Massachusetts General Hospital for what was known casually as "stomach-stapling" surgery. There was nothing routine about the procedure. The surgery had turned out disastrously, and a supposedly simple operation had become life-threatening for Weis. He had internal bleeding for two days and required a blood transfusion of seven pints. He faded in and out of consciousness, at times being alert enough to recognize his wife, Maura, and sometimes looking near his bed and seeing Brady. It was dire. He was given last rites by a Catholic priest.

Fortunately, his condition began to improve and, after a month in rehab, he was sent home. It was time for training camp now, and Weis wasn't well enough to rejoin the coaching staff full-time. He watched film from his Rhode Island home and constantly checked in with Belichick and the quarterbacks. He still had a burning sensation in his legs and feet, from nerve damage, and he knew when he got back to the team he'd have to use a golf cart to get around. It was still good news that he could coach again, and doctors were encouraged by his progress.

In fact, September in New England was brimming with the positivity that was there during the run through the play-offs. The Patriots had won their final nine games, and the entire region had responded in kind to the success. Now it seemed that many of the stale and ineffectual things in the city were shifting, too. The Red Sox, who had been either owned or controlled by one family since 1933, were sold to a group led by a man named John Henry. Henry was a risk-taker, and he promised changes to the team that had flattened more dreams over the years than any franchise in the region. Rumors were that the Celtics were for sale as well, and two lifelong fans, Wyc Grousbeck and Steve Pagliuca, were prepared to present a $360 million offer.

There was a lot to celebrate and the venerable Rolling Stones were up for it. They planned to go on a fortieth-anniversary tour, with Boston as the kickoff city. One day while the Patriots were in meetings preparing for their game with the Steelers, they heard start-and-stop pulsing through the Gillette Stadium walls; the Stones had to practice, too. They were still the hard-living Stones, though, so it wasn't a shock when the *Herald* reported that during one of their nights out in Boston, Mick, Keith, and some of their friends got a private room in a restaurant and drank $13,000 worth of booze in two hours. The drinking was left to others on the night of the show, and after going through all the hits, including a "Satisfaction" encore with fireworks, it felt like the perfect time to start the season.

Two weeks before the first game, there was some contractual business to handle. Brady was up for a huge raise. He had been the league's lowest-paid starting quarterback in 2001, making $375,000. In 2002, he signed a four-year extension worth $30 million. There were still a few people who said that he was a fluke and a "system quarterback," but the feelings about him in New England were now in print. He was being paid like the top quarterbacks in the game.

If there was any doubt about the legitimacy of Brady in his first full season as a starter, it went away after an easy 30–14 win. Brady threw three touchdown passes, all to new guys: Fauria, Branch, and Donald Hayes. After the Hayes score, a forty-yarder that was made possible by a beautiful Branch block, assistant coach Jeff Davidson yelled to receivers coach Brian Daboll through the coaching headsets, "Make sure you congratulate his ass! That was a GREAT block." Weis and his staff loved receivers who had the ability to block, so this kid was going to be all right.

The early part of the season, three wins in three games, was a test against human nature. And the Patriots were human. There was no way they could avoid connecting the seasons. Those of them who had been on the championship team knew that they had won twelve games in a row since November of 2001. Brady and receiver David Patten, chatting on the field before the fourth game in San Diego, even talked about going undefeated.

And that's where the slide began, with the Patriots afflicted by a different plague each week. They were gashed on the ground by the Chargers; denied the ball for two-thirds of the game in Miami; mentally slow at home against Green Bay (Belichick was aghast that the offense stood unaware as a live ball rested on the turf and was recovered by a Packer who had been thirty yards away); and unable to move the ball against Denver.

This was what previous champions talked about, in retrospect. They talked about the difficulty of the next season, in which the ability to sneak up on people goes away. The first-place schedule guarantees a stiffer challenge, as does the adrenaline from the opposition, eager to prove itself against the best. But even after blasting Bledsoe and the Bills by 31 points, the Patriots' excellence was in what they had done in New Orleans, not who they were in the present.

Sometimes after games at home, Belichick would retreat to his office and educate his football-loving sons, fifteen-year-old Stephen (named after Belichick's father) and ten-year-old Brian, on the basics of the game. They were all happy in there, totally satisfied by a whiteboard, a couple of Sharpies, and some formations. It was a side of Belichick rarely seen, and what made it even more touching was his ability to compartmentalize. Because whatever his considerable happiness was with his boys, the inverse was true of the team. He didn't like how it played or practiced. He questioned his own coaching, as well as the instruction of the assistants. It wasn't unusual for him to criticize himself and his staff during team meetings. Even the players who gave him everything they had, the true professionals, a few of them were too close to the end to make a difference on the field.

Defensive end Anthony Pleasant, thirty-four, a respected locker room evangelist and counselor, was one of those guys. So was cornerback Otis Smith, thirty-seven, who was a master of defensive positioning in the secondary. Even a couple of new additions, thirty-two-year-old Victor Green and thirty-one-year-old Rick Lyle, proved that they had the high football aptitude that would easily translate to coaching one day. But this was a young man's game, and those ages told part of the story about the defense: not fast enough, not youthful enough. It was mid-December now, and the Patriots were technically in contention for the division title and the play-offs. Technicalities are tricky. These Patriots were average, and if they were fortunate enough to slip into the postseason, they'd be pushed aside humbly.

As for the Bills and Bledsoe, they were the only team in the division less happy than the Patriots. Bledsoe had a good season. He passed for 4,359 yards, roughly 600 more than Brady, and twenty-four touchdowns, which was four fewer than Brady's league-leading total. He went 0-2 against his old team, though, and the Bills finished last in the division. The Patriots, just one game better at 9-7, found no consolation in that. They learned that they had missed the play-offs late on a Sunday evening. There was a team meeting the next morning at nine. Later that afternoon, Belichick was joined in his office by Pioli and Ernie Adams, the coach's multifaceted adviser. Each man had a legal notepad, filled with team needs. The short-term focus that the players saw was on display here, too. On to the offseason.

Belichick thought about his defense constantly. One day in late January, while he was driving from Foxboro to Annapolis to visit his parents, he was haunted by bad routes to the ball, missed tackles, and a lack of speed. And that was just on the field. The economics of his secondary were also impractical: He had large cap numbers for Lawyer Milloy and Ty Law, and an upcoming contract for Tebucky Jones, who was going to demand a salary much greater than his performance warranted.

Normally, a 400-mile drive is perfect for untangling and problem-solving issues. But in this case, it was probably about 350 miles more than necessary. No question, there was going to be a makeover with the defensive backs. The options, through free agency and the draft, could be franchise-altering.

There was one safety from Southern Cal that the scouts couldn't stop talking about. His name was Troy Polamalu and, if it were possible, his play seemed to reflect both joy and fury. He was excitable and aggressive. More than that, the scouts gave him the highest possible special-teams grade, too. He was a Belichick guy if they ever saw one. But the Patriots had two first-rounders, numbers fourteen and nineteen, and the first pick was going to be used on a defensive lineman. It was unlikely that Polamalu would be available for the selection at nineteen.

Things started to become clearer at the end of February. One of the best and most hated safeties in the league, Rodney Harrison, was released by the Chargers. He had once lost over $100,000 on a single hit, a helmet-to-helmet shot on Jerry Rice. He was big and aggressive, an underdog spirit housed in a linebacker's body. Belichick wanted him. He'd figure out the secondary shuffle later, but he knew Harrison would fit as a Patriot.

The team also got lucky with what became, inexplicably, a slow market for Rosevelt Colvin. In the language of Patriots scouts, he was a "projection" player, meaning that he had played one position in college and was expected to do something else in the pros. Tedy Bruschi and Mike Vrabel had done that, going from collegiate defensive end to pro linebacker. So had Colvin. He could rush and cover, he was twenty-five, and he was surprisingly affordable. The Patriots signed both Harrison and Colvin in March. They also added another cornerback, Tyrone Poole, who was released by the Colts.

Milloy was watching closely. He knew his agents and the Patriots had talked about restructuring several times, and those conversations hadn't gone well. Harrison had said he looked forward to playing with Milloy, but he was a player. That's how players talked. The decision-makers saw players in terms of production and dollar signs. Besides, Milloy had been in Boston long enough to have an edge. He was often defensive and suspicious, especially now. Anticipating a fight, he changed agents and hired Carl and Kevin Poston, brothers known for their fierce, pro-player negotiating style. They also represented Ty Law, had gotten him that $50 million contract, and were opposed to any type of contract restructuring that even mildly resulted in a loss for a client. Milloy had no problems letting his teammates know each progression, or lack thereof, in negotiations.

With that said, the new players were made for the Patriots' competitive culture. Colvin was doing some work at the team facility one day when he saw Brady and the other quarterbacks going through some passing drills. They would take three or five steps back and zip footballs into a square that was surrounded by netting.

"Ah, that's nothing," Colvin shouted when he saw the drill. "You're supposed to be able to make *that* throw. You're quarterbacks!"

"Let's see what you've got, then," Brady challenged.

"What are the stakes?" Colvin replied.

They agreed on $1,000. The linebacker admitted that it was a fluke, but he had been able to hit the square from a farther distance than Brady. Pure luck. The next day, Colvin went to his locker and found a thousand one-dollar bills stacked neatly in the stall.

In a way, Belichick and Pioli got the equivalent of a cash shower on draft day. It was their best overall work since their arrival in New England three years earlier. They played chess with their draft picks, and they played it so often and so quickly that they usually made their partners do something regrettable. It started before the draft, when they traded Tebucky Jones to New Orleans for three draft picks, the highest one being a third-rounder. They then took that third from New Orleans, number seventy-eight, and traded it to Miami for a 2004 second-rounder. In other words, they moved up at least fourteen draft slots simply by waiting a year for the pick.

As the scouts had said for months, the Bledsoe first-rounder became a defensive lineman, Ty Warren, a three-hundred-pounder who was difficult to run against. The other first-rounder was sent to Baltimore in exchange for a 2003 second and a 2004 first. Already, then, the Patriots had two firsts and two seconds for the following season. They added potential starters in the later rounds with cornerbacks Asante Samuel and Eugene Wilson, as well as center Dan Koppen.

It was a brilliant day of trading, but it was too dizzying to be seen that way by the local football columnists.

"If the non-NFL draftniks are to be believed, and they have developed a deep reservoir of credibility over the years, the Pats didn't come close to getting the best bang for their buck," Kevin Mannix wrote in the *Herald*. At the *Globe*, Ron Borges continued his trend of healthy Patriots skepticism. "To paraphrase a statement once used by Ronald Reagan to defeat Jimmy Carter in the 1980 presidential election: 'Is your team better off today than it was four months ago?'" he wrote. "How you answer that should tell you how you feel about what went on in Foxboro yesterday."

What went unnoticed was how the Patriots were beginning to affect their division. Before the draft, they made no effort to quell rumors that they were looking to move from the middle of the first round into the top five. They never considered it. Belichick didn't think it made financial sense. But they didn't mind the unfounded rumors; misinformation at draft time was good for the Patriots poker game. The Jets did move up, however, selecting a defensive tackle named Dewayne Robertson. They vacated the spot that Pittsburgh used on the dynamic Polamalu. The last-place Bills had already conceded their first to the Patriots. And Miami, in its desperation, had made the foolish your-third-for-our-second trade, a deal that would be vetoed in most fantasy football leagues.

Not only was the team better off than it had been four months earlier; the division was worse. Belichick still believed that he needed a nose tackle, though, and he eventually traded for the most massive one available in comic-book character Ted Washington. He was six feet five inches, at least 375 pounds, and hilarious. He loathed the media, but he'd often recite one-liners for his teammates and try to convince them what a fashion model he was.

The Patriots were feeling good about their direction, but that nagging piece of business remained. The Milloy situation still hadn't been resolved. Anyone listening to the conversations between the respective sides, player's and team's, knew what was coming. It always begins under the guise of a business conversation. Then there is a stalemate. Then there is one insult, followed by a misunderstanding, followed by true conviction that a fair contract can't be reached.

Then there is the good-bye.

So on September 1, five days before the beginning of the regular season, Belichick walked into a team meeting and broke the news. Milloy had been released. He said it plainly. There was no dramatic pausing, and the players didn't sense that he was wrestling with this transaction. In fact, that was the problem for many of them. This was all business. Cold. Economical. But no one was willing to let it pass that easily.

Chapter Six

THE PELTS OF SUCCESS

It's a strange thing to say, and most people wouldn't want it to be said of them, but it was true: Bill Belichick was good at being called idiotic. Experienced, too. It was a claim that even the reality stars and entertainment villains couldn't honestly make. Everyone knew that they were acting. They were just playing the character who, when confronted with scowls and slings, goes about his normal business, unaffected.

Not Belichick. He wasn't pretending to be the boss who could give sentimentality a sharp elbow on the way to an unpopular decision. He had done it many times, in multiple cities.

The angry fans outside one of his 1993 press conferences in Cleveland had been real. They pushed, pounded, and tried to tip a trailer that they knew he was in and screamed, "Bill must go." That was shortly after he had fired local hero Bernie Kosar, the quarterback who smiled with gritty Cleveland when it was fashionable to laugh at it. Kosar wasn't a good player anymore, and Belichick said it. The fans didn't like the message, the messenger, or his curt delivery.

The president of the New York Jets had truly been a critic, albeit a passive-aggressive one, when he psychoanalyzed Belichick in front of the New York media in January 2000. His diagnosis was that Belichick was in "personal turmoil." That was after Belichick had gotten all dressed up in a suit and tie to resign, when everyone thought he was there to accept the job. "The Tuna," Bill Parcells, learned about the switch at the last minute and went back to his office. The headline writers went into a frenzy: BELICHICKEN, BRING BACK TUNA, and WE NEED TUNA, NOT TUNA HELPER.

Rodney Harrison was appearing as himself in September 2003 when he commented, "This is supposed to be about winning games, and I can't say we're better without Lawyer. You'd have to be an idiot to think we're a better team without Lawyer Milloy." That was when the release of Milloy had gone public, when Belichick had every reason to feel like the loneliest man in New England. There weren't many friendly spaces where he could go and have people sympathize with his way of thinking. The opinions about him were everywhere, in his own locker room and beyond, and they were forceful.

Duplicitous. Arrogant. Megalomaniacal. Pond scum. And that was all from one *Herald* article at breakfast. Elsewhere, one popular thought was that it was only a matter of time before something like this happened to every Patriot. Another was that at least one team leader had lost his sense of devotion to the franchise since, indeed, it was the franchise that had kicked a player like Milloy "to the curb." A straightforward angle was that Belichick's move was a major distraction to a team trying to win. And those weren't the reactionary analyses from the talking heads. They were in-house quotes from Tom Brady, Tedy Bruschi, and Damien Woody.

This was the part of Belichick's unusual talent, as it were, that frustrated so many people. He'd stand there and get crushed, without the expected or desired wince. He'd get ripped apart on sports-talk radio, in the sports pages, or just down the hall in the locker room, and it didn't move him into a mode of self-advocacy or correction. Whether that was a personality flaw or a divine gift was for others to decide. Maybe this was one of the reasons he encouraged his assistants and scouts to logically disagree with him. He'd had entire metro areas angry with him, often well past the boundary of logic; having a few employees do the same in a conference room was, by comparison, a massage.

The fear in New England was that he was in a crisis, the kind that would result in an inability to lead this particular team. After all, he had cut one of his captains just five days before the start of the regular season. And as bad luck would have it for the Patriots, not only had that captain joined Drew Bledsoe and divisional opponent Buffalo; the Patriots' first game of the season was against Buffalo. It was going to be tough to move on from this when they'd have to relive it again in five days.

"I understood the business side. But I think from a respect standpoint and a moral code of ethics, if it was going to go down like that, do it earlier," Ty Law says now. "Give him an opportunity because he was a good soldier, a Pro Bowl player, and a team captain. The vocal leader of the defense. Plain and simple. No question about it. Do it earlier. He bled Patriots. If you look at the Super Bowl win, Lawyer is the only one who started to look for Belichick afterwards.

"It hurt him. I got more upset because I could see how hurt he was by it. It was all over money. We were pissed. You didn't do that to a team captain. He always had something to say, motivating the team. He was passionate. He loved the team. The way they did him at that time, that was some disrespectful stuff. It was bad. We tried to go on like normal, but it wasn't normal.

"Lawyer was the first situation where I was like, 'They really don't give a damn. This is a business for real.' That was the real wake-up call. I thought, 'Who's next? That can happen to me.'"

There were several reasons the head coach didn't see things the same way the crowd did. For one, he saw his players in a way that they hadn't seen themselves. Many of them, along with members of the media, continued to say that Milloy was the heart and soul of the team. Belichick saw a team that couldn't be defined that simply. Over the span of his controversies, Belichick had heard "The Arrogant" before his name so often that it became a royal prefix. He was labeled arrogant for a range of things, including his unpredictable approach to team-building. He never paused to point out the irony: He was called arrogant for making uncommon decisions that built up this team in the first place, and now he was being called it for making moves that the masses either didn't agree with or didn't understand.

He thought his team was superior to last year's version, and that clicked into place for him less than two weeks before Milloy's release. That's when the trade for nose tackle Ted Washington was made. He was ecstatic to have an anchor like the thirty-five-year-old Washington, who confidently told his teammates that he'd retire if an opposing team didn't honor him with constant double teams. He had the most predictable and accurate nickname in the league: "Mount Washington." His listed weight should have been a range, anywhere between 365 and 390.

This was also a quality of Belichick's that was tough to grasp. While the conversation often focused on the players that the TV cameras follow, either for sound bites or highlights, Belichick spent a lot of brainpower under the hood of the team. A valid criticism was that sometimes he stayed under there too long with the mechanics, at the expense of occasional common courtesies. Many people who saw him daily noticed that he could go to subterranean levels with his thoughts, and he'd be so deep in them that he'd walk by without so much as a hello. Leading up to the opener, that weakness of his was actually a good thing because there wasn't much that could be said that would reverse what he'd done. They just had to win some games.

On a perfect September afternoon in western New York, it appeared that Belichick's tinkering had gone too far. Milloy was energized wearing his familiar number 36 uniform, and the Bills' game operations crew played up the drama by saving the safety's introduction until the very end.

Not only did he look like the same disruptive player that Patriots fans had seen in 106 consecutive games; he was making a case for another item on his résumé: defensive coordinator. There was absolutely nothing, not a single thing, that the Patriots did that the Bills weren't ready for. The natural thought was that Milloy had arrived in Buffalo and poured out every detail that he had learned in fifty-one games under Belichick. Of course, that wasn't the reality. But what difference did that make? This was an afternoon for instant story lines, not the steady rigor of a football season.

The Bills won easily, 31–0. Brady threw four interceptions, one of them caught by a defensive tackle with a patriotic name and Patriot ties: Sam Adams. He wasn't quite as big as Washington, but it was close. So imagine ol' Sam Adams, whose father, Sam Sr., played for the Patriots in the 1970s, picking off a ball and running toward the end zone. Just before the goal line, the big man did a dance after which bellies and the stadium shook. It was hysterical. As afternoon turned into evening, Milloy was in the parking lot hanging out with tailgating Bills fans. He'd had a lot to say before he got there, and so did many others in Buffalo and Boston.

"I got some stats now," Milloy said after the game, referring to his lack of forced fumbles and interceptions the year before. "That was one of their tactics. They made sure I ended up with no stats and then they used it against me. Belichick is so worried about himself and his own stature. There's more credit that goes to his game plan than goes to his players. He doesn't play on the field. He had a game plan today, didn't he? How'd it work out?"

There was a reference to Milloy daily. Usually a new development would come along to knock the previous big story off its perch. Not this time.

On Monday, *Globe* columnist Dan Shaughnessy wrote that the Bills were division favorites and Brady "won't be eager for a rematch with Takeo Spikes and Friends in Foxboro December 27th." It was Ron Borges's turn on Tuesday, and he not only sensed the void of Milloy; he questioned the effectiveness of the Brady–Charlie Weis offense. "Has the NFL caught up with Brady and Weis? Have defensive coordinators who get overpaid to devote their lives to solving these kinds of problems succeeded?" he wrote.

Wednesday was relatively quiet. Oh, except for the rumor that Belichick had banned his players from attending a Milloy fund-raiser in downtown Boston. The team's public-relations director hurriedly denied the rumor. It was safe to conclude, then, that the appearance of several Patriots at their ex-teammate's night of bowling, wings, and airing of grievances was either inevitable or normal.

Thursday was for analogies and apologies. Cris Collinsworth, on HBO's *Inside the NFL*, compared Belichick to "a great doctor with a bad bedside manner. For him to completely misread the pulse of that team and not understand what Milloy meant to the locker room, I can't believe he was that far removed from it." Bruschi apologized for saying his all-out commitment to the team had wavered. He explained that he had been emotional when he made that comment and, now, there wasn't another team that he ever wanted to play for.

Things started to settle a bit on Friday, with Karen Guregian writing in the *Herald* that it was time to focus on the players, not Belichick. "Shame on them if they're still wallowing in the fall-out from losing Milloy. Shame on them if they look comatose in another game because of something that amounts to a business decision." Saturday was for the *Buffalo News* and an ode to Milloy. In the piece, Milloy admitted that Robert Kraft called him, and that he had hung up on the Patriots owner.

No one in New England was ready for what was said on Sunday, and it's something that actually unified the locker room after two weeks of anger, insecurity, and mistrust. ESPN had just aired a story headlined HAS BELICHICK LOST HIS TEAM? Analyst Tom Jackson looked at the story, and then turned to look directly at the camera. "I want to say this very clearly," he said. "They hate their coach. And their season could be over, depending on how quickly they can get over this emotional devastation they suffered because of Lawyer Milloy. Belichick can't get them back. They'll have to do it on their own and win in spite of him."

The Patriots were playing a late-afternoon game in Philadelphia that day, and many of them had seen the bold statement before busing to the stadium. They were surprised by the message and the authority with which it had been delivered. Belichick heard about the report as well. His official response, publicly, was that he didn't want to dignify the comment with a response. But there was something about this report that penetrated the usual iron wall.

There was evidence in Philly that the Patriots were still alive. They won 31–10, and Bruschi sealed the win by returning an interception for a touchdown. The worst news of the day wasn't the commentary of Tom Jackson. Rather, it was that linebacker Rosevelt Colvin, playing just his second game as a Patriot, would have to watch the rest of the season from the sideline. He suffered a serious hip injury on what initially looked like a routine play. The Patriots split their games the next two weeks, up against the Jets and down against Washington, although some members of the offense believed that the Washington loss featured an atypical Tom Brady. The Patriots were the more talented and disciplined team, but they were struggling against a team led by made-for-college coach Steve Spurrier. Brady had his all-around most inaccurate day as a pro, throwing four interceptions and, surprisingly, calling the wrong plays in the fourth quarter.

"He'd make the call and I'd look at him like, 'What the fuck?'" Christian Fauria says. "These were easy plays, too. They were supposed to be to the left and he'd call them to the right. It was the only time I ever questioned him."

After the game, as Fauria and Brady talked on the bus, the on-field confusion made sense. Brady had been concussed and stayed in the game. The NFL was still years away from enlightening itself and its players on head trauma, and years away from the issue being documented by one of Brady's teammates.

It was early October in New England, and by using ordinary logic, it was understandable why the focus was not on the 2-2 Patriots. This was when all hopes were brought to the altar of the Red Sox. They seemed different from their teasing, heart-stopping ancestors. The new owners had hired the youngest general manager in baseball history, twenty-eight-year-old Theo Epstein. The team bonded over shaved heads, karaoke, and a catchy slogan, "Cowboy Up." The region was so fixated on the Sox and their possibility of greatness that many were slow to recognize the football brilliance that was happening in front of them.

When the Patriots beat the Titans for their third win of the season, the game was viewed as a warm-up act. That same evening, Fenway Park was the stage for a wild Red Sox comeback win over the Athletics that extended the season. The next week, after a

17–6 shutdown of the Giants, the Patriots were put on the waiting list again. The attention now was on the Yankees, whom the Sox had played and fought the night before. There had been baseballs thrown high and inside, profane words and gestures, a fight in the bullpen between two Yankees and a Sox groundskeeper, and, an image for the ages, star pitcher Pedro Martinez, thirty-one, being bull-rushed by Yankees coach Don Zimmer, seventy-two.

By the time the Patriots arrived in Miami the next week, no one at home was talking about the players. They were talking about a controversial management decision, and this time Belichick was not the target. Everyone was enraged that Grady Little, the Sox manager, had refused to take a tiring Martinez out of game seven against the Yankees. A 5–2 lead was blown, and for the eighty-fifth consecutive year, there would be no World Series title for Boston.

Belichick had been opposed by cities and regions before, but at least his opponents had all been alive. Little was forced to defend himself against the present and the past. The rage directed at him was for not only what he had done at Yankee Stadium, but what his predecessors had done to frustrate fans in 1986, 1978, 1975, 1967, 1946...all the way back to Babe Ruth being sold away in 1919. Even Belichick would have had a hard time surviving that. And Little didn't. He was the main character in a modern-day Western, the unwanted visitor given a generous severance package and a one-way ticket out of town.

While this was going on, the Patriots quietly won two more games, against the Dolphins and Browns, good for a 6-2 record.

Every week, though, there seemed to be a major Sox story that hid just how good the Patriots had become. One day, Belichick-like, GM Theo Epstein placed high-maintenance outfielder Manny Ramirez on waivers. He and the remaining $104 million on his contract were there for anyone in the league to pluck and claim as their own. The next day, there was a report that Boston was interested in acquiring Texas Rangers shortstop Alex Rodriguez. And if they got him, that meant their own previously beloved shortstop, Nomar Garciaparra, would be playing somewhere else. It was all sports theater, and it was the leading discussion topic in town.

The Patriots enjoyed the drama from afar. How things had changed; the Sox were the region's most public dysfunctional family now and the Patriots were their drama-free, bookish alter egos. Finally, eight weeks after the release of Milloy, they were able to recognize the vision that Belichick had seen for them late in the summer. They possessed style and substance in abundance.

They knew they had a superstar in Brady, who was a young Paul Newman and Joe Montana rolled into one. He had a full celebrity life, from getting the attention of Hollywood actresses, to judging beauty pageants, to posing on magazine covers, to hinting that a career in politics could be possible one day. Through it all, he realized how important it was to be one of the guys. He was just Tommy to them, and sometimes they teased him mercilessly. He competed intensely in practice, and when he got upset his voice would rise to soprano levels. "C'mon guys!" he'd exhort, his voice squeaking. The defensive players would mimic him, and the intensity level would increase for everyone.

Similar competitions would happen in the meeting rooms, where players competed to see who was hydrating the most. Willie McGinest started it by drinking a twelve-ounce bottle of water. Someone else would come in another day with seventeen ounces. McGinest would counter with a gallon and make a production of drinking it slowly in front of the entire team. The practice field was littered with water jugs inscribed with the players' names. Players would look at one another and tease, "I'm gaining on you." They competed in their unpredictable fine system, where one could be fined for being late, telling an unfunny joke, or wearing an outfit that represented poor style and judgment. They even had competitions to prevent being a dullard in practice. They'd watch the practice film and blurt out when someone missed an assignment. "That's one," a player would say. "Oh, there's another one..." It went on and on until the end of the film. The number of mental errors would be tallied, and then someone would head to the weight room for the big "prize" that no one wanted: a championship belt, which was really just a weightlifting belt, for the king of mental errors.

The message was drilled in daily. You've got to pay attention or risk being called out by your peers, long before Belichick got to you. It was all instructive to the injured Colvin, who had been to the play-offs just once in his first four seasons in the league with the Bears. "Tom had it and a lot of other people did, too. Mike Vrabel, Richard Seymour, Willie, Tedy. It was an attitude of winning," he says. "It's a culture. You've got to sacrifice. On defense, you can't just run up the field and get sacks. It takes a lot more than that. And if you did something wrong, you'd get called out. It didn't matter who you were, even Tom. When you do things wrong there, you get called out."

Showing that he had learned from raw linebacker Bryan Cox two years earlier, Tedy Bruschi would remind his teammates what he needed on "rush" calls. He'd scream out, "Butch! Butch!" which translated was, *Hey, make sure you hit that running back and knock him off his route as you're on your way to the quarterback*. In moments of selfishness, sometimes guys didn't want to hear "Butch." It didn't always provide the glory of a sack. Bruschi would still insist on it, and if there was any problem, he'd give them the same advice that Cox had given: *Take it to the coaches*.

It rarely came to that. Most players were so well versed in the game plans that they knew what to do before Bruschi, Brady, or anyone else said it. A great example of their player-to-coach alertness happened on *Monday Night Football* in Denver. They were trailing the Broncos 24–23, backed up to their most extreme position, at the one-yard line. After three incomplete passes and just under three minutes remaining in the game, Belichick decided that it was best to take an intentional safety. That way, the Patriots would still be able to tie it with a field goal, and they could get out of this risky situation by executing a good free kick.

It was a move that worked flawlessly, and it culminated in a late touchdown pass from Brady to receiver David Givens. Ironically, the winning pass in front of a national audience was an illustration of how underrated Brady was. He was so smooth at the line of scrimmage that he didn't give hints at how quickly he was processing and adjusting before the snap of the ball. He made it look too easy. Even after the snap, on the winning play, Givens had run the wrong route. Brady noticed it when he looked Givens's way and instantly made the adjustment. The Patriots had won their fifth straight game and were now 7-2.

Belichick was amazed by what Brady routinely saw, and impressed with the intelligent way that he maximized each play. One of the defensive coaches, Rob Ryan, had begun calling Brady "Belichick with a Better Arm," and the description was as precise as a Brady throw.

While Tom Jackson had said that the players hated Belichick, many of the players were starting to notice the opposite. He was informative in team meetings, with the right dose of self-deprecation, and the mixture always made them feel prepared for anything. "He gave me every aspect of the game. I had never thought of it in such detail from a defensive lineman's standpoint," Seymour says. "Bill's approach was, 'These are their weaknesses; we're going to take away their strengths.' He'd talk about the plays that were run when the tight end or fullback was on your side. He'd have you think about the tendency of an offense out of a one-back set versus two backs. He covered it all. Your awareness level went way up."

Belichick knew that the big story for the next game, against the Cowboys, would be his relationship with the new Dallas coach. Guy by the name of Parcells. The players smiled when he told them, "Don't get distracted by irrelevant aspects of this game. Belichick versus Parcells? We're both assholes." They roared and shook their heads knowingly when he pointed out that he and Parcells last coached together five years earlier and, "What were you doing five years ago? And what people were you doing it with?"

He had put them at ease during the week. On game day, the Patriots' league-best defense took care of the rest. They shut out the Cowboys, 12–0, and no one was writing about Tuna Helper anymore. In fact, one of the daring assistant coaches with a sense of humor had ribbed Belichick by leaving a stuffed animal, a tuna, on his desk. Those kinds of things could be done after six consecutive wins. It was seven in a row after an overtime win in Houston. The next stop was Indianapolis, where the Colts had the identical record as the Patriots, 9-2.

The Patriots had led 31–10 in the second half, but Manning never believed that he was in a hopeless situation in the temperature-controlled comfort of his domed stadium. The Colts had come back to tie the score at 31, given up a touchdown to trail 38–31, and then gotten a field goal to draw within four, 38–34.

Now they were in a situation where they seemingly couldn't lose: They had the ball at the two-yard line, first-and-goal, with forty seconds to play. The only mystery was how they were going to win this. Their first try was on the ground, and that netted a yard. Second-and-goal from the one. They tried a run again, but Mount

Washington had positioned himself to cut off any creases between the guard and center, and it was as if the play never happened. No gain. Third-and-goal from the one. Eighteen seconds left. Manning threw a fade route to one of his lesser receivers, thus resulting in a low-percentage play and an incompletion. On fourth down, there were no surprises, and the Patriots blew up a running play to win just before time expired.

There were very few questions with Patriots games now, especially when they played at home. After giving up those 34 points in Indianapolis, they shut out the Dolphins, 12–0. That win gave them the division title for the second time in three years, and it should have been the celebratory topic on sports-talk radio. But there had been much speculation about the Red Sox and popular shortstop Nomar Garciaparra. So as Seymour prepared to do a radio interview on WEEI, he was put on deck by a caller, Nomar from Southern California.

The shortstop, still on his Hawaiian honeymoon, was calling in to the station to say that he didn't want to leave town. The hosts apologized to Seymour, giving him the *Hey, you know we have to take this call* treatment. He smiled. Belichick always told his players that regular-season wins don't get you much in the NFL. He was right. Nine wins in a row and the division title got you put on hold on local radio.

The team was so steady and consistent that one *Herald* columnist, Michael Gee, even said that they should lose *because* they were so steady and consistent. "The only motive for suggesting New England might want to finish 13-3 and not 14-2 is one man's devout belief in arithmetic," he wrote. "All winning streaks end, and the longer one goes on, the more likely it is to end. For the Pats to run the table to a title, their winning streak must reach 15 games. That's not just a long run, it's an historic one."

Losing games? On purpose? Even the harshest Belichick critics who had said that the coach was doing just that with the release of Milloy didn't mean it literally. Anyway, if a fifteen-game winning streak is what it would take to get everything they wanted— no more losses and another Lombardi Trophy—that's what they believed they would do.

They went into their final game of the regular season against the 6-9 Buffalo Bills. The Bills were quieter and less optimistic than they had been in September. Instead of people in Buffalo talking about the Super Bowl, they wondered about rebuilding. Their head coach, Gregg Williams, was likely to be fired. Moving on from Williams would mean that Belichick would be competing against his third different Bills head coach in four seasons. The new coach would likely want a new quarterback, too. Bledsoe had been much worse than he was in 2002. He had thrown more interceptions than touchdowns, and it was hard to believe that those joyful stories in the *Buffalo News* about the players who had "come from New England wrapped in a bow" were written in the same calendar year. It was a wrong-way dynasty; the Patriots were methodically turning their division into a wasteland.

Milloy had played well for the Bills, but those who knew him well could see it and hear it. He didn't always see his Buffalo teammates on off days because he was in Boston, seeing the guys from the team that was still in his heart. He missed the city, the Patriots, and even the exacting eye of Belichick.

Brady had been asked to participate in a movie by the Farrelly brothers, the Rhode Island natives behind the outrageous Hollywood comedies *Dumb and Dumber, Kingpin,* and *There's Something About Mary.* The quarterback accepted and got a spot for Milloy as well. The title of the movie, *Stuck on You,* was perfect for the story on the screen and the one in the Bills' defensive huddle. But the final game of the regular season just didn't seem believable, even in the Farrelly brothers' world. It had nothing to do with the Patriots' win, their twelfth in a row, completing a home schedule where they allowed an average of 8 points per game. It was that final score, which seemed scripted by someone who had gone too far with the revenge theme. It was 31–0 at the end of the regular season, just as it had been in the beginning.

As the play-offs began to unfold, it was obvious what the biggest sacrifice of being a 2003 Patriot was. Sometimes, when you played for this team, your talent could be hidden, right before thousands of people in the stands and millions watching on TV. A quarterback like Brady, gifted as well as studious, might be overlooked when compared to Peyton Manning. On this team, sometimes the game plan would call for forty-five passes, and sometimes it was half of that. Maybe it's why the perception of the quarterbacks was so different. Manning and Tennessee's Steve McNair shared the league's MVP award, while Brady received no consideration for it.

No one, not even in the White House, questioned Brady's leadership qualities. He was invited to watch the State of the Union address with First Lady Laura Bush. He looked the part there in the box, in a classic suit, clapping at appropriate moments during the speech. Strangely, he didn't get as much credit for his leadership and expertise *in* football as he did outside of it.

On this team, a wide receiver wasn't guaranteed to get the same amount of targets every week. Here, defensive tackles would sometimes exit a game with a tackle or two, applauded by the coaches and met with indifference by the media. You have to be secure in your talent on teams like these because you'll be known as a football player's football player, and sometimes even they would miss what you were doing.

"This is what we started to do: We slowly accumulated winning stat guys as opposed to the high-sack, high-interception guys," former Patriots linebacker Matt Chatham says. "Willie McGinest, Mike Vrabel. Those guys are way more valuable if they get eight sacks rather than sixteen. Dominating the edge, getting on the tight end, blowing up wide receivers and never letting them get into the pattern. That's way more valuable than sixteen sacks.

"I think that the world thinks that the sixteen-sack guy is more valuable, but the Patriots don't think that, and you can get into the economics of this: The sixteen-sack guy costs twice as much as the other guy. And once you get to a certain point, it's saturation. It's just sixteen plays and when you play five hundred snaps, it's not that important. It just isn't. Who are the best rerouters among outside linebackers? Who are the best edge-setters? Does anyone in the media know that?"

It wasn't just the media in 2003. The Patriots' first play-off game was against Tennessee and McNair. On the coldest day of the year, with a game-time temperature of four degrees and a windchill of minus ten, the Patriots got into a frostbitten street fight with the Titans. There were no comfortable moments in the game, whether it was warmth or aesthetics. Consecutive win number thirteen was secured when Tennessee receiver Drew Bennett dropped a ball on fourth down. A catch would have put the Titans in field goal range. Instead they lost, 17–14. And one of their guards, Zach Piller, guaranteed that the Patriots wouldn't win the Super Bowl.

The next week, the Patriots were visited by the other side of the split MVP award, Peyton Manning.

This was what it meant to be a Patriot; winning had to be satisfactory enough, because the hype and awards weren't always going to be there. Brady should have known that better than most. He had grown up watching Montana, his generation's symbol for winning. Montana had won his first Super Bowl at age twenty-five, but he didn't win his first MVP until he was thirty-three. Sometimes it took a while for people to catch up.

The president of the Colts, Bill Polian, watched the conference championship from the press box. Members of the media could see and hear him pounding the table and cursing. He hated what he was seeing out there. As Chatham mentioned, there were lots of jams and reroutes by linebackers. Lots of instances where receivers were obliterated at the line of scrimmage before they had a chance to give Manning a clean target. The Patriots called it suffocating; Polian called it holding.

"Throw the flag!" he bellowed several times.

He was an influential member in the league when it came to shaping policy, and so was head coach Tony Dungy. The Patriots weren't going to be able to play like this during the 2004 season. But that season hadn't arrived yet, and Manning still had to try to pass his way to the Super Bowl. He seemed surprised at just how good Patriots corner Ty Law was. Four interceptions later, three of them to Law, and the Patriots were conference champions.

The fourteen-game winning streak didn't hover because they hadn't been coached to think that way. Belichick was all short-term focus and living in the moment. The criticism never distracted him, and he encouraged them to follow his lead. "Ignore the noise," he'd often say. It needed to be ignored. The Patriots were scheduled to meet the Carolina Panthers in Houston, and some wondered how their offensive line, without the injured Damien Woody, would be able to block the Panthers. Warren Sapp, the Pro Bowl defensive tackle, went on national TV and said that it couldn't be done, and he singled out Patriots backup Russ Hochstein.

"He couldn't block either of you two," Sapp told ESPN's Michael Wilbon and Tony Kornheiser.

Even on the day of the game, with the Patriots in position to claim their place among the greatest teams in pro football history, there was noise. Some of it came from the Panthers, who wanted the Patriots to know that they weren't afraid of them or their mystique. Some of it came from Justin Timberlake and Janet Jackson, who performed at halftime. The nation and the FCC were shocked when America was exposed to Jackson's breast. The game itself, entertaining as it was, couldn't compete with the conversations about nudity and multi-million-dollar fines.

Still, Hochstein and his friends on the offensive line found a way to block the Panthers. Brady threw the ball a season-high forty-eight times and wasn't sacked. He tallied 354 yards and three touchdown passes. He ceded the stage, briefly, to allow Adam Vinatieri to kick another winning field goal, this one from forty-one yards. The 32–29 win, the fifteenth in succession, had been like so many others. Close yet convincing. Dramatic yet locked into the same ending.

That's what their team was for the season, and that's what they were going to be as long as they continued to win. In a way, Brady and his teammates had been correct to lament the release of Milloy. Tough decisions would have to be made to ensure more parades, more rings, and more kid-like moments when they'd press their fingers on the shining Lombardi Trophy and see all their fingerprints winking back at them.

It was natural to become emotional in these moments and want to keep everybody. So the players were angry when it was time to say good-bye, because that wasn't their strength. They weren't big-picture economists the way their coach was. It was a necessary and basic trait for those who wanted to be dynastic architects. Be clear, be thorough, be decisive, be bold. Be unpopular. And, sure, be a heartbreaker as well. A big parade was certainly awaiting the Patriots again in Boston. So was another tumultuous, controversial offseason.

CHAPTER SEVEN

ROLLING

There were many similarities between this outrageous regional party and the previous one, two years earlier. Just like the last time, having a car in downtown Boston was useless. The roads surrounding the parade route were closed as the day's traffic patterns were all made on foot. Once again, some children and their parents decided that school on this Tuesday afternoon was optional, ignoring the advice from Mayor Tom Menino, who had said of the kids, "They can go home and watch it on the news at six o'clock."

The mayor said it and, based on the numbers, everyone did the opposite.

This time the crowd was slightly bigger, from 1.2 million New Englanders in February 2002 to 1.5 in February 2004, but the dancing was just as strong. Ty Law had dominated this postseason, just as he had the last one, and the cornerback once again convinced Tom Brady, Bill Belichick, and Robert Kraft to show a wild side. Tedy Bruschi saw the moves of his coach and quipped, "If I was a member of the scouting department, I would say he's a little stiff in the hips."

The biggest difference could be seen and heard in Brady. He had been very much in the background the first time around, playing the happy-to-be-here role to the hilt. He was a star now, riding in the lead duck boat with Belichick, Kraft, and the latest Lombardi Trophy. He now had two Super Bowl titles, two Super Bowl MVP awards, and a career record of 40-12, including 6-0 in the postseason. He'd gotten the blessing of "The Godfather," Bill Walsh, who'd said that Brady was "as close to Joe Montana as anyone I've ever seen." According to *People* magazine, he was beautiful; according to roughly half of the people here, he was beautiful and a dream-ender because word had just leaked that he was dating actress Bridget Moynahan. In nearly three full seasons as a starting quarterback, he had gained access to a space that New Englanders were hesitant to open. It's the legends' suite of Bobby Orr and Bill Russell, Ted Williams and Larry Bird. And now, Tom Brady.

"We're baaaack," he announced in a singsong to the crowd, and the mass of them roared in return. What he didn't say, and what they all understood, was that they were back and still getting stronger. They would begin the next season as the best team in a disintegrating AFC East. They'd be looking to extend their fifteen-game winning streak, and they'd do it led by a twenty-seven-year-old Brady.

Still, some of the differences were hidden by the excesses and joys of the parade. Law was charismatic and funny in front of the crowd, but he was starting to believe that it was time for him to play somewhere else. People would soon be shocked to learn that it wasn't the first time he'd had that thought. He was a few weeks away from revealing that he'd asked Belichick to put him on the expansion draft list two years ago. Law had the same agent as Lawyer Milloy, and the safety's abrupt September release had been on his mind for months. If they could do that to a captain like Milloy, why wouldn't they do it to him, especially since his cap number was twice as large as Milloy's?

Law was still under contract, so whether he could return or

play for a new team wasn't up to him. The talent drain had begun, however, for some of his coaches and teammates. Rob Ryan, who had coached Patriots linebackers, left to become the Raiders' defensive coordinator. In a major blow, he was followed there by Mount Washington. The big man saw an opportunity to cash in for the last time in his career, and the Raiders were willing to pay twice as much as the Patriots.

One of Belichick's favorite students, Bobby Hamilton, also departed for Oakland. Once frustrated by the inability of his interior defensive linemen to play the correct technique, Belichick inserted the undersized-by-comparison Hamilton for proper demonstration. Indeed, as Jerry McDonald observed in the *Oakland Tribune*, Hamilton was just a winning player, one who "shows up in the jewelry box more than in the boxscore."

Another coach on the move was Jon Hufnagel, recruited by the Giants to be their offensive coordinator. Hufnagel had coached Brady and the quarterbacks, and his impressive résumé had begun when Josh McDaniels was in elementary school. Belichick still believed that McDaniels, a three-year apprentice, was more qualified than anyone in the league to replace Hufnagel and become Brady's tutor and confidant. McDaniels was twenty-eight, just sixteen months older than his quarterback. His promotion created an opening for a new coaching assistant, and the job went to a rocket scientist. Matt Patricia had an aeronautical engineering degree and the credentials to develop aircraft and space stations. Instead, he toted an inflatable mattress to his closet of an office in Foxboro, hoping to prove himself to Belichick.

The polite thing to say to someone charged with managing the postchampionship exodus is, *Well, it's a nice problem to have.* And that's partially true. If the downside to winning a Super Bowl is navigating some tricky financial and emotional obstacles, most people in the league would take it. Their reasoning is simple and usually correct: The Super Bowl is difficult to get to, let alone win; do everything possible to win it, and figure out the damages in the morning. It was that type of desperation that led some general managers to trade away future assets for a chance to win right now. It's why some coaches, feeling the pressure from their owners and general managers, opted for short-term solutions rather than a panoramic view of the team and franchise. Honestly, it's why some players got their rings and then started looking for the cash piles.

Belichick was on the other side of that reasoning, though. When he was an assistant coach with the Patriots in 1996, he would often run into team president Jonathan Kraft at five a.m. They'd either be in Foxboro in the stadium weight room or, if they were on the road, some hotel's fitness center. Sometimes their conversations would last forty-five minutes to an hour after the workout and Kraft, who has an MBA from Harvard, would listen to Belichick school him on maintaining excellence in the league. He'd talk about financial discipline, the strength of the draft, finding undervalued players, and the importance of the lower half of the fifty-three-man roster. Belichick didn't buy the premise of the system. He thought, even with a salary cap, that you could build a winner that could consistently be in the championship conversation.

"He clearly got it," Kraft said of Belichick years later. "It was certainly different than talking to Bill Parcells and Pete Carroll. It was on another plane, another dimension." Parcells and Carroll may have thought of the game in multidimensional ways when they coached the Patriots, but they didn't have those talks with the younger Kraft. His sense was that their expertise was in coaching the game, not coaching it along with a deep understanding of the game's finances.

From a player's perspective, there were two paths for free agents with Super Bowl rings, and the discount path was the road less trav- eled. The Patriots' best offensive lineman, Damien Woody, was faced with his own free agent decisions shortly after the parade, and one of them seemed obvious.

"Let me ask you this," he says now. "If you work for a good com- pany and another company comes along and says, 'We're going to double your salary,' what are you going to do? Some of my team- mates were upset with me, but I told them that I enjoyed what we accomplished together. We won our rings, but are those rings going to pay my bills when my career is over? I'm thinking, 'I have my whole life to live, not just my life in football.'"

Woody and Brady were the same age, and the lineman had been among the quarterback's trusted group of protectors since Brady took over the job in 2001. Woody had gotten used to Brady's com- plete authority of the huddle, how he would tell the team what was going to happen and then look at each guy "as if he was looking right through you and into your soul. He'd give you that look like, 'Are *you* going to bring it?'"

But with that said, the Detroit Lions were calling and they had millions of dollars to spend. The only problem was that they were awful. They'd won a combined ten games the previous three sea- sons, a win total that the 2003 Patriots had reached by November. It didn't matter. They offered Woody $31 million, the largest deal ever for an interior lineman. So after getting a $9 million signing bonus, a $2 million first-year base salary, and a $500,000 roster bonus, Woody was a Lion.

Belichick already had plenty to consider, and the flight of Woody complicated the to-do list. It was clearly money season in the NFL, for linemen and everyone else. It got Law's attention and, on a Saturday morning in March, Patriots fans were surprised to see the following headline trumpeted from the *Globe*: LAW OUT TO END

DAYS AS A PATRIOT. The fun-loving cornerback had sat down with beat writer Michael Smith for wings and drinks. The only question after reading the story was when did Law find time to eat? He had an arsenal of memorable one-liners in each paragraph. "I no longer want to be a Patriot," he asserted. "I can't even see myself putting on that uniform again, that's how bad I feel about playing here."

Law's teammates always said how entertaining he was, and linebacker Rosevelt Colvin referred to him as football's Richard Pryor. Law was just starting to warm up. He compared himself to a stock: "I'm Coca-Cola. I'm Microsoft. You know what you're going to get. Yeah, it's going to have its ups and downs, but I'm steady. And I'm the best. I'm just like that good ol' stock that you can depend on. I ain't that type, like Enron, to sit there and blow up, and next thing you know, you're bankrupt."

He said Belichick and Scott Pioli lied to him and therefore he was "drop-dead serious" about wanting out. "I am willing to pay them to let me go," he told Smith. "I told them, 'Instead of you paying me a $7 million salary, I'll pay you.'"

Based on Belichick's history of doing business, there was a good chance that Law would remain on the New England roster despite his fighting words. The reasons were simple: production and economics. Salaries were rising for all free agent players, and they could sometimes be astronomical for great players. Law was a great player, and he was under contract. Belichick didn't just thoughtlessly move on from talented, high-salaried players; any transaction would have to make sense. Releasing Law didn't. Yet the player still seemed to be searching for the phrase that would jab the most.

All of this was stunning and infuriating to Patriots followers. They had embraced the selfless identity of the team and, in heavily collegiate New England, the brainy profile of Belichick and his players was valued deeply. The *Jerry Maguire* NFL, all about the money, was for other teams. They were different.

But Law's unburdening was just a preview of things to come. The Patriots weren't *always* different, and they didn't *always* seek team-first guys. Belichick and his staff had engaged in innumerable discussions about who the team was and what risks it could afford to take. It had several pillars of performance and leadership, standing firm throughout the locker room. Brady was one of many. He was joined by Bruschi and Troy Brown, Richard Seymour and Rodney Harrison, Willie McGinest and Roman Phifer, Law and Larry Izzo and Adam Vinatieri. Belichick had been correct when he rejected the popular thought that Milloy, or anyone else, could solely represent the heart and soul of this team. It was too varied for that, and its power was derived from multiple sources, many of them overlooked.

There was a new question going into the 2004 season, and it had nothing to do with Law saying, "The team I've busted my ass for the last nine years doesn't realize or can't see that they're not giving me the proper respect or the contract that I deserve." Belichick knew that he wasn't going to trade or release Law, and that training camp was four months away. He was going to let him talk. He didn't offer a single word in response. Nothing. Even when Law said that the coach "lies to feed his family," Belichick was silent. Because that wasn't the big question for 2004.

Neither did it have anything to do with Bill Polian and Tony Dungy, from the rival Colts, lobbying the league. Polian was a team-building wiz with a volcanic temper. He had watched most of the 2003 conference championship with his teeth and fists clenched and his veins bulging. He and others were convinced that defenses were getting away with holds, so the offseason priority was to tailor the game to passing offenses.

That added a layer of intrigue to the critical question for the Patriots, because it was an issue on the ground. Could their culture absorb and correct a character like Corey Dillon? And even if it could, why would it want to?

It was the major topic of draft weekend when the Patriots took the easy second-rounder from Miami and traded it to Cincinnati for three-time Pro Bowl running back Dillon. In terms of reputation, he represented an athlete that the Belichick Patriots had tried to weed out, not bring in.

People said he ran angry, and that made sense because that was said of him away from football, too. He *was* angry. Once he'd been arrested for fourth-degree domestic assault. Another time it was for driving under the influence and driving with a suspended license. A staggering nine other times, as a teenager, it was for various offenses.

"The thing about Bill is that he not only knows what kind of players fit his system, he can get in people's heads," Lionel Vital, the longtime scout, says. "He's the best in the business at working with personalities; Bill can work with anybody. He'll reach you. If you're a different bird, he'll reach you in his own way."

Belichick traded for the twenty-nine-year-old back, believing that the change would revive him and that the locker room would restore him. If Belichick and Pioli were correct, they'd have themselves an All-Pro running back. If they missed, they would move on from him. The cost of doing business in this case, a second-round pick, wasn't even a factor, since the Patriots owned four draft selections among the top ninety-five slots.

They hadn't just been helped by the extra pick from Miami. They also owned Baltimore's first-round pick, twenty-first overall, in addition to their own pick at thirty-two. Their idea was to draft running back Steven Jackson at number twenty-one, bring him along slowly, and then have him in position to take over as the lead back when Dillon's inevitable decline began in a few years. But the draft took a strange turn. Jackson was still available as the picks got into the teens, but so was a superb nose tackle from the University of Miami named Vince Wilfork. For all the draft homework that the Patriots had done, this was a surprise. They thought he could go to Chicago at fourteen, but the Bears took a defensive tackle named Tommie Harris instead. Wilfork was officially a slider.

Belichick knew that as much as he loved Jackson, he'd take the nose tackle over the running back. He already had a back; but with the departure of "Big Ted," the coach needed a young player who could be groomed for the dirty work of interior line play. So as the draft marched on to fifteen, sixteen, and seventeen, the Patriots were on the phone. They were trying to package their second first-rounder with another pick so they could be in position for Wilfork and Jackson. It didn't work. The Rams moved up for Jackson at number twenty-four, leaving the Patriots with Georgia tight end Ben Watson.

The euphoria of the Patriots' good fortune selecting college players didn't last long. Two days after the 2004 draft, there was a tragic story in Columbia, South Carolina, a domestic dispute that ended in a murder-suicide. According to police reports, Richard Seymour Sr., fifty-one, fatally shot his girlfriend, thirty-six-year-old Coretta Myers, and then shot himself. His son, twenty-four, was out of town when he heard the halting news. He didn't recognize the man described in the reports, and he spent hours upon hours in counseling and prayer and reflection, trying to grasp it.

They had spent so much time together, at home and at work. They shared everything. He had been there on draft day. He had been there for the birth of his grandson, another male in the family carrying his name; the child was nicknamed "RJ." The elder Seymour, proud and smiling, had been in New Orleans for the first Super Bowl title, in Houston for the second. He had shown his son how to work hard with no excuses, as they both carried bricks in the blazing South Carolina summers. And now he was gone.

"We were best friends as I was growing up," Seymour says now. "He's the one who taught me the game of football. When it happened, and it took a lot of great books and great people to help me get to this point, I tried to look at the blessings and the foundation that he had given me. He'd been able to spend time with his grandkids. We'd spent time together at Super Bowls.

"I've always been strong in my faith, and everything went back to that. From a spiritual perspective, everything happens for a reason and you try to pull the good from anything that happens to you. I thought, 'I have a wife and kids and mom, and they're looking up to me. I can't crumble.' There's a passage in the Bible, Second Chronicles, that says, 'The battle isn't yours, the battle is the Lord's.' I did try and have tried to stay mindful of that."

As the Patriots began training camp, Seymour was there and he looked the same. But the tragedy had changed him, and not just by shrouding him in sadness and, at times, leading him to feel sorry for himself. It also strengthened his faith. He believed, more than ever, that the ability to play football was larger than the NFL and truly "an opportunity to give God glory," as well as, he says "God building me up for my story to tell."

On the field, there was no pending controversy. Law had been seen and heard on multiple media outlets in the spring, but he was a different man in the summer. He said he wanted to finish his career with the Patriots and that he had no problems with Belichick. Law was instinctive on the field, and his reversal with Belichick proved that he was the same way away from the game.

He wasn't going to win a PR fight with the head coach in New England, and neither was anyone else. The coach had power, championships, a winning record in debatable decisions, and the overwhelming support of ownership and the fans. He had not only changed football in the region; he'd changed the contents of sports debate. Many conversations about Belichick's unusual moves often devolved to shrugs and the phrase "In Bill We Trust."

"From the experiences I'd seen with Drew and Lawyer, I conducted myself the way that I did accordingly," Law says now. "Maybe it wasn't always right, but I was trying to think, 'Hey, this is business. This is where I have the leverage and this is where I may not have the leverage. I'm going to conduct myself this way and know my worth even if the Patriots don't.'

"I had a man-to-man conversation with Coach Belichick. I admitted it then and I can admit it now: I could have handled things differently. Sometimes emotion takes over. You get caught up in it. I've always been one who takes someone at their word. It could be something simple like, 'Ty, we're going to work this out.' I'll take you at your word; we've got the basis of a deal. And when things changed I just said, 'Liar.' I used that particular word because I thought that I was lied to. There were no promises made, but I thought I was lied to. I could have used a different choice of words and not done it as publicly."

These days, the scathing analyses were for the other three sports teams who had yet to deliver what Belichick and the Patriots had. The Red Sox, for example, had spent wildly in the offseason and had hired a new manager, Terry Francona. They'd even had the gall to trade Nomar Garciaparra, the franchise shortstop who was friendly with Ted Williams and hit like Joe DiMaggio. Theo Epstein, the Sox's youthful general manager, admitted that he was so unnerved by his franchise-altering trade that he took Ambien so he could sleep. Even with all the activity, the Sox were ten games out of first place in mid-August.

All the attention was on the Patriots a month later when they unfurled their second championship banner at Gillette Stadium. Elton John, a friend of the Kraft family, was performing along with Mary J. Blige, Lenny Kravitz, Destiny's Child, and Toby Keith. On the field, the entertainment was almost guaranteed to be satisfying due to the opponent: the Colts.

Both organizations tried to be diplomatic about it publicly, but they couldn't stand each other. Polian had helped shape three franchises into championship contenders, the Bills, Panthers, and Colts, but he'd never been a part of a Super Bowl champion. One of his best teams, the 1990 Bills, was slowed down just enough to earn rings for the Giants and their defensive coordinator, Belichick. It wasn't just that Polian and Belichick were opposites. Both of their franchises were, from the facilities they played in (outdoors versus a dome) to the players they scouted (bulkier for the Patriots versus leaner for the Colts) to the quarterbacks who led them.

In Brady's first two seasons as a starter, no one thought to compare him to Manning. He was seen as a quarterback who stayed out of the way, one who respectfully turned the game over to his defense when he got into trouble. Manning was the line-of-scrimmage control freak, conducting and directing, making sure everything was just right before he allowed one of his precious plays to be activated. His father had been an NFL quarterback. Just five months earlier, his younger brother, Eli, had been selected first overall in the draft. He was royalty, and Brady was the grinder.

That perception began to change in 2003, when the Patriots became that winning machine, on the strength of the defense and Brady. He was not a quarterback of extremes; he was inclined to give the game what it needed. Manning put up dazzling statistics almost every game, and those numbers promised to shine brighter due to the politicking that Polian had done on his behalf in the spring. The Brady-Manning debate always followed a pattern: It would be about quarterbacking in the beginning, winning in the middle, and by the end it was often a contentious and judgmental conversation about what a person found most valuable, individual award tours or excellence within a collective.

As usual, the first Patriots-Colts game of the season was decided in the fourth quarter. It actually had some humor to it. Colts kicker Mike Vanderjagt was known for his strong opinions and self-confidence, and had even criticized Manning and head coach Tony Dungy for not showing enough emotion. They kept him around because of his talent, as he had made an NFL-record forty-two consecutive field goals. With twenty-four seconds to play and the Patriots leading 27–24, Vanderjagt lined up for a forty-eight-yard attempt that would have sent the game into overtime. Moments before the attempt, he looked at the Patriots sideline and rubbed his fingers together, indicating that this one was easy money. He kicked it, the ball sailed to the right, and one streak ended while another one survived.

The Patriots had won their sixteenth game in a row.

It was only September, but people talked about the postseason when they analyzed the Patriots. Everyone, including their rivals, knew it wasn't worth pretending that someone in the AFC East could challenge them. Since that was the case, the team knew but never publicly acknowledged that there would be at least one game at home in January, maybe even two. The only mystery was how high this winning streak would go.

It reached seventeen in the desert, with a messy win over the Cardinals. Turnovers annoyed Belichick, and the Patriots already had five in two games. The positive thing was that they were displaying a dimension that had been missing for two years. Dillon got the ball twice as often as he had against the Colts and more than doubled his production: thirty-two carries, 158 yards. He was going to be a problem for some teams. Clearly, there were moments when defenders turned down opportunities to tackle him. The next game was in Buffalo against the Bills and their new head coach, Mike Mularkey. The new guy tried to motivate his team by purchasing copies of *Patriot Reign*, a book in which Belichick had been quoted dismissing the Bills' offensive line as "horseshit." It gave the Bills a jolt, but not enough of one. They lost, 31–17, and the Patriots' streak reached eighteen in a row.

Back at home, the Patriots were scheduled to play the Dolphins, the worst team in the league. Sometimes Miami was able to make things difficult for Brady, and there was some truth to that in this game. The quarterback completed just seven passes, but two were for touchdowns, and the Patriots had their NFL-record nineteenth consecutive win. They hadn't lost a game in 377 days. Their celebration was low-wattage. Richard Seymour and Rodney Harrison doused Belichick with ice water and the head coach, staying in character, wasn't too flowery in victory.

There was a palpable anger, which had been hammered into depression, lingering over the region before the game with the Seahawks on October 17. It had nothing to do with the Patriots. The Sox were in the American League championship series against the Yankees again, and it had been a disaster. They were coming off an embarrassing 19–8 loss in game three, trailed the series three games to none, and were now in sweep-prevention mode. They hadn't won a World Series title in eighty-six years, but they were the Sox, and they still had the ability to affect the moods of everyone. The Sox made you paranoid, always waiting for the slapstick moment when you learned that there was a cosmic joke being played and that it was on you. The Patriots were the opposite. Efficient and steady, they won again, for consecutive win number twenty.

From a New Englander's perspective, the world changed after the Patriots beat the Seahawks. Later that night, the Sox avoided the sweep against the Yankees with a succession of unlikely occurrences: They trailed by a run in the ninth, down three games to none, facing all-time great closer Mariano Rivera; a batter walked; a pinch runner got a steal; a single tied the score; and a slugger who had been signed for just over $1 million a year earlier, David Ortiz, hit a two-run homer in the twelfth to win it. They won again the next three nights, too, including Curt Schilling's bloody sock game in game six and a blowout in game seven, completing the most improbable comeback in sports history. The *Globe*'s Dan Shaughnessy was the author of the 1990 book *The Curse of the Bambino*, detailing the Sox's post–Babe Ruth absurdity. He wrote that the curse wasn't over until the Sox won the World Series. The region disagreed. Streets were filled with revelers on the night of the twentieth and well into the morning of the twenty-first. Finally, it seemed, the baseball team was on the verge of tasting what the football team had already done twice.

Fittingly, consecutive win number twenty-one for the Patriots came against New York. The 13–7 victory over the Jets was a reminder of how quickly things can change. In the tabloid "Belichicken" days, the Jets had four first-rounders, Bill Parcells as general manager, and no indication that Belichick would have a clue of what to do on his own with the keys to a franchise. Parcells was long gone from New York, and although he was now coaching in Dallas, the consensus was that his quirky defensive scientist, "Little Bill," died a few years back in New Orleans. Belichick had outgrown the nickname and was now the premier strategist in football.

Sometimes, though, strategy gets crushed by injuries. And runs out of luck, too. The Patriots went to Pittsburgh on Halloween, and the Steelers were eagerly waiting. One of their running backs, Jerome Bettis, had been watching the Patriots on TV a week earlier, rooting for them to win so that the Steelers could be the team to snap their streak. He got his wish, and it wasn't even theatrical. Dillon missed the game with a foot injury, and the drop-off was so pronounced that the Patriots managed just five yards rushing all day. They lost 34–20. Streak over after 398 days.

If there is such a thing as a good weekend for a loss, this was it. It followed the most expensive, mind-altering, life-changing sports party in Boston history. The Curse of the Bambino was officially over—the Boston Red Sox won the World Series. And it was as if the attendees from the Patriots' first two parades agreed to merge. The official parade count was 3.2 million people, and the celebration didn't just rock. It rolled. Literally. In the interest of public safety, Mayor Menino introduced the "rolling rally" for champions. The idea was to ride the duck boats through the city, touching all aspects of it, but not gathering at one main stage. The Patriots deserved some credit for this festival for, among other things, teaching the city how to parade, twenty-first-century style. Of course, with the third Boston celebration in four years, the corporate types got involved. So it wasn't just a rolling rally; it was a rolling rally sponsored by Budweiser, Verizon, Home Depot, Dunkin' Donuts…Several businesses got on board and figured, after eighty-six years of waiting, why should the city have to pay? Corporate gifts to the city totaled $750,000.

Everyone had a good time two weeks later when the Sox brought their elaborate World Series trophy to Gillette Stadium. It was November, the weather was turning, and the thought was in the air: What if the Patriots won it again and starred in a rolling rally of their own? It wasn't a wild thought. The Patriots had just that single loss, to the Steelers, and looked better than they had last year. Their constant winning had turned the region into a bunch of expectant champions.

When the Sox pursued free agents in the offseason and moved on (or tried to move on) from stars previously thought to be untouchable, it was expected. That's what Belichick would do. When a Celtic or Bruin talked about himself more than the team, or complained about his contract, the expectation was that management had to handle it swiftly and convincingly. Because Belichick would do that.

It was all over the locker room, where players had mastered the art of thinking and speaking like Belichick when the conversation was on the record. It was all over boardrooms and schools in the city, where kids copied the coach's slovenly chic look, a gray hoodie with the sleeves cut off, and CEOs and CFOs explained things with *It is what it is* and *That's not what we're looking for.*

The expectation reached its highest point at the end of the season, with the Patriots finishing 14-2 for the second consecutive season. There were some natural motivators in place, too, which promised to make the play-off games interesting. One of them was that the Patriots did not have home-field advantage throughout the postseason. The 15-1 Steelers did. The other was the Polian-Manning effect. As predicted in the spring, the renewed emphasis on penalizing defensive contact had wildly benefitted the Colts. Manning was the runaway league MVP, with a league-record forty-nine touchdown passes. The Brady-Manning debate had become a regionalized thing; everywhere else, overwhelmingly, Manning was seen as the best quarterback in football.

Going into the postseason, there was the familiar excitement, but finality as well. Charlie Weis had already been hired as Notre Dame's head coach, and he would go to South Bend, Indiana, as soon as the season was over. Romeo Crennel was likely to get a head coaching job, too, with some speculating that he would go to Cleveland. There were always new players, new challenges, and seemingly the annual personnel surprise from Belichick. If the players ever were going to mimic the head coach, now was the time to copy his short-term focus, his obsession with recognizing the moment and dominating it.

That spirit could be felt long before the beginning of the divisional play-off game against the Colts. The Patriots were playing at home, but they had an underdog's edge, and a lot of it had to do with their depleted secondary. Ty Law, the corner whom Manning had a difficult time solving, was out for the season with a broken foot. He would most likely end his Patriot career watching the team's Super Bowl run. He had seen up close, with some of his best friends, how Belichick and Scott Pioli thought; it was probably going to be a story of economics. In the absence of Law and Tyrone Poole, the corner depth was so scant that Troy Brown, a receiver, had logged an incredible 250 snaps in the secondary.

Imagine, the MVP of the league, owner of the best passing season in NFL history, scanning a secondary that included Brown, a couple of second-year players in Asante Samuel and Eugene Wilson, and Harrison. It seemed like a terrible idea until it began to snow shortly before kickoff. This was one of the Patriots-Colts talking points on the compare and contrast list. The Patriots loved the elements and bad-weather games. Manning had never won in Foxboro, and the thought was that snow and wind and sleet, typical winter weather in New England, bothered him.

That certainly appeared to be the case throughout the game. Brady consistently gave the ball to Dillon, who didn't look much smaller than the Colts' linebackers and safeties. He had run hard all year, piling up a team-record 1,635 rushing yards. The locals had given him a rhyming nickname: "Clock Killin' Corey Dillon." He ran hard against the Colts as well, staying in bounds and accepting hits when he didn't have to. And that was the thing. He wanted the hits and the contact. This was going to be a long day for Manning, maybe the longest of his career. The crowd ridiculed him, randomly chanting lines from his popular TV commercials. *Cut that meat!* Why were they saying it? It didn't matter. They had held Manning and the Colts to a field goal. Their 20–3 win gave them a return trip, with Dillon this time, to Pittsburgh.

The last time the Patriots were in western Pennsylvania for a play-off game, the city swelled with Super Bowl pride. Lawyer Milloy had noticed it and was ready for a fight. Law, who was from nearby Aliquippa, had noticed and had vowed to shut down Pittsburgh's receivers. Damien Woody sensed what they did, and couldn't wait to hit somebody. Drew Bledsoe had been ready to bounce into the game and, just like in the make-believe world of animation, had arrived in the nick of time to save his teammates.

This time, all those guys were gone. Only the foolish were surprised by the Patriots, this machine of a team that had, remarkably, a quarterback who had never lost a play-off game. And he had played seven of them, going into the conference championship at Heinz Field. He played the whole game this time, and one of his early throws seemed to be a taunt to his critics. Some of them said he couldn't throw deep, so he faked a handoff to Dillon, and then dropped back for a sixty-yard launch to Deion Branch. Touchdown. It was 10–0 then, and 24–3 at halftime.

There were no tears this time over the Lamar Hunt Trophy, which goes to the AFC Champion. There was just expectation. They had won, again, 41–27, and were on a run in which they had been victorious in twenty-seven of their previous thirty-one games. Now they were headed to another Super Bowl. On their way there, Tedy Bruschi and Roman Phifer looked at each other and thought the same thing. Phifer was the one who dared to break the silence.

"Man, if we win this thing, we'll be like the teams we watched as kids. We'll be like the Steelers and Cowboys. We'll be a dynasty."

CHAPTER EIGHT

BONDS AND BREAKS

Two days before his team's biggest game of the season, Bill Belichick had an idea that he was excited to share with his defensive players. He wanted to add a wrinkle for the Philadelphia Eagles to consider, a wrinkle that they wouldn't have seen anywhere in the New England film because it wasn't there. The Patriots hadn't run the scheme, called Dolphin, all year.

The players were so used to seeing this experimental side of Belichick that none of them paused to raise points and ask questions. Such as a glaring one: Why now? The team had dominated its competition in the postseason, including its silencing of the Colts. The defense had been elite for two years now, finishing first in the league in 2003 and second in 2004. Why mess with a good thing? Why overthink it?

For Belichick, questions like those are signs of fear and mediocrity. His players understood that he was constantly searching for the perfect matchup. They trusted that he had put the film work in to justify whatever unconventional concept he offered them. They had seen him in action with the clicker in his hand, analyzing the film, and they knew they were watching the best in the industry. Bar none.

Many of them had come to New England feeling good about their ability to detect tendencies on film, but he was much more detailed and analytical than all of them. He'd let the film run for a second or two, reverse it, and then go forward again to the first couple of seconds. They all thought they were seeing what he did, but they weren't. They'd be looking at the point of attack, and he'd go somewhere else, to an infinitesimal place that he believed was the glue of the entire play. He was amazing that way. And he approached new plays reasonably: If there's any delay in "getting it" in practice, it won't be a part of the game.

Dolphin certainly was going to make it into the core of the Super Bowl game plan. It called for Tedy Bruschi and Mike Vrabel to fill the "A" gaps, the areas between the center and the guards, while Roman Phifer took advantage of a favorable matchup he had against tight end L. J. Smith, who wasn't a strong blocker. The linebackers picked up the defense quickly, and it was as if this twist had been a part of their repertoire the entire year.

"We prided ourselves on being intellectuals and students of the game," Phifer says. "And obviously that's a reflection of Bill."

Each of the linebackers knew the defensive signals, even if Bruschi was the official signal-caller. They lined up according to Bruschi's instructions for the sake of order, but they already knew what to do. Bruschi was similar to the leader in a familiar call-and-response exercise; everyone knew his lines as well as their own, yet they respected the tradition of having a song leader. Sometimes defensive lineman Richard Seymour would tell the linebackers that he was going to tweak his stunt, and the 'backers would in turn adjust the call based on Seymour's freestyle. It was advanced communication, and they had refined it through years of practice competitions, pop quizzes, and play-off wins against record-setting players and teams and, sometimes, in record-setting conditions.

This was a close group, a brotherhood, and they all knew enough to anticipate playing in the Super Bowl and to dread the ending of the game, too. They always expected to win these games, and who could blame them? Twenty-two of them were playing in their third Super Bowl in the last four years, and they had an eight-game post-season winning streak. That wasn't normal. The last team to do that was Vince Lombardi's Packers of the 1960s, an era when there was no salary cap or unrestricted free agency. Those elements were the lifeblood of the modern game, and that's what made each of these championship runs so emotional. It's not like the group was going to return as a whole next year.

The coordinators, Charlie Weis and Romeo Crennel, were definitely leaving. Joe Andruzzi, whom Tom Brady once teased as a "little, fat guard," was a free agent and in line for a fat contract, probably on the open market. David Patten's contract was expiring, and some team out there was likely to look past "fiscal responsibility" and all the other things the Patriots said, and pay for Patten's speed and championship profile. Ty Law wasn't going to have to ask for his release this time; the Patriots were almost guaranteed to move on from the cornerback and his $12.5 million cap number. Seymour had completed his second consecutive season as a first-team All-Pro and wasn't going anywhere. But a protracted vacation wasn't out of the question. He was twenty-five and had far outperformed his contract. He was one of the few Patriots who had the leverage and temperament to hold out for a better deal.

Phifer, now thirty-six, wanted to return but knew it wasn't going to be in New England. He had been pulled aside by linebackers' coach Dean Pees after the fifth game of the season. He was told that Belichick didn't like what he was seeing on film, and that if his play didn't pick up he'd be cut during the season. Phifer knew what Belichick was seeing. The linebacker looked at himself in those film sessions, and he saw a player who was stiff and a step slow. He was supposed to be a guy who could stop the run and cover, but there was a play in that fifth game, a win over the Seahawks, that had bothered him and Belichick. Seattle quarterback Matt Hasselbeck had faked a toss to running back Shaun Alexander, and the back had almost lounged there as if he were out of the play. Then he suddenly ran full speed up the sideline, where Hasselbeck hit him for a big gain of twenty-four yards. Phifer was supposed to be on Alexander. He wasn't close.

After the warning from Pees, Phifer's play picked up markedly. In the play-off win over the Colts, he got a big hit on Edgerrin James and immediately felt something pop in his right shoulder. Torn labrum. He didn't play much in the conference championship game in Pittsburgh. But with a chance to start in the Super Bowl, to be a contributor to this team that could be remembered as a dynasty, there's no way he was going to miss the opportunity. He was a right-handed player who couldn't lift his right arm, but he still had full range of motion with his left. He'd get the job done that way. Not many people in the game as long as he'd been in, fourteen seasons, gave much thought to the condition of their postcareer bodies. If you thought about that too much, you'd never make it to year fourteen, or even half that long. But there was no question the game wore you down, at times in life-threatening ways, and players were starting to think of that more than ever.

Everyone, regardless of their age, knew that the NFL's year to year was akin to real life's generation to generation. Time moved at warp speed here, with no space for gradual and thoughtful change. It had been only a year ago, minutes after the Super Bowl win over the Panthers, when Belichick had asked Phifer, "So are you gonna keep playing? Or are you gonna call it a career?" The coach had asked in a hopeful way, as he appreciated the skill and professionalism of the linebacker. Phifer had replied, "I'm in." Just one year later, he knew there wouldn't be any polite asking. He was at the point in his career when a private meeting with the boss wasn't likely to produce good news.

On the day of the game, with Dolphin fully committed to muscle memory, Bruschi roamed the Alltel Stadium field in Jacksonville and began to look into the stands. He saw his wife, Heidi, there along with two of his three sons. It was hours before the game and they were already in place. He knew the kids would be restless, so he ran over to them with a plan in mind. He took a boy in each arm and they all made their way to the field. Then he slowly backpedaled as they chased after him, and he went down in a heap as he let them playfully pile on and tackle him. He and Phifer had talked about becoming a dynasty and now here they were, on February 6, a couple of hours away from making it happen. They couldn't possibly know all the reasons why this would be their last game playing together, but they had a feeling that this was it.

Brady was excited for the game to begin, and his reasons were different from those of his teammates in their thirties. He had talked about winning a third title at the previous year's parade, and he hadn't been pandering. He always believed that he should win, and he had a case with the best offense of his career. He had a particularly strong relationship with Deion Branch, the receiver who shared a mastery of the offense with him. Branch was finishing his third season in the offense, and he had gained his quarterback's total trust by knowing his assignments on his first day as a pro.

Branch was always in tune with Brady, so when the quarterback would begin to scan the defense and eventually identify the player who is the "Mike," primarily the linebacker who keys the defense, Branch would know what to do. "All of your sight adjustments are based on that call," Branch says now. "If you miss that call, you're going to miss the whole play. Tom is expecting you to make the adjustment off of what he's just identified. You have to see it the way that he does. It can be very complex."

It was simple for Brady and Branch. They almost always saw the defense the same way. In the win over the Panthers, Brady was the MVP and Branch was his leading receiver, securing ten catches for 143 yards. They expected tight coverage from the Eagles, who had given up exactly the same point total as the Patriots during the regular season. Their defense was coordinated by one of Belichick's friends, Jim Johnson, with the two men often chatting during the season to compare notes about opponents. Brady and Branch weren't surprised when they often faced what they called a Cover 2, Man Under defense. The Eagles had their safeties protecting everything over the top, with linebackers and corners underneath taking away the passing game. "One of the toughest defenses to throw against," Branch says.

It didn't matter. Brady was determined to get his receiver the ball. They had only one miscommunication the entire game, on a third-and-nine. Branch was certain, based on his read, that Brady was going elsewhere. He got the message when Brady clarified on the sideline. "Hey, I'm just trying to get you the ball."

Over and over, that's exactly what happened. Brady would see the creases in the Eagles defense and Branch would run to them. He'd snag the ball out of the air, run as much as he could, and then smartly go to the turf just before an Eagle had a clean shot at him. Branch tied a Super Bowl record with eleven receptions for 133 yards. This time, he got the game's MVP trophy and Brady got to deliver on the promise that he had made to all of New England a year earlier.

The communication between Brady and Branch was flawless, but the same could be said of many relationships on the team. It had been like that in the Super Bowl and during the entire season. They knew they were no longer being judged by division titles or appearances in the play-offs. They were chasing the ghosts of the game now. A lot of the communication was unspoken during the season, like when players would look at Rodney Harrison in practice and see the intensity and speed he brought to it. Not wanting to be shown up, they did the same thing. Or maybe it was not wanting to be the first one to leave the facility. Or to not be the first one to miss an answer on one of Belichick's tests.

Not much had to be said after the game, when there was a three-man huddle with Belichick, Crennel, and Weis. This wasn't even year-to-year transformation; it was moment-to-moment. They had gone into the game as one staff and, as soon as it was over, they were in that huddle as head coaches of the Patriots, Browns, and University of Notre Dame. They weren't a trio at that moment, and they were unlikely to be that again.

There were other sweet, unspoken moments at the end of the 24–21 win. Bruschi, naturally, was drawn to a beautiful father-son snapshot. His time had come before the game, a thirty-one-year-old father and his preschool-aged sons. Now he noticed Belichick on the sideline, with his arm draped around his eighty-six-year-old father, Steve. It couldn't have been more perfect than this for Belichick, winning the Super Bowl next to the man who taught him the game. He could remember being eight years old and hearing Steve's typewriter as he composed his scouting book, *Football Scouting Methods*. It was his mother who edited the book; Bill was the one who wanted to be a part of the life that the book described. This was a family affair, and Bruschi punctuated it with a celebratory douse of father and son. The Belichicks loved it.

After the game, Bruschi could be seen on the field smiling and holding up three fingers. Dynasty. Just as he and Phifer and many others had imagined. The night would be full of music, laughter, dancing, and wine. They would savor it as long as they could, and then prepare for the departures. The veterans thought they had steeled themselves for this, so there was nothing in football that could sneak up on them. But that was football, not civilian life.

Nine days after the Super Bowl, Bruschi was back at home and he still couldn't get enough of the season. Heidi and the boys were asleep and he was awake in the master bedroom, watching football. He had come across the NFL Network, and a replay of the conference championship game in Pittsburgh was on. He had played in the game, replayed it in his mind several times, and now he wanted to watch it again. He looked at it for a while and then he began to doze. He was in a deep football dream, or so he thought, trying to wrap up Jerome Bettis in a tackle. He was acting out his dream, though, and when he awoke at four a.m., his arms were in the air.

Several hours later, he and Heidi realized that he'd had a stroke. It was tough to settle the contrasts. In the Super Bowl, just a week and a half earlier, his boys had run after him on the field. Now, in North Attleboro, Massachusetts, he could hear their tiny footsteps behind him as they were curious about the flashing lights of the ambulance that he was being carried into. He heard them behind him only because he couldn't see them; there was darkness in his left eye.

It seemed that his career was over.

As Bruschi underwent surgery and rehab, the Patriots went about their expected football business. Bill Andruzzi called in to a local sports radio station, angry that his brother couldn't generate interest from the Patriots and had reluctantly signed with Cleveland instead. "If the Pats had offered him anything decent, he would have stayed," his brother told the station.

Patten indeed got triple the money that the Patriots were offering, and happily took a $3.5 million bonus from Washington. Law was released. Seymour decided to hold out. Troy Brown, who had been a receiver, punt returner, and defensive back for the team, didn't have his option picked up and was encouraged to test the market. Belichick's first Patriots draft pick, Adrian Klemm, signed with the Packers. And Phifer had that private conversation with Belichick, the one where Belichick said there were no hard feelings and Phifer said he wasn't ready to say good-bye to football yet. So the Patriots released him.

The math was adding up quickly. More than one-third of the Patriots with three rings were now either leaving or in limbo. There was a pattern starting to emerge, and most people on the team either didn't see it or didn't want to say it aloud: These Patriots, under Belichick, were capable of breaking up with just about anybody, with the exception of one player. Brady.

If the Patriots were known for their study habits, then they knew the reason Brady was one of the guys yet not like them at all. For example, his agents were never heard from on contract issues, and he and the team agreed to deals long before the media started countdown clocks on his expiring contracts. In the spring of 2005, Brady's contract was extended six years for $60 million. He got a $14.5 million signing bonus. He further endeared himself to New England because he made it clear that he wasn't interested in every available dollar. Locally, he got a halo from fans for not demanding as much as Peyton Manning ($34.5 million signing bonus in 2004) and Michael Vick ($37.5 million).

Good quarterbacks were hard to find. Great quarterbacks were untouchable. Quarterbacks who understood the cap game and how to motivate their teammates were perhaps one of a kind.

"There's just so much to consider at that position," Louis Riddick, currently an ESPN analyst, says now. "It starts with decision-making and accuracy. But it's more than the physical aspect of it. Can he make decisions under pressure? On third down? How about if his left tackle gets knocked out of the game; can he still be consistent? I've been on the headsets and heard coaches change the play call because they didn't think the quarterback could bounce back from a negative play. The position is about physical ability, communication, and leadership."

Brady was a quarterback; he'd allow Belichick, Scott Pioli, and Kraft to stock the team. For all that Belichick didn't give to the media in press conferences, he certainly made up for it in daring personnel moves.

Previously, Belichick's media management, or even his media awareness, had been viewed as a weakness. He now understood that he could use the media to his benefit by knowing what they were saying about him, other teams, and his own players. The latter point interested him most of all: another way of knowing just how on-message players were could be gleaned by seeing, hearing, and reading what they had to say to the public.

Reporters would have been surprised to know how much time he spent doing elements of their jobs. That is, he spent a significant amount of phone time, talking with various football sources, trying to get information. He did more questioning and listening than talking, which was the opposite of his one-dimensional profile in the media. Part of his homework was taking notes from other coaches in town, such as Doc Rivers with the Celtics and Jerry York, Boston College's championship hockey coach.

He had a few issues to manage just after free agency and before the draft. The departures of Weis and Crennel meant that he'd have to replace two significant staff positions in the same offseason. Eric Mangini, a Wesleyan graduate like Belichick, would take over the defense. Although Belichick didn't give Josh McDaniels the official offensive coordinator's title, the job belonged to him. He was confident that both men, studious and bright, had the intellect to be successful on the job. The only thing lacking was their experience.

Belichick also offered advice to Bruschi, who had already walked into his office and tearfully retired. The linebacker had intentionally gone to the locker room first, put all of his locker belongings in a huge trash bag, and placed them near an exit before going in to talk with Belichick. He'd asked Heidi and his sons to wait in the car, and as soon as the meeting was over, he grabbed the belongings and left the building for what he believed to be his last time as a player.

Bruschi didn't have all the information on stroke recovery, and Belichick had even less information than Bruschi did. But Belichick's tendency to impartially ask questions was a strength in this case. He continued to tell Bruschi to be patient and see how he felt in several weeks before he made any hasty decisions.

In the meantime, there was a draft to get ready for and, per usual, Belichick was trying to catch up as quickly as possible.

Many were surprised and confused when the Patriots drafted a cowboy from Fresno State. His name was Logan Mankins, and he grew up on a cattle farm. He was big and strong and wanted to be a professional roper. He was good at football, so he played at Fresno, playing both tackle and guard. He was the definition of a Patriot with his low-maintenance lifestyle, on-field toughness, and suspicion of the spotlight. In a comical and organic exchange, the Patriots had asked Mankins to wear his "Sunday best" to his first press conference. He was prepared to go with a cowboy hat, dress shirt, jeans, and his doing-business boots. Learning that, the team directed him to a Men's Wearhouse so he could purchase his first suit.

Since none of the draft experts had Mankins going to the Patriots, and very few of them had him being drafted in the first round at all, the pick was not initially well received.

"The Pats' decision to take offensive lineman Logan Mankins and pass on much higher-rated players like safety Brodney Pool and linebacker Barrett Ruud seemed even 'woise' a day later," wrote Kevin Mannix in the *Herald*. He used the analogy of boxer Jake LaMotta being bloodied even worse than he imagined. "Nobody was expecting the Pats to walk away with 'Best in Show' hardware. Not many Super Bowl champs get that honor. Picking at the end of each round and without the benefit of multiple picks in the early rounds pretty much eliminates that chance. But even when you factor in the position of the picks, the Patriots came away looking barely average because they blew the chance to get a playmaker with that first pick."

No one seemed to consider the timing of the poor review. While Belichick was being ripped for supposedly making a bad draft pick, he was being forced to problem-solve the situation with Seymour, another onetime "bad pick" who was now holding out because he was one of the best defensive linemen in football. Seymour was in the fourth year of a contract that had since become illegal. The deal was for six years, and the Players Association had argued, successfully, that such long contracts had allowed teams to take advantage of players who had outperformed those deals. Seymour was a perfect example and he knew it.

"I wanted the business side to be taken care of," he says. "For a team to just rip up a contract was seen as business. But if a player asked for that, he was being selfish. I looked at it as business from my perspective, and it was one of my proudest moments. I never compromised who I was as a man to fit in."

At the beginning of the 2005 season, perhaps as an indication of what was to come, Belichick seemed to trade one set of problems for others. He had resolved the contract dispute with Seymour by giving him a $1.5 million salary bump, and Bruschi had enthusiastically come to him saying that his career wasn't over after all. But now there were impending contractual issues with Branch, McGinest, David Givens, and Adam Vinatieri. It was going to be difficult to keep all of those players at the numbers they were requesting.

Even if they could, was it practical? He truly wanted to sign Branch, who was young, productive, and shared a football brain with Brady. But the sides couldn't seem to agree on the receiver's value, and they were at a stalemate halfway through the season. Bruschi had returned, miraculously, from a stroke—the first NFL player who had ever done that. Wasn't that an indication that it might be time for a real youth movement on defense, if not the entire team? Harrison was out for the season, having torn three ligaments in his knee. On offense, tight end Christian Fauria had been told, in a candid conversation with tight ends coach Jeff Davidson, that this was likely his last year in Foxboro. The young tight ends, Daniel Graham and Ben Watson, needed more time to play. Fauria sulked when he heard the news and then, he says, "I told myself, 'You're such a baby.' I was pissed at myself for acting that way. In that instant, I decided to change my attitude."

Belichick was so engrossed with team-building, so prepared with any football situation about which he was asked, sometimes it was easy to forget how he got that way. He was doing what he did only because of his mother and father. He studied and taught football, he researched and collected dozens of football books, only because of what they valued. His father was to college scouting what Belichick was to pro coaching. He covered every situation so no player on his team could possibly complain that he didn't see something coming.

The senior Belichick had a way of being funny, too, even during tense times. In 1962, with the United States and the Soviet Union in the thick of the Cuban Missile Crisis, Steve Belichick noticed that his Midshipmen football players were overwhelmed. Earlier in the week, they had heard President Kennedy's warning that the Soviets had put themselves in position for "nuclear strike capability against the Western Hemisphere." They were stunned and a little scared, and Steve Belichick knew it as he scanned the players' faces before a team meeting. He talked about these important world leaders, President Kennedy and Nikita Khrushchev, and joked, "I don't think those guys realize that we are playing Pittsburgh this weekend."

The team laughed and relaxed. And they also beat Pitt, 32–9.

Bill Belichick wasn't as loquacious as his father, at least not publicly, but he was an observer of people and moods. He knew when a team was too tight or too casual, and a lot of that insight came from his father. Steve Belichick had been on the sideline for all three Super Bowl victories, including the most recent one over the Eagles. His mind was still computer-quick, and there genuinely wasn't anything in the game that he hadn't seen before. But he loved the modern game, especially college football. He watched college football every Saturday, in the same house where he and his wife had raised their only child.

On Saturday night, November 19, Steve Belichick was watching college football when his heart stopped. Bill Belichick heard the crushing news and didn't share it with many people. The Patriots were playing the Saints the next day, and Belichick planned to coach the team. All of the players didn't know the details until after the Patriots had defeated the Saints, 24–17.

Belichick was presented with a game ball after the win, and a line of Patriots offered hugs and kind words. The team was 6–4. But for the first time in Belichick's head coaching career, preparing for the next game was not the most important thing to do. As the team devised a plan for Kansas City, Belichick was on his way to Annapolis to eulogize his hero.

On November 23, usually the first day of game-plan installation in Foxboro, the head coach of the Patriots was in the Naval Academy Chapel. He had been there many times, and he had been married there nearly thirty years earlier. Now he and hundreds of others from the college and pro football world were here to memorialize a man who devoted his life to his country, his family, and football. Patriots owner Robert Kraft was in attendance, along with Charlie Weis and Ernie Accorsi, who had worked with Bill Belichick in Cleveland and was now the general manager of the Giants.

Everyone in attendance could feel and see the impact that Steve Belichick had on those he met. He was able to balance a love for rigor and discipline with an earnest love for the uniqueness of people. He liked to joke that in the house intelligence rankings, he was a distant third behind his wife and son. But on the day he said good-bye to his father, Bill Belichick also honored his mother, saying, "You were the real strength behind two coaches in this family, and I love you." He may have cried during this time, but the public didn't see it. What Bill Belichick wanted the world to know, and remember, was that Steve Belichick represented all that was good about fatherhood, coaching, and football.

When Belichick got back to New England, he was in business mode again. He talked about the challenges of playing the Chiefs and the difficulty of dealing with the raucous atmosphere at Arrowhead Stadium. Those difficulties could be easily seen a couple of days later when Brady had one of the worst days of his career. He threw four interceptions in a 10-point loss.

Typical of their season, the Patriots followed the loss to Kansas City with a win. The rhythm of the season had been erratic, and it wasn't clear what the identity of the 2005 Patriots was. The same could not be said of their opponent after Kansas City, the Jets. They had a new, playmaking cornerback, Ty Law, who had signed with them to reestablish his market value after teams had concerns about his injured foot. His individual season had been great, with five interceptions through twelve games. His team had been miserable; the Jets were 2-10 after a 16–3 loss to the Patriots. The two teams played again, the day after Christmas, and the Patriots walked away with a 10-point victory. One of the few highlights in the game for the Jets was Law picking off Brady and running seventy-four yards for a touchdown. It was his seventh interception in what would eventually become a ten-interception season. New York would soon be looking for a new coach. But that was next year.

A couple of days after the game, Law got a phone call. He recognized the number, the voice, and the question.

"Hey Ty," Brady said. "What did you see on that interception? What did I give away?"

Three titles and two MVPs later, he was still searching the way he had when he was trying to take the job from Bledsoe.

"Tom, I played with you longer than anybody over there, right?" Law explained. "It's obvious what you do: You do this exaggerated throwing motion and I knew you were coming back the other way. I played with you long enough to know that. As soon as I saw that motion, it's not a real throwing motion, I just stopped. You threw it right there."

The flaw would be corrected for the play-offs, where the Patriots were headed. Law was going to be looking for a new team and, truly, there were no hard feelings for New England. He wanted to return to Foxboro.

Since the Patriots were in season, and had cobbled together a wobbly 10-6 division winner, they didn't have time to reflect the way Phifer did. Since being released by the Patriots in March, he had searched for a job until finding one, briefly, with the Giants. But something wasn't right. He'd taken a hit in practice, nothing out of the ordinary, and twisted his knee. He'd had it drained a couple of times, yet it wasn't responding to treatment. He was living in a Jersey hotel at the time, and one day he lay there on his bed and looked at the ceiling. He was away from his family, and he was down about that. He was forever aware of that problematic knee, and he knew what his body was telling him. This was it. It was over. He called his wife and cried.

"It felt like a breakup after a long relationship," Phifer says. "The game has done so much for me and my family. It's the only thing that I really loved. It gave me passion. It's something that I was blessed to do since I was eight years old. It's something that I shared with my father. And you know, there's nothing like that locker room. The relationships. Going to work on a winning streak with guys you care about and admire. It's hard when that's taken away from you."

That was Phifer's story for the end of his career. But there was a larger truth to his words about the end, and several Patriots were going to have similar feelings after a tough night in Denver.

CHAPTER NINE

UNEXPECTED ENDINGS

It ended just before midnight on the East Coast, and the New Englanders who watched it finally understood what they had been envied over and warned about for years. It's one thing to comprehend that your team can lose in the postseason, but when it doesn't happen in ten consecutive games, do you truly believe it?

If there is a problem with winning (imagine that), this is it: The ability to earnestly listen becomes difficult. You go over all the cliched checklists, recite all the things you've been programmed to say. How it's hard to win games in a league where the difference in talent is as faint as a whisper. How it's challenging to just drop into someone's city, mute their stadium, and erase their football season. And, best of all, from the wise ones: how the current run of success should be appreciated now, because the future most certainly will have troubled paths.

It would have all made sense, if not for the results in that ten-game stretch. The first win had come in 2002, one month before the Winter Olympics in Salt Lake City. The tenth win had come in 2006, one month before the Winter Olympics in Turin. In between, there had been anomalies, too many of them to be called anomalies anymore. The Steelers were a combined 17-3 at

Heinz Field during two dominant seasons, and two of those three home losses were delivered by the Patriots. Peyton Manning had thrown fifty-three touchdown passes in seventeen games, an average of three per, and in game eighteen, against the Patriots, he led his team to just a field goal. A fumble recovery by the Raiders had become a Tom Brady incompletion. A kicker, Adam Vinatieri, had become a rock star. A guy who was once on the 2002 expansion list, Willie McGinest, set a league record with four and a half sacks in a play-off game in 2006.

A ten-game winning streak in the worst conditions, against the best competition; it's not supposed to happen. So even though the 2005 regular season had not been great, and the odds of winning a January game in Denver were low, the winning memories were powerful. Humility usually comes from experiencing the bitterness of failure, not being lectured about it. You hear the words, clear and thoughtful, about what you can't do and still expect to win. But the tug of memory says, *It won't happen to us. It never has.*

Late in the game, when they had often worn out opponents by wit and will, the Patriots finally felt it. They trailed 17–6 in the fourth quarter, and Vinatieri missed an easy field-goal attempt. Still trailing by the same score, with ten minutes remaining, the Patriots were about to get the ball and would no doubt cut into the lead. Then Troy Brown muffed a punt and lost the ball. Three plays and two minutes later, it was 24–6.

This was that bogeyman, all dressed up in Broncos orange. Bill Belichick didn't have a special move in his game of football chess, Brady didn't coolly position the offense for an improbable win at the end, and there was no fit of nerves from the opposition, melting down on its own before the Patriots even approached. No, this was consistent with what the rest of America knew about play-off frustration. These kind of games got into your head and made you

replay each of the five turnovers, including one forced by, of all people, their punter. These losses took away your graciousness and elo-
quence, leaving you with a vocabulary of excuses. *If* the refs hadn't
called that pass interference on Asante Samuel; *if* Brady had run the
ball in near the goal line instead of forcing a pass that was intercepted; *if* the league had cameras near the goal line, they'd have
had a better look at a legendary hustle play by Ben Watson, and the
Patriots would have gotten the ball back...

Excuses.

It was over now, the first postseason loss in Brady's career. He
had thrown a seventy-three-yard pass to Deion Branch, proving
again just how natural their chemistry was. But late in the game and
well after it, Branch cried hard because he knew that the business
of football was going to prevent this group from being maintained.
Brady had thrown a touchdown pass to David Givens, a rugged
receiver who had been drafted in the same class as Branch. Givens
had worked hard, done the dirty work on special teams, and pushed
his way up from a marginal seventh-round draft choice to a number
two receiver who had earned Brady's trust. He was a free agent,
though, and he and his teammates had already seen this economic
snapshot, over and over. He was going to be a rich man, but it wasn't
going to happen in Foxboro.

McGinest, thirty-four, would be perceived in the open market as an old veteran who could teach a young team; Eric Mangini,
thirty-five, would be coveted as a young coach who could refresh a
veteran team.

In a way, the loss was a good thing for Belichick and Brady.
They would never say it like that, but if they thought about the way
the region had deified them, maybe they would see that losing a
game would remind people that they were just men. The 10-0 story
line never gave them space for that, though. The streak emboldened

people, and it elevated Belichick and Brady beyond elite performers, which they were, into something that they weren't and no one ever could be. The qualities that they were given started on the field, but they didn't end there. And that was the problem. They didn't end anywhere. There were no boundaries, no ceiling, for either of them, and as a result there was no cap to any expectations.

A *Globe* editorial, figuratively one million miles away from the good humor and hyperbole of the sports pages, had compared the Patriots to Microsoft and Michelangelo's work at the Sistine Chapel... all in five paragraphs. The prolific and titanic David Halberstam, who had authored fourteen consecutive bestsellers, announced that he was turning his eyes to the Patriots and Belichick. So the author of *The Best and the Brightest* focused on the NFL's version of that title, Belichick, and penned *The Education of a Coach.*

Brady had not only spent time at the State of the Union address, clapping knowingly and compassionately; he had knelt before and presumably been blessed by the pope at the Vatican. His dating life, with actress Bridget Moynahan, had led him to red carpets and galas. He seemed to fit in perfectly at these black-tie affairs, moving about confidently in his velvet jacket among famous designers, actresses, musicians, and comedians.

The feeling was that Belichick and Brady could do just about anything, in their field or otherwise. Turn average players into good ones; reset the games and mores of wayward personalities; teach knuckleheads the Patriot Way; defeat superior talent with brains and hard work; stare down and defy the media in spite of withering criticism; give seminars on composure under pressure, business restoration, and, in general, overall success. They displayed aspects of those elements on TV, weekly, during football season. They became part of the long-running, highly rated local drama, and just like in the world of plots and scripts, sometimes it was hard to distinguish the real person from the character he was portraying. Belichick and Brady were winning, so the descriptions of them as winners at everything weren't necessarily dangerous, just unrealistic.

One of the people who didn't treat Belichick like a celebrity was Eric Mangini. He was an independent thinker who didn't automatically do things the way his boss did.

He was never disrespectful of the head coach, but he had a way of pushing back, with an edge, that other coaches rarely did. In 2005, his first season as a coordinator, sometimes the resistance could be felt in the defenses he asked his players to execute.

"The complexity level kicked up a bit," Tedy Bruschi recalls. "Sometimes it got too complex and we'd tell him to scale it down, and he would. I didn't feel that he was trying to do his best Belichick impression; he did the best job of pushing his stuff on Bill. He had a lot of ideas. He had new stuff that he wanted to do, new adjustments that he wanted to do.

"We'd have double calls, sometimes even triple calls in the huddle, based on certain formations. 'If it's two by two, it's one defense. But three by one is something else, and if they motion to three by two we gotta switch...' We got it down the best that we could. We liked being pushed intellectually."

Immediately after the loss in Denver, the rumors began: Mangini was a leading candidate to be the next head coach of the Jets. From Belichick's perspective, a Mangini departure for another team in the division was going to be a problem, particularly *that* team. He despised the Jets. The situation got worse with office gossip. Some people said that Mangini was trying to recruit and build his staff even before the postseason game. He denied it passionately, but it was out there, just like the opportunity to triple his salary was out there. Mangini took the Jets job, with its $2 million annual salary, and the line was drawn. He was officially cut off by Belichick. It was going to be hard, if not impossible, to ever reenter the inner circle.

In mid-January 2006, the tone was already set for the rest of the year. Mistrust. Deception. Betrayal. Heartbreak. The "complexity level" was there on the field, and in several relationships, too. The timing was incredible. It had all begun with just one play-off loss, the first one in four years, and now the filter was gone from everything. Before that loss, the Patriots appeared to be different from everyone else, not just immune to the play-off follies that chased other teams, but immune to organizational dysfunction. They had spent four years in that protective bubble, and now it was time to truly feel the heat.

It was time to say good-bye to McGinest, who got a $12 million contract to join Romeo Crennel with the Browns. Givens had managed to turn a fifty-nine-catch, two-touchdown season into a $24 million offer from the Titans, including an $8 million signing bonus. Neither move was a surprise. And even though there were reports that Vinatieri was visiting Green Bay, no one thought there was any chance that he'd leave the Patriots for the Packers.

It turned out to be worse than that. The Patriots didn't want to set the market on any player, even a kicker. It didn't matter to them that the dollars it would take to sign Vinatieri were scant compared to the numbers being discussed at other positions. They believed in financial discipline, and there was a level they weren't willing to go to sign Vinatieri. That was fine with the Colts, who had struggled to beat the Patriots in the postseason. They were excited to extend a $3.5 million signing bonus to the kicker, and that did it. The rare kicker, one who got autograph requests and commercials, the main object of framed photos in which he was punctuating big play-off wins, the man to see at closing time, was now a Colt.

The parade watchers heard the news and went straight to the polls. According to Boston.com, more than half of the region's residents claimed that they no longer subscribed to the "In Bill We Trust" mantra. Vinatieri was one of the most popular players in team history, and he had been the symbol of something that had eluded the region in the fifteen-year gap between Larry Bird's last championship and Brady's first. He was reliable. He was dependable. When big moments arose and he was asked to perform, there was nothing to dread.

On the day the Vinatieri news broke, NFL commissioner Paul Tagliabue announced his retirement. He had just presided over a new collective bargaining agreement, one that the owners ultimately deemed too generous to the players, and said it was the right time to turn the job over to someone else. He was viewed with warmth in most markets, including New England, and he had faith in a handful of owners, such as Robert Kraft, to find a strong successor.

"It's a very complicated job," Kraft told writer Judy Battista. "The skill set required to do this job is unbelievable: legal, media, sponsorships. And really, you have thirty-two members of the board of directors."

The emphasis for the new commissioner was youth (under fifty), the ability to balance the concerns of thirty-two owners, and a strong financial plan that would help the league take advantage of international opportunities and new media. Most people agreed that the league's chief operating officer, forty-seven-year-old Roger Goodell, might be the perfect candidate.

While the league was trying to maintain its run of success, the Patriots had the same mentality. It was becoming more difficult to counter the talent drain, on the field, on the coaching staff, and in the front office. Belichick's system of promoting from within was a tribute to his eye for talent, but it was also an indication to the rest of the league that anyone chosen by Belichick was worthy of attention. In the past two seasons, three coordinators had left for head coaching jobs. He had installed Josh McDaniels as offensive coordinator; Dean Pees to replace the enemy, Mangini, as defensive coordinator; and the rocket scientist, Matt Patricia, to take over for Pees coaching the linebackers. How much longer would he be able to keep a cadre of talented personnel evaluators in scouting? Many teams had expressed an interest in Scott Pioli, and if he didn't answer their calls, then one day Thomas Dimitroff, Jon Robinson, and Bob Quinn would.

Preparing for the 2006 season was a struggle, for multiple reasons. There were intense contract negotiations with Richard Seymour. Going into his sixth season, Seymour was recognized as one of the best defensive linemen in the game. He had already made four Pro Bowls and had been an impact defender on three championship teams. The Patriots couldn't treat him like other players and move on in the name of value. He was too young, just twenty-six, and too good; he needed to be paid. They agreed to a three-year extension, for $10 million per season.

The talks with Deion Branch weren't nearly as smooth. The sides were millions upon millions of dollars apart. The Patriots wanted the receiver to accept an $18 million contract; he wanted more than twice as much, $39 million. He was prepared to hold out, which would mean that Brady would start training camp without his two favorite receivers from the previous season.

Ty Law had left the Jets as a free agent coming off a ten-interception season, best in the NFL, and he had the power to pick the team of his choice. He was still young enough, at thirty-two, to play corner effectively. He went to visit Kansas City, and when he was on his way to meet with Chiefs coach Herm Edwards, he got a call. It was Belichick. He wanted Law to return to the Patriots, too, but New England wasn't offering what Kansas City was: five years and $30 million.

Even drafting high-end players, a Patriots strength, was contentious. The benefits of a gifted and opinionated scouting staff are obvious. The underside of it is that as young scouts grow into veteran ones, as inexperienced evaluators become seasoned ones with their own team-building principles, reaching a consensus can be messy. That was the case in the Patriots' draft room, when some were very high on University of Minnesota running back Laurence Maroney, while others questioned his maturity. Those contrasts were normal in the scouting process, and, eventually, aggressive debate would lead to a clearer understanding of who the player was. But that didn't happen here. There were factions on Maroney and University of Florida receiver Chad Jackson, also a player who left school after his junior year.

Belichick preached that the past was no predictor of things to come. He gave that message to the team and to the media. It was also true of his personal life. He had been married in 1977 to a girl, Debby Clarke, whom he knew from high school. They had been separated for three years and now, in the summer of 2006, they divorced. It was hard enough for anyone, in any profession, to manage the emotional weight of it all. There were the three kids, who were actually either young adults or in their late teens now, and their feelings about it. There were friends and family and colleagues, lawyers and accountants and documents. All of that was bad enough, and that was without the scrutiny of the public. But stardom like this, in a year like this, made any hope for a quiet divorce a fantasy.

The year was barely half over, and it was already heavy. The Branch talks were regressing, to the point where the sides began making their arguments to the media. Branch was being fined $14,000 for each day of camp that he missed, and his agent said that it didn't matter. He had been paid a base salary of $500,000 the year before, and the number had doubled only because he had reached a performance incentive. He was a former Super Bowl MVP, his quarterback's favorite receiver, and one of the best route runners in the business. He wanted out of a contract that he had outperformed; the Patriots didn't see his value the way he did.

Brady and Branch had once showed off to Steve Kroft in a feature for *60 Minutes*. They wanted to prove to him that they could know exactly what to do without saying a word, and they went to the practice field and did it. That's how connected they had been. But they were both raised as Patriots, and they knew that this was not the land for sentimentalists. It wasn't going to last that long for them, or anyone else. Branch was traded to the Seattle Seahawks in exchange for a 2007 first-round pick.

"We never let business get in the way of our personal relationship," Branch says now. "I told him that I loved him and to keep doing what he was doing. I said, 'I hope to be playing against you in the Super Bowl.'"

Seattle gave Branch the $39 million contract that he was looking for, beating out the other team that was willing to do the same thing: Mangini's Jets. In fact, the Year of Disruption couldn't head into September without Belichick and Mangini continuing their feud. The Patriots filed tampering charges with the league because they felt that the Jets had weakened their bargaining position with Branch. Long before any other team had been granted permission to speak with Branch, the Patriots argued, the Jets had illegally done it. The league didn't agree with the Patriots' position, but it wouldn't be the last time the new commissioner in New York would have to mediate conflicts between the Patriots and Jets.

As expected, the new guy was Goodell, a former Jets intern and longtime league employee. He wasn't a lawyer like his predecessor, opting for economics during his undergraduate days. He was from Jamestown, New York, less than an hour from Buffalo, but that didn't please Bills owner Ralph Wilson. The owner, who believed that the league rigged the process to usher Goodell into the job, claimed that the new commissioner had forgotten his roots and hadn't been to Jamestown in years. Most owners weren't as personal as Wilson, and instead were excited by Goodell's business acumen. Before the commissioner was selected, Kraft couldn't have spoken more piercing and prophetic words.

"If we choose the wrong person as commissioner, it will be two or three years before we find out," he told the *Globe*. "A lot of damage can be done in that time."

As the season began, Brady was facing the biggest test of his career. He'd become used to the gradual change in Foxboro, with age, new opportunities, and phaseouts affecting some of his offensive teammates. He'd never before faced losing his two top weapons, both in their twenties. He'd have to figure it out with a new receiver, Reche Caldwell, who was solid but nothing like Branch and Givens. The tight end that he renamed "Motoring" Christian Fauria was in Washington and miserable. "As soon as I got there, I knew: They don't get it," he says. "Their style was antiquated. [Head coach] Joe Gibbs would be in team meetings listening to Clinton Portis bitch about wearing white shoes versus black shoes. I knew I was on borrowed time." Fauria's old teammate in New England, Troy Brown, was expecting to play a reduced role. But the lack of gumption from the rookie Chad Jackson meant that the veteran Brown would be needed to give more than expected.

The people Brady was handing the ball to were also changing. Corey Dillon had been record-setting in his first season with the team. In his second season, starting in November, things weren't quite right. Before a game in Miami he told new running back Heath Evans, "Hey, my calf feels funny. You better get ready." Evans did and ran for eighty-four yards in a spot start. Dillon's production was off all that year, and that's what led to the drafting of Maroney in Dillon's third and probably final year with the team.

One thing that wasn't changing in 2006, despite the personnel changes, was the expectation level of Belichick.

"When Bill would deliver tough messages to the team, they were all delivered with a purpose," Evans says. "They were very rarely pleasant messages from Bill, but they were purposeful. There's nobody like him in mastering the whole operation. It can be uncomfortable when you first witness it, and it was for me. I was paranoid. I was writing down every critique, every coaching point. But the nervousness calms down when you realize that he's giving you the answers to the test. You're getting prepared so you can play free in the games."

Brady had just turned twenty-nine, and he was at the point in his career where organizations would be adding to their quarterback's repertoire, not taking away pieces from it. He was in a different place in his life as an athlete and as a man. Moynahan was part of a TV show called *Six Degrees* that she filmed in New York. Speculation was that he had her in mind when he made a stunning $14.5 million purchase. His new three-bedroom condo was on the seventieth floor of the Time Warner Center at Columbus Circle. Moynahan, seven years older than Brady, often mentioned in interviews that she had a strong desire to start a family. Given all the circumstantial evidence, everything seemed to be aligned.

Even though the new characters around him were different, and often insufficient, Brady didn't suffer much. He clearly was manufacturing everything he could from the offense, and he was helped by a defense that was on its way to the best season in team history.

By early December, the Patriots were positioned atop the division with a 9-3 record. The season, on the field, had been drama-free, except for another Belichick versus Mangini episode in November. In that one, leading up to the Patriots-Jets game, Belichick refused to refer to Mangini by name. There would be "he" or "him" or "they're well coached," but no "Eric" or "Mangini."

What the audience didn't know at the time was that the organizations were fighting over cameras. Mangini knew that as part of their research to detect signaling trends, the Patriots liked to film coordinators giving signs, and he didn't want it done to him. He interpreted it as a power move by Belichick, maybe even a test to see what he would do. Belichick didn't see it that way, and so the taping continued. Mangini, in turn, planned to tape the Patriots. This, along with the Branch tampering charges, as well as the gossip about how he took the job, and just the fact that it was the Jets, accelerated the relationship to irreconcilable status.

The Jets were 7-5, a huge improvement from where they had been after week twelve in 2005, so Mangini was doing something right. He was mentioned as a Coach of the Year candidate, and some writers had begun calling him "Mangenius." He may not have been talking to Belichick, but he was acting like him as a team-builder. He went heavy on the offensive line in his first draft, selecting tackle D'Brickashaw Ferguson and center Nick Mangold. In free agency, he was interested in some familiar ex-Patriot names: Matt Chatham, Bobby Hamilton, Hank Poteat. With the way the division was unfolding, the Jets had a chance to make the play-offs and see the Patriots as their first opponent.

Brady didn't seem to have the postseason on his mind when he and the team went to Miami for their thirteenth game. The only good thing about the day, for the Patriots, was the plentiful sun. Brady kept dropping back and looking for the players he trusted. It wasn't accidental that he targeted Brown and Kevin Faulk, his guys, more than anyone else. He was desperate and frustrated. The Dolphins limited him to twelve completions and seventy-eight yards all day, winning 21–0.

Maybe the offense just didn't get it, or maybe he was simply out of it. Moynahan was in Miami, too, but she didn't visit him, nor did he visit her. It was surprising for the couple that had been spotted at NBA play-off games, galas, and random spots around New York and Boston. But there was a reason Brady didn't see Moynahan at her art show event and she didn't see him against the Dolphins. The relationship was over. Brady was the only quarterback in the league who could be the subject of the sports pages and *Us Weekly*. According to the magazine, and to Moynahan's publicist, "They amicably ended their three-year relationship several weeks ago. We ask for your respect and consideration of their privacy."

But this wasn't 2001 anymore. Privacy was no longer an option for Belichick or Brady. That would be fine with both of them if the public had just been gripped by the games and the cerebral matchups on the field. They had been too successful for that narrow gaze. Too handsome and too smart as well. Halberstam's book on Belichick had become the writer's fifteenth consecutive bestseller, and corporations and magazine photographers had reported no lack of interest in Brady's brand, his body, or his face. Belichick and Brady were going to have to learn what some celebrities meant by the paradoxical statement that, sometimes, there's deep loneliness in being famous.

For a brief window, it seemed that the worst public relations were over for the coach and the quarterback. There wasn't anything written about Belichick's divorce, and the society columns didn't share anything out of the ordinary about Brady. The first play-off opponent, the Jets, and the circus that they brought to Foxboro was refreshing compared to the pop-culture curiosity that the public craved.

Mangini hadn't spent all those years with Belichick in vain. He knew that the Patriots had greater talent, greater intangibles, and a greater quarterback. He would be able to junk up the game, defensively, for a while. Then talent was going to take over, which is exactly what happened. The Patriots won 37–16. With extra attention on the handshake between Belichick and Mangini at midfield, camera operators and photographers swarmed the would-be meeting point between professor and former student.

One of the photographers there was a perennial award-winner named Jim Davis. He knew sports as well as he knew photography, which gave him a skill for capturing some of the most provocative images in the city. But as he stood there trying to line up the shot, he was the one who was provoked. By Belichick. The coach pushed him out of the way and wrapped Mangini in a bear hug.

There was no coaching animosity between Belichick and Marty Schottenheimer, head coach of the Chargers. The only issue, beforehand, was the Chargers' 14-2 record. But when the Patriots upset San Diego, and subsequently danced on the Chargers' field, running back LaDainian Tomlinson attributed it to a lack of "class" and posited that it began "with the head coach."

There was so much accusing, name-calling, and finger-pointing after the game that not many people observed Brady's visitor. She was tall and thin, striking actually, and was much more comfortable talking about *fútbol* than the American version of it. It was Gisele Bündchen, the Brazilian supermodel, and perhaps for the first time in her adult life, most people didn't immediately notice her.

The calm of the moment, the sliver of privacy, was temporary. That would all change later in the year, when everything about the Patriots was public and wrong. That would all change next week, in Indianapolis. It was hard to believe: Despite the hellish year, the Patriots still had a chance to return to the Super Bowl.

CHAPTER TEN

TO CATCH A PATRIOT

In retrospect, Bill Belichick and Tom Brady's first play-off game together was easy. The opponent that night, the Oakland Raiders, had been tough, along with the weather. It had taken a painstaking film review, slow frame by slow frame of Brady's right arm, to reverse a game-ending fumble. After all that, a man who wasn't wearing winter boots in a nor'easter was expected to keep his footing and kick a football forty-five yards.

And that was only good enough to force overtime.

At least it was just about football then, and nothing else. At least they didn't have to put on armor before facing the local and national media because, for the most part, the media came in peace. They had learned to appreciate the coach, sometimes brainy and boorish, who was prep school classmates with Jeb Bush and Buzz Bissinger. They were smitten by the charismatic quarterback who always did and always would refer to Belichick as "Coach Belichick." Their story had sold dozens of times in American history, and it would sell again. Overcoming the odds. Redemption after mockery. The power of teamwork. The rejection of groupthink.

That Raiders game had been just five years ago, but it truly was from a different era. There was no such thing as Facebook or Twitter or TMZ then, and even if there had been, Belichick and Brady would have been too square for the format. But the years and a dozen additional play-off games had made them national celebrities. It was great for name recognition and the bottom line, although it also required profound self-awareness; if you're a celebrity who doesn't care about creating a public image, the public will scrutinize every piece of information about you and take over your self-portrait.

January 21, 2007, wasn't purely about football for Belichick and Brady, but it was one of the last times they'd take the field without having the legitimacy of their play-off wins and Super Bowl titles questioned. More pointedly, it was one of the last times they'd appear in public without having their characters probed and debated. The previous year had been accented by conflict at every turn, so much so that the default response of focusing on football was no longer valid. Their football world had been laced with conflict as well, and 2007 was going to be much worse.

For the moment, in an overheated domed stadium in downtown Indianapolis, there was still respect for both men. While it was going to be Brady's ninth career start against the Colts, it was only his third game in Indianapolis. According to the statistics, this was far from Brady's best season, but the fact that Brady could draw twenty-four touchdown passes and 3,529 yards from this leaden receiving corps was a tribute to his talent. Belichick, meanwhile, had not only fought with Eric Mangini, the exiled disciple; he had improved the defense with his replacement. New defensive coordinator Dean Pees relied heavily on a concept that was known as a Cover 4. It was a conservative, big-play-prevention defense, but when his players complained about it he would give them a simple response: "Win on first and second down, and we can get exotic on third down." They answered by winning a lot on the early downs, and they had finished with the fewest points allowed average, 14.8, in team history.

Pees couldn't have been happier in the first half, with the Patriots leading 14–3. That's when Asante Samuel, an elastic corner who was proficient at anticipating routes, made eye contact with Peyton Manning before his receiver, Marvin Harrison, did. Samuel intercepted the ball and ran thirty-nine yards for an easy touchdown and a 21–3 lead.

Adam Vinatieri had given the Colts five field goals the week before in Baltimore, and that was enough to get by the unimaginative Ravens offense. History suggested that the Colts wouldn't be able to do that while facing Belichick and Brady. What the New England head coach and quarterback understood was that this team wasn't like the others that had tormented Manning. Belichick had been nervous about the Colts' speed, so he had inserted a young linebacker, Eric Alexander, to match up with Dallas Clark, the quick Indianapolis tight end. It was a reach, and Manning was smart enough to recognize it and exploit it.

On offense, the problem for the Patriots was not complicated. They had a lone star, Brady. Two years earlier, Corey Dillon had run at the Colts, daring anyone to challenge his mix of fury, muscle, and speed. He was now in steep decline and not a consistent threat. Neither was his soon-to-be replacement, rookie Laurence Maroney. Troy Brown was the smartest player on the field, but this was going to be the last meaningful game of his career. Jabar Gaffney was fearless and athletic, a third option for a great offense, a primary option for this one.

As for Reche Caldwell, he was the first exhibit for the prosecution that argued *against* the Patriot Way and its good-value principles. Indeed, he had come up with a season-saving fumble recovery in San Diego. It was telling, though, that his most memorable play had not come as a receiver. In this game, the most important one of the year, Caldwell had twice dropped passes with no one covering him. The costlier one, with just under nine minutes to play, was maddening. The score was tied at 28, and Manning was on the sideline nervously chewing on a Gatorade towel. Brady and the offense were set up at the Colts' eighteen-yard line, and in a shocking defensive lapse, no one was lined up across from Caldwell. He waved his arms to alert Brady, and Brady saw him with his peripheral vision. He lofted a perfectly catchable pass to the receiver, who briefly touched the ball with both hands and then watched it fall to the turf. Nineteen-year-old Steve Belichick, the older of the coach's two sons, put his hands on his head in disbelief.

"It's hard to explain," Jim Nantz said to his TV audience on CBS.

They settled for a field goal on that drive, which everyone in the building knew wasn't going to be enough. Predictably, the Colts scored with a Vinatieri field goal, and the new kicker in Foxboro, rookie Stephen Gostkowski, responded with a forty-three-yarder for a 34–31 lead with 3:53 left. Unfortunately for the Patriots, they couldn't take advantage of another gift, a three-and-out by the Colts. They had the ball with 3:22 remaining, and all they had to do was sweat out the clock and force Indianapolis coach Tony Dungy to use his timeouts.

The strategy didn't work, and sixty-five seconds later, the ball was in Manning's hands again. This was where sweat came into play. The dome, with its arid heat and the relentlessness of Manning, was wearing down the defense. It didn't look like a historic unit at all. One of Tedy Bruschi's former coaches, Bo Pelini, used to have a meeting room saying when he was critiquing film with his players. The saying stuck with the linebacker during tough times. "The longest play in football is eight seconds," Pelini would begin, "and if you can't go hard for eight seconds, get the fuck out of my room!" They were going hard for those eight seconds, but they'd walk to the line of scrimmage with their hands on their hips.

Manning was aggressive now, scanning a defense that didn't have the loping Willie McGinest, who would practically pick up Manning's receivers and change their routes. There was no Rodney Harrison, injured at the end of the regular season. Harrison was a thinker and a hitter, so every play in his direction was a surprise. There was no Roman Phifer, who could stick with Manning's tight ends and punish them, too. There was no audacious Ty Law, who was now in Kansas City.

Eleven yards here to Reggie Wayne. Thirty-two yards there to Bryan Fletcher, who ran past Alexander, the so-called speed option. Fourteen more yards to Wayne, who bobbled and nearly lost the ball on the catch. It wouldn't have mattered if he had, because there was also a Patriots' penalty on the play.

The Patriots were wheezing. There were just under two minutes to play, with the ball at the New England eleven and the Patriots close to expiration. This was going to end their hopes of going to their fourth Super Bowl. Their run was not going to end, but their story was. This was their fourteenth play-off game since 2002 and, even if you didn't root for them, there was no reason to view their accomplishments with disdain. That would soon change. This was the end of a no-snark, no-scandal era for them.

So in the fourteenth and final act of the play, a production featuring the brilliant, cost-efficient, and authentic Patriots, they lost. Colts running back Joseph Addai ran up the middle, untouched, for a touchdown, and with twenty-four seconds to play Brady threw an interception.

All sorts of things had shifted now. Dungy and Manning, who had been the foil to Belichick and Brady, were finally getting a chance to go to the Super Bowl. Manning could figure out a way to beat Brady and the Patriots when it was important after all. The next time the Patriots played a game here, the Colts would be defending

Super Bowl champions while the Belichick-Brady public-relations stock would have fallen from hero worship to Hades.

The first hit of the offseason arrived courtesy of the *New York Times* and *Boston Globe*, with both newspapers publishing stories containing biting quotes from Ted Johnson. The former Patriots linebacker, a member of all three Super Bowl teams, claimed that Belichick made him practice in 2002, knowing that he was concussed. Johnson, thirty-four, said that his postfootball life was in shambles and added, "There's something wrong with me. There's something wrong with my brain. And I know when it started."

He said that he was anxious and forgetful, full of disappointment and shame. In his view, Belichick had "played God" with his health. Johnson's comments were a follow-up to a *Times* piece one month earlier, in which the paper reported that the 2006 suicide of former Philadelphia Eagle Andre Waters was caused by brain damage from football injuries. Belichick told the *Globe* that he would never ask an injured player to participate in anything physical. "If Ted felt so strongly that he didn't feel he was ready to practice with us, he should have told me," the coach said.

Within a week, in an interview with ESPN's Wendi Nix, Johnson backed off his story and said that he didn't want to blame Belichick or anyone else for his struggles.

It was never a good time to be accused of ignoring concussions, but PR-wise, this was the worst stretch of Belichick's career. The resignation from the Jets, outside of New York, had a *Saturday Night Live* feel to it and wasn't seen as egregious in all corners. The press conferences, as awkward as they could be, weren't always criticized by the public due to the public's contempt for the media. Some fans found it fascinating watching the watchdogs squirm as they were given long pauses and minimalist answers. The controversial moves with Drew Bledsoe, Lawyer Milloy, and Adam Vinatieri could be interpreted as doing good business. There were even some who defended Belichick's hearty push of *Globe* photographer Jim Davis following the play-off win over the Mangini-led Jets.

But the testimony, under oath, from Morristown Family Court in New Jersey was hard to fathom. This was a multilayered nightmare for the coach: It was a story that he couldn't control or even counter; its contents were explosive; and it gave the public a gateway into aspects of his personal life, of which he was fiercely protective.

A New Jersey construction worker went to the court to request an amendment to his alimony payments. He said that he shouldn't have to pay $350 per week because his wife was already receiving lavish payments, gifts, and services, and that they could only be coming from someone wealthy. And that's when Belichick's name became a part of what was supposed to be a routine no-fault divorce case. The woman, a former New York Giants receptionist named Sharon Shenocca, testified that she was the beneficiary of numerous gifts from Belichick, including a $25,000 rental for the summer on the Jersey Shore; help with an $11,000 retainer for her attorney; $3,000 per month; trips to Disney, Puerto Rico, and Jamaica; furniture; chartered flights; a personal trainer; a health-club membership; Giants season tickets; a trip to the Super Bowl; and use of a $2.2 million Belichick-owned brownstone in Brooklyn's Park Slope, a historic neighborhood adjacent to Brooklyn's version of Central Park, filled with trees, kids, dogs, and strollers.

The records for Belichick's own divorce were sealed and impounded, but the Morristown case was antithetical to everything he envisioned, media-wise. New information about the case was trickling out weekly, in New York and Boston, and the only way to stop it was for Shenocca to settle with her ex-husband, which she eventually did.

In early February, Brady put the $14.5 million Time Warner Center condo that he had purchased five months earlier on the market. He bumped the price to $16.5 million. It was thought that he purchased the space to be closer to Bridget Moynahan, but the couple's relationship ended late in 2006. Through a mutual friend, the quarterback had been introduced to one of the savviest and most successful supermodels in the world, Gisele Bündchen, who had her own palatial space in Tribeca. *Rolling Stone* once referred to her as the most beautiful girl in the world, and perhaps she showed the magazine's phrasing to some of her classmates in her Brazilian hometown; back then, in the small city of Horizontina, she was nicknamed "Olive Oyl."

As a five-foot-eleven-inch international symbol, her modeling nicknames were a little different and much more suggestive, such as "The Body" and "The Boobs from Brazil." She was discovered when she was fourteen. By nineteen, she was considered a star. At twenty-six, when she and Brady quickly fell for each other, she was known for making any cover she graced or clothing she modeled fly off the shelves.

She and Brady also had a lot in common, beyond their Hollywood exes (actor Leonardo DiCaprio once went so far as presenting Bündchen with a $500,000 engagement ring). They were both physically attractive people whose smarts were overshadowed by their looks. They also had similar views of celebrity, which Bündchen summarized one year into her superstardom: "I know that if I had a normal job, I wouldn't make as much money, but if you have a normal job, you can go home and be normal. I love my job, but I don't love all of it. And I don't love being famous."

The rich and famous were forced to live differently, such as releasing good news via publicists. That's what happened on February 20, when Moynahan announced that she was three months pregnant and the father was her ex-boyfriend, Brady. It wasn't long before Brady's agent, Don Yee, was announcing that Brady "and his family are excited about the pregnancy."

This was one of the downsides of fame that Bündchen mentioned, the speculation of what might have happened and then the subsequent judgment based on the speculation. One thing quickly became clear, through publicists and sources: Bündchen and Brady were staying together and Moynahan, with cooperation from Brady, was going to raise the child alone. It was mind-bending news in Boston because the reputation of Brady was nothing short of angelic.

"Brady never has ripped a coach, turned on a teammate, shoved a cameraman, whined about money or forgotten to send a card on Mother's Day," Gerry Callahan wrote in the *Herald*. He continued, "Bottom line: The guy has been virtually perfect since the day he stepped in for a severely wounded Drew Bledsoe more than five years ago. It is hard to believe the first bump in the road turns out to be a baby."

Dan Shaughnessy took a similar tack in the *Globe*: "Brady was going to be the Boston superstar athlete who'd get in and out of town without being touched by scandal or controversy. No police blotters…No diva demonstrations. No steroids. No suspensions. No palimony suits. No taking money under the table while at Michigan…Now he has taken a hit—something far more bone-rattling than any blind-side tackle delivered by Dwight Freeney or Shawne Merriman."

Brady was used to having his quarterbacking scrutinized, and even his appearances at expensive dinners and galas. Now his potential to parent from another household was a debate point, along with some sleuthing to find out when exactly he ended things with Moynahan and started things with Bündchen. He was a cover boy, often described as a sex symbol, although it was clear from TV and radio shows, blogs, and conversations locally and nationally that few people believed that he would actually have unprotected sex.

There was some harsh criticism of Brady, but it was mostly national voyeurism of how three wealthy people planned to handle an issue that affects more than one-third of the country.

Belichick had coached the AFC in the Pro Bowl in February, and he'd hit it off with a couple of players. One of them was free agent linebacker Adalius Thomas, a man who claimed to have no position. He wanted to be called, simply, "a football player." In Baltimore, Thomas's bombastic defensive coordinator, Rex Ryan, had called him a cross between Lawrence Taylor and Carl Banks. He had played corner, safety, linebacker, and defensive end.

Belichick had coached Taylor and Banks, so he knew Ryan was exaggerating, but he lived for players with the 270-pound Thomas's skills and mentality. He returned to Foxboro excited about the big football player's intelligence, speed, and character.

With their first chance to get the twenty-nine-year-old Thomas, the Patriots overwhelmed him. They gave him $18 million in guarantees and $24 million in the first three years of his contract. They also bought their receivers in bulk: They agreed to deals with former Saints first-rounder Donté Stallworth; Wes Welker, a twenty-five-year-old slot receiver that they were getting in yet another heist from the Dolphins; and Kelley Washington, a receiver whom they also projected as a special-teams ace.

The Patriots were in the middle of a shift, and so was the league. The new commissioner, Roger Goodell, was getting stellar reviews just seven months into the position. It didn't seem to concern anyone that Goodell, with an economics background and an economic platform to get the job, seemed to be magnetized to discipline and legal matters.

The tough-talking sheriff played well in Football America, and when he took the stage on draft day he was well received by the Radio City Music Hall crowd. The Patriots held two first-rounders, with the extra one coming from Seattle in the Branch trade. Far ahead of the Patriots' first pick at number twenty-four, Eric Mangini had pulled off a Belichick-like maneuver for a player he craved. It was University of Pittsburgh cornerback Darrelle Revis, whom Mangini had personally worked out and given the highest possible grades in several categories. He felt that Revis was one of the best prospects he'd ever seen and was ecstatic to get him at number fourteen.

The Patriots, meanwhile, approached this draft tepidly. They drafted Miami safety Brandon Meriweather with their lead first-round pick.

They traded their second first, number twenty-eight, to San Francisco for the 49ers' top pick in 2008. It was a patented Belichick move, exchanging a current asset for a future one that had the potential to be much greater. Overnight, the Patriots also had conversations with one of the most exciting receivers in NFL history. Randy Moss, thirty, was desperate to play on a winning team, and he expressed that to Belichick and Scott Pioli in a candid and emotional conversation. He was introspective and tearful, and he even agreed to rip up the deal he'd signed with the Oakland Raiders, reduce his cap number from over $9 million to $3 million, and prove his worthiness on a one-year contract.

The next morning, the slender six-foot-four-inch receiver was riding in Josh McDaniels's SUV, headed from Logan Airport to Gillette Stadium. The Patriots traded a fourth-round pick, number 110 overall, for the right to gamble on the resurrection of Moss.

Moss was a prodigy at the position when he was in the right space, and when that happened the field was wide open for everyone. Belichick and McDaniels were pinning their hopes on that version of Moss, and it was part of the reason the offensive coordinator had picked him up from the airport. They were going to need to talk about the possibilities of the new offense.

"You're going to really see some things that you've never seen before," Moss boasted to the local media in his first conference call with them. "And when it does happen, don't say I didn't tell you."

Briefly, there was no controversy with the Patriots, or any other local team. Belichick, not known for his outward displays of affection, was seen in Boston and on Nantucket with his new girlfriend, Linda Holliday. They'd gone to Celtics, Red Sox, and college basketball games together. They'd held hands on Nantucket, drinking wine and listening to romantic piano ballads. The coach looked happy. When he went to those games around town, there was a lot to be cheerful about. The Sox had been in first place all season, and at the start of training camp on July 27, they led the Yankees by eight games. A few days later, the Celtics, coached by Belichick's friend Doc Rivers, announced that they had acquired future Hall of Fame forward Kevin Garnett from Minnesota. The addition of Garnett to a team that already included All-Stars Paul Pierce and Ray Allen meant that there could be another year of multiple rolling rallies in downtown Boston.

Belichick taught on-field restraint and media understatement, but it was hard to keep the 2007 Patriots in the box. McDaniels was quickly seeing how a routine play and the mere whiteboard theory of it could explode into artistic greatness when players such as Moss and Welker were executing the assignments. They were going to be hard to stop, and there weren't going to be many opponents, on the field, capable of doing it. This was quite the offensive wake-up call from last year's camp.

"Randy was the type of guy who would light up a room," Richard Seymour says. "He was such an amazing talent. Everyone else was pros, but he was like a Greek god. He had the ability to do whatever he said he was going to do."

On August 22, a Wednesday, Brady wasn't there to answer a question about Moss, the possibilities of the new offense, or anything else. He wasn't spotted during the fifteen-minute period when the media could view practice, and the Patriots were offering no clues about where he was. But it was obvious. Moynahan had announced her pregnancy, at three months, in February. It was just over six months later. Brady was on his way to Los Angeles to see his newborn son. The healthy baby was given a good Catholic name: John Edward Thomas Moynahan. Tongue in cheek, the critics astutely noted that the baby's initials spelled "JET."

Brady and the Patriots were now focused on the beginning of the season, which was two and a half weeks away. They'd be opening against the other Jets, certainly not the cuddly kind, and there was plenty of work to do on them. They didn't have time to study news trends and the opinions of American sports fans. But if they had, they would have found an angry sporting public, disappointed by a year that had already represented fraudulence and broken trust.

The summer pushed many people over the threshold, which in part explained the early popularity of Goodell. The public wanted someone to be firm in the face of unethical and criminal behavior. Michael Vick had been accused of bankrolling and gambling on dogfighting, and equipment for the crude sport was found on his Virginia property. Investigators found whips, injectable drugs, chains, and treadmills. Sixty pit bulls were found, many with scarring and broken limbs. Vick was likely going to prison and his Atlanta Falcons and NFL career was in jeopardy. An NBA official, Tim Donaghy, had been found guilty of betting on league games.

There was already suspicion about the league's officials, who had to fight the perception that they looked the other way when superstars fouled, traveled, carried, complained, or did anything negative that might interfere with the predestined result of the game. It wasn't that simplistic, but that was the perception, and the criminal actions of Donaghy fueled the urban legends and conspiracies.

And then there was Major League Baseball, with the saddest and most legalistic record-breaking chase ever. Barry Bonds, who unconvincingly claimed he never knowingly took performance-enhancing drugs, was in pursuit of Hank Aaron's all-time home run record, and no one wanted to see or hear him break it. Literally. The year before, when Bonds passed Babe Ruth's 714th home run for second on the list, the microphone of play-by-play man Dave Flemming went dead just as he was saying, "A drive deep to cen—" That was number 715, and no one on San Francisco's KNBR radio heard it. This year, commissioner Bud Selig sent someone else to witness historic number 756 and Aaron sent a video tribute. Except even that wasn't really a tribute. A Giants executive had asked Aaron to do it a month earlier in New York, and the slugger agreed only after he was able to have his statement carefully written and vetted. That was sports in 2007; even the heartfelt moments needed copywriters and lawyers.

Which explains how the Patriots stepped right into the spirit of the cheating times, twice in the span of two weeks, and found themselves on a rotary with no exit. They had always been seen as contrary to the age, in every way. Players behaved badly elsewhere and their crooked paths became straight in Foxboro. Commentators measured talent individually through Pro Bowls; the Patriots countered by speaking collectively about Super Bowls. In a culture of shortcuts, they went the long hard way, and you could see it with receivers playing cornerback, linebackers playing tight end, and everyone chipping in on special teams. Isn't that why they were celebrated as the model organization? Isn't that why the clever coach and analytical quarterback were celebrities? But then Rodney Harrison, one of the captains, admitted that he purchased human growth hormone online. He had been injured the year before, and he said he took the NFL-banned drug not because he wanted a competitive advantage, but because he wanted to get back on the field.

It sounded hollow. It sounded like a rationalization for cheating. It was easy for Goodell to make the call. He suspended Harrison for the first four games of the regular season.

The Harrison news created a buzz, but it didn't invalidate the accomplishments of the entire team. That would happen just over a week later, after the Patriots displayed their new look to the NFL in New York. The game itself was fine, with Moss gliding past Jets rookie cornerback Darrelle Revis and a fleet of others on his way to a fifty-one-yard touchdown reception from Brady. The whole defense chased Moss, and it was a reminder of how fragile schemes can be when they try to contain a virtuoso. *You're going to really see some things that you've never seen before*...Moss had been right; this was supernatural. The Patriots won 38–14, and that was a footnote within hours.

There had been a report after the game that Patriots employee Matt Estrella had ventured to the sideline, with a camera, and begun filming Jets coaches. The teams had argued about this for more than a year, and the league had sent a memo explicitly detailing the restrictions on camerawork. The Jets had expected the videographer, Estrella, to try this. They took him and his camera off the field and alerted the league.

As more information was gathered in the days after the game, an undeniable picture was starting to take shape. Belichick had broken the league's rules on the use of cameras. This was no border-line cruise through the caution light; he had blown through the red, undoubtedly. It was tough for many in New England to accept, and there was a segment of media and fans who claimed that the violation was strictly about location of the taping and not the offense itself. It wasn't true.

The league didn't want teams to videotape the signals of other teams, no matter where they were. A friend of Belichick's, Jimmy Johnson, suggested that the practice was commonplace when he was coaching. That defense didn't resonate with the league, the public, or even thousands of embarrassed Patriots fans. The seemingly contradictory nature of what was happening in front of eighty thousand people—coaches giving signals!—and the restrictions on taping those signal-giving coaches was not lost on members of the competition committee.

"See, not everybody does it," Jeff Fisher, Titans coach and chair of the competition committee, said. "That's the misunderstanding. When you say everybody does it, not everybody is recording. There's not a bylaw against sitting up in a press box and taking notes with binoculars as fast as you can. But there is a bylaw as far as videotaping signals, and that is the issue. We just have to be very careful when we say everyone does it. To my knowledge, this is the only team that videotaped coaches' signals."

Belichick and his players tried to use their Ignore the Noise template to deal with the story, and it worked for them in the cocoon of football operations. But there was a national avalanche outside those doors, and it wasn't going to slow down all year. It was hard to go anywhere without hearing voices. Current and ex-players. Current and ex-coaches. Players in Philadelphia and Pittsburgh saying they deserved to have rings because the Patriots were cheaters. Aha moments from the Rams and Panthers, who now had an explanation for how the Patriots beat them in Super Bowls. Suggestions that the Patriots taped practices. And taped walk-throughs. And even taped microphones to their jerseys to pick up the audio of quarterbacks. There were whispers about equipment always failing at critical times in Foxboro. There were those who wondered if three titles, won by a total of 9 points, would have been achieved without those cameras. Was Brady truly a smart quarterback or someone who was clandestinely told everything an opponent was doing? Were those original Belichick game plans? Or was he just a gifted spy, trying to gadget his way to the Hall of Fame?

It was an onslaught, unforgiving and unstoppable. It even had its own catchy moniker: Spygate.

The Patriots had to reconcile this and live with it, perhaps forever: They might be able to defeat an opponent on the field, but they would never defeat Spygate. Never. It was impossible. It was fueled by valid criticism as well as irrationality. It got air in its lungs both from the disobedience of Belichick and the discontent of silver, bronze, and non-medalists. It got its muscle from justice and jealousy. There were so many obvious truths, such as the sledgehammer language the league used when it sent its memo about the purpose of cameras. The tone was just short of all-caps: "Videotaping of any type, including but not limited to taping of an opponent's offensive or defensive signals, is prohibited on the sidelines, in the coaches' booth, in the locker room, or at any other locations accessible to club staff members during the game." There were half-truths as well. There were only so many seconds to diagnose an offense or defense and call a play; Spygate was many things, but it was no open-book test.

But what was it? Why did Belichick put so much at risk for something with such a minimal payoff? Only time would tell if it was his secret weapon, but the reasonable voices in the symphony knew that he didn't have to do it, which made his decision to do it so infuriating. He had created a raging, complex, multidimensional beast.

When Goodell sorted out the information, he slammed Belichick with a league-record $500,000 fine. He fined the organization $250,000. He took away a 2008 first-round pick. He ordered all tapes and notes in the Patriots' library to be handed over to him. Some critics complained that Goodell hadn't been harsh enough, arguing that a suspension should have replaced the draft pick. But the commissioner, an economist himself, knew how to hit at the knees. Belichick's understanding and manipulation of draft picks had helped him suffocate the AFC East and set the Patriots' foundation. The penalty was crushing.

When asked for specifics about the incident, both Mangini and Belichick offered no insight. Belichick released a statement that suggested he'd had a different interpretation of the league's memo. His position was that he was never taping for use in that particular game. Even so, the league found the practice of taping coaches objectionable.

The rules for the 2007 season needed no special interpretation: It was Football America versus the Patriots. Last one standing wins.

The Patriots, talented and extra temperamental now, got a sprinter's start. The first game after Spygate, against the Chargers at Gillette Stadium, Belichick was shown on the video board and received rousing applause from most of the sixty-eight thousand fans. They cheered all night in another 38–14 win. It got silly the next week with another 38 against Buffalo, and then back-to-back 34s against the Ohioans, the Bengals and Browns. It was Patriots lotto. Call out a number higher than 30 and see if it's reached. How about 48 against the Cowboys? Raise that to a 49 in Miami. You really want to show off? Try accepting the worst field position possible, force yourself to have three scoring drives of eighty-five yards or longer, and score 52 at home against Washington.

That was good for 8-0 at intermission, and America needed some halftime adjustments. Honestly, the Boston thing was becoming burdensome. The football team wins in a blowout by day and the baseball team sweeps through the World Series at night. The Sox were champions again, winners of eight consecutive Series games between 2004 and 2007.

Brady's numbers were more absurd than those. He was completing 74 percent of his passes, and he'd already set his career high with thirty touchdown passes. His sack and interception numbers were nearly identical, three and two respectively. Moss had unveiled a modest touchdown celebration, in which he parted his hands, signifying that he could still split and get behind a defense. He had done that dance, to the delight of his teammates and fans, eleven times.

The return trip to Indianapolis ended with another Spygate swipe and Patriots win, the usual daily double. Colts coach Tony Dungy had used an analogy linking Belichick to Bonds, so there was no surprise postgame when Dungy got the Mangini treatment from the Patriots coach. The final score there was actually football-like, 24–20.

Not many people nationally had to like what the Patriots were doing, but they couldn't resist watching and talking about it. Not all of their critics believed that they were cheating, yet it was still shorthand for all of the things they detested about the team. They were as villainous now as they had been embraceable in 2001.

"Bill Belichick sickens me," Rick Telander wrote in the *Chicago Sun-Times*. "And, no, it's not because his New England Patriots have won three Super Bowls in the last six years or that he's widely saluted as a sports 'genius.' This is not about jealousy, envy or anything that has to do with his ratty sweatshirts or suspect personal skills or coldheartedness (ask longtime Patriots linebacker Ted Johnson, currently brain-damaged, about Belichick's empathy)... This video-camera sideline recording of the New York Jets' defensive signals was no 'mistake'... It was a conscious, overt act of deception and a blatant middle finger to the essence of fair play."

That was going to be the story for many, no matter what the dizzying results on the field.

A four-touchdown *half* for Moss in Buffalo; a clinched division title in November; a good-fortune win in Baltimore, where former Dolphins coach Don Shula openly rooted against the Patriots in the *Monday Night Football* booth. Ravens defensive coordinator Rex Ryan called a timeout a split second before his team had made a game-ending stop on fourth down. After that, three easy wins over the Steelers, Jets, and Dolphins.

They were 15-0 returning to Giants Stadium for the first time since this lopsided race began. America, yes, the whole country, had decided to take them on and they hadn't backed down from the challenge. So who was the underdog here, a nation of millions or one team called the Patriots? A superficial reading had the United States losing on all cards. After all, everyone was watching this game because Goodell had declared it worthy of three networks. He didn't want there to be a chance that anyone would miss it. For a team that was so disgraceful, America found the Patriots irresistible.

The former Patriots were watching, too, and were rooting for the team to do something that was realistic in high school and college but certainly not the pros. "Nobody ever sets out to go sixteen and oh," Deion Branch, who was watching from Seattle, says. "Sixteen and oh is crazy. I can't imagine what those guys were thinking week to week. I was proud of them." Branch, in a different offense with the Seahawks, could still identify what the Patriots were doing.

The principles of the system were the same, but instead of David Patten as the "X" or downfield receiver, it was Moss. A younger version of Troy Brown, Wes Welker, was now in the slot. Fast receivers who could alternate between the slot and perimeter, where Branch used to be, were now named Donté Stallworth and Jabar Gaffney.

Roman Phifer, two years into retirement, was able to sit back and hear some of the conversations about the team that was marching through the league. It didn't take long to take the national temperature. "People just do not like the Patriots outside of New England," he says. "Usually it's people who don't understand what it takes to get to that level. They look for excuses for why you were so good. They always try to tarnish it."

That was the theme for many former Patriots, either on other teams or out of the league. It wasn't just the current team being questioned. They felt an attack on their careers and their rings. They were insulted.

"I've never once seen a tape of somebody else's walk-through or practices. I didn't know what the hell they were talking about," Ty Law, who was in Kansas City at the time, says now. "I was really oblivious to the situation. You're not going to take away my Super Bowl interception. I was thinking, 'You all are full of shit.' I thought it was just a thing because it was the Patriots and Bill Belichick. They wanted to stick it to us somehow or some way."

The other numbers, not just the ratings, said that the Patriots were winning. They had won all fifteen of their games, and with flair. Brady had thrown forty-eight touchdown passes, and Moss had caught twenty-one of them. There were over one hundred catches and one thousand yards from Welker, whose new team in New England had as many wins as his old team in Miami had losses.

So what was the problem? There was nothing discernible against the Giants, who played well in a 38–35 loss. Brady finished the regular season with fifty touchdown passes, one for each state in the country. He was thirty years old and was finally going to get an award, the MVP, that he'd deserved years earlier. Moss's twenty-third touchdown reception, a league record, came on Brady's fiftieth touchdown pass.

There was nothing wrong with 16-0, a miraculous achievement in any year, and especially one in which there were open calls for authentication. The problem wouldn't be obvious until after there were two play-off wins over the Jaguars and Chargers, setting up a rematch against the Giants in the Super Bowl.

The Patriots, as sublime as they were, should have known the rules better than anyone. Never let your opponent define what the game is about. Throughout the season, as the games got tighter, the Patriots put more pressure on themselves to be perfect. They had always been able to use different media reports for an Us versus Them straw man, but it wasn't a straw man this time. It was real, and as much as they tried to reflect the steel and indifference of their head coach, it got to them; it turns out that more than a few of them wanted to be liked.

As the game got closer, Spygate, the insatiable dragon, started breathing again. Senator Arlen Specter told the *New York Times* that he wanted a congressional investigation, and the *Boston Herald* reported that it had a source who claimed that the Patriots taped the St. Louis Rams walk-through before Super Bowl XXXVI. At a time when they should have been focused on the history they were going to make in Arizona and the game they were going to play against the Giants, they were thinking about their critics. Belichick met with his captains the day before the game and asked them if he should mention the *Herald* report to the entire team. The captains told him no, although they could acknowledge that going through the entire season with their hands up was exhausting.

This was not their style, their fight, or their game. All of those regular-season numbers were gaudy, but the old Patriots were never concerned with the numbers. They were the first ones who would point out that the definition of success was championships, not sending three offensive linemen to the Pro Bowl, or league records from the quarterback and one of his wide receivers.

They should have known, early, that something was amiss. The Giants defensive coordinator, Steve Spagnuolo, had hoped to keep the Patriots' offense in the twenties for the entire game. He wanted to be realistic, and that number was just about right. But at half-time it was 7–3, Patriots, and the Giants were dominating the line of scrimmage. There was no need to concede the twenties. Playing like this, the Giants might be able to keep the game in the teens and win it.

It was a scoreless third quarter, and the Giants went ahead, 10–7, early in the fourth on a touchdown reception by receiver David Tyree. A touchdown catch in the Super Bowl is a highlight for most players, but it would be far from Tyree's most significant play of the night. With just under three minutes to play, finally, the most feared duo in the league connected. It was Brady to Moss, on a short touchdown pass, for a 14–10 lead. On the sideline, Tedy Bruschi hugged teammate Junior Seau, thirty-nine, who had never been this close to a championship. In his previous Super Bowl appearance, a dozen years earlier, his team never had a chance. That night, against the 49ers, it was due to Seau's Chargers' lack of talent. On this night, his team was the favorite but didn't have a chance, either, with some of the things that were happening in the final minutes.

The definitive play was a third-and-five with seventy-five seconds to play. New York quarterback Eli Manning appeared to be lost in the arms of Richard Seymour and Jarvis Green. He escaped, though, and threw a long pass downfield. In one of the most extraordinary plays in Super Bowl history, Tyree reached above his head, trapped the football against his helmet, and brought the ball to his body for a thirty-two-yard reception. All the while, Rodney Harrison tried to swat and wrestle the ball away from him.

America was rallying.

"I haven't watched the game to this day," Seymour says. "If you think about all the things that happened, from almost getting Eli in the grasp, to Asante [Samuel] almost getting a pick, to Tyree catching the ball on top of his head. If you think about all that, you have to say that they deserved it. I played in four Super Bowls and we won three of them. But it's the one that you don't get that you agonize over."

With Tyree's catch, the Giants had great field position but not a lot of time. With forty-five seconds remaining, they converted a third-and-eleven that gave them the ball at the Patriots' thirteen-yard line. The Patriots' best cornerback was Samuel, and this was his last game in New England. He had agreed to sign the franchise tag in 2007, but he had been assured it wouldn't be applied in 2008. The Patriots liked his ability to cover, although they questioned his versatility due to his discomfort with playing left and right cornerback. He was more at home on the left side, which is why five-foot-nine corner Ellis Hobbs, who was playing with shoulder and groin injuries, was matched up with six-foot-five-inch receiver Plaxico Burress.

"I thought that for who he was on the team, The Guy, The Cover Corner, Franchise Tag Corner, Asante should have been on Plaxico," Law says. "And I'd tell him that. He was my young pup. I was a mentor to him when he was there in his young days, playing behind me.

"Everybody in the stadium, everybody at home, knew where the ball was going. You've got a six-foot-five receiver down in the red zone. You knew it was going to be a fade. Everybody knew that. Hobbs bit on the worst move I've ever seen in my life. It's no need to bite on something like that because you know it's a jump ball situation to Plaxico Burress. Asante should have went over there and said, 'Ellis, I got this. Take the other guy. We gonna win or lose the ball game on me. I'm getting the big bucks, I'm gonna show everybody that I'm the best.' You didn't have to ask that with Deion Sanders. You didn't have to ask that with me. You don't have to ask that with Darrelle Revis."

It wasn't just Samuel. Everyone had a moment or two from the game that would be mentally played and replayed, over and over, for weeks, months, and years. As Law said, Burress put a move inside on Hobbs and then ran to the corner of the end zone. It was an easy completion for the winning touchdown.

The Patriots had their first loss of the season, 17–14. They were 18-1, ridiculed for that loss, and suspect-in-perpetuity until they could win another Super Bowl, something that 40 percent of the league had never done.

The early days had been easier. America had caught up to them, finally, and won.

CHAPTER ELEVEN

THE OUTSIDERS

One of the things that drew Tom Brady's teammates to him was that he never said the things that they were thinking. Once, for example, Mike Vrabel had been talking with reporters about the Patriots and their ability to overcome injuries to Rodney Harrison and Matt Light.

"Those are great players," Vrabel said that day, "but nobody is too good to be replaced around here." He quickly corrected himself. "Well, besides Tom."

They all knew it was true, and they also knew it wasn't a part of Brady's personality to say it. Not even while joking around in the locker room or during a guys' night out. He was a natural observer and team-builder, quickly diagnosing what the situation needed and then delivering it. He was gifted, and it went far beyond his knowledge of the game and his photogenic face.

When a lot of people started to talk and be concerned about identity theft in 2004, Visa wanted to make that the centerpiece of a thirty-second commercial that would air in 2005. The idea was to "talk about layers of security without getting too deep in the weeds," says John Van de Brook, who worked on the spot for six months. It was the perfect situation for Brady. This was an opportunity to do a commercial and involve his teammates. So five of his offensive linemen became the five layers of security sitting around a table in a fancy restaurant in full pads and helmets, while Brady played the handsome bachelor out on a date who was constantly surrounded by their "security" and one-liners. It was his commercial, technically, but it had played out exactly the way he wanted.

"It took us three or four hours to shoot the commercial, and Brady and the guys were cracking up the entire time," Van de Brook says. "Lots of laughs and jokes. It was clear that he loved his linemen. Brady was great and affable, but he was not the star of that spot. The strength was in the interaction of the linemen, their warmth and humor."

Off camera, he wasn't even good at playing the demanding superstar of a Visa commercial. Contractually, he had the right to request whatever he wanted in his greenroom. He chose Gatorade and Skittles.

That same year, DirecTV wanted to do a commercial with Brady.

"He called me and said, 'Let's go do this commercial,'" says Deion Branch. "It didn't surprise me at all. That's just Tom. He wants to be one of the guys."

It wasn't an easy task, mostly because it required cooperation by Brady and his teammates. It had been simple in 2000 when he was a backup, and in 2001 when he was an emerging star and not yet the leader of the team. But what about now, in February 2008? He needed to be an interactive leader for many reasons, beginning with a basic point: The majority of the team hadn't seen him when he was just Tom, hanging out by his locker and teasing Damon Huard for carrying what appeared to be a purse. They didn't all know him, the real him, so part of his quarterbacking was to guide them away from the celebrity and toward someone who had a lot in common with them.

This wasn't the old days anymore. The Super Bowl loss to the Giants was illustrative of just how fast the league moved. When Brady walked off that field in Arizona, he was one of just nine Patriots who had been around for all three Super Bowl titles. He was going to be thirty-one at the beginning of the season, and thirty-one meant he was old enough to hear some of his teammates say that they had been watching him play since they were in high school. It was a good reminder that his leadership style couldn't be a disengaged *I'll just lead by example.*

That had never been his way, even when he was their age. There was dexterity to his intelligence, so he was comfortable in multiple settings. New teammate Christian Fauria, six years older than Brady, noticed his maturity in 2002. Fauria was married at the time with two young children, and Brady was single and twenty-five. They were hanging out at Huard's house, and Fauria's wife, Rhonda, began breastfeeding their infant son. Instead of being awkward, Brady initiated a conversation about breastfeeding and the benefits of it.

"It made me think, 'He's real,'" Fauria says. "He felt it was important for him to show her the respect and attention she deserved. He wasn't weirded out; he saw the situation as natural. It wasn't the typical reaction of a twenty-five-year-old man. I know it sounds strange, but that's actually the moment when I realized how special he is."

Three years later, it was Brady's thoughtful letters and texts to teammate Tedy Bruschi that made the linebacker wonder aloud in amazement, "Who is this guy? Is he real?" Brady was checking in on and encouraging him after Bruschi's stroke. He and his sisters brought him food. He went to church with him. He even helped his wife, Heidi, plan a surprise party for Bruschi's thirty-second birthday.

Two weeks after the stunning loss to the Giants, a loss that had a team wondering how it could improve on an 18-1 season, Brady was at it again. This time he was doing a favor for a friend in Suffolk County Superior Court. He was testifying in Charlie Weis's medical malpractice trial in downtown Boston. Patriots fans wanted what was best for their former offensive coordinator, but they weren't focused on anyone except for the tall man who climbed out of a black Volvo wearing a pin-striped suit, a crisp white shirt, and a neatly folded white pocket square.

Court officers attempted to maintain order, all the while trying to get a glimpse of Brady themselves. In anticipation of his appearance, the courtroom was packed tighter than Gillette Stadium. Some people even tried to go with stadium rules and create standing-room-only positions. They were told to leave; many of them didn't listen. A sixty-one-year-old woman named Gail Whittier, who ran the courtroom coffee shop, got to chat with the quarterback and get his autograph. Whittier, who is legally blind, told the *Boston Herald* that Brady had a firm handshake ("He was no wimp") and that he smelled the way everyone thought he looked ("Nice and clean").

Vrabel was right. The Patriot Way did not apply to Brady. He was unlike any athlete in Boston history. Many of the greats had aspects of what he had, but not in totality like Brady. Ted Williams had been a war hero, an expert fisherman, and genuine hitting scientist. But Ted never won a championship and often found himself fighting with the media. Larry Bird was a three-time champion and three-time MVP, but he wasn't nearly the heartthrob that Brady was. Bill Russell won eleven titles and five MVPs; Bobby Orr was the greatest defenseman who ever lived; David Ortiz slugged away at the curse and helped the Red Sox win two World Series in four years after winning none in eighty-six. But no one combined style, substance, local and national pop-culture appeal, and public relations like Brady.

"Tom is a special dude," Ty Law says. "It's a little bit different for him now because he's such a celebrity. Such an icon. Such a, you know, living legend. It's hard to go out and move about and do things like a normal person. But he has such a sense of normalcy when you're with him. And long before all this stuff, it's what made us like Tom so much. With Tom, we were all there and it was just like being with one of the guys.

"It's hard to do, but he did well with it. He *can't* be like the rest of us. He can't do the same things that the rest of us do. He ain't gonna be able to enjoy himself. I've always said in life, 'F the fame, give me the fortune.' I don't need the fame. Anytime you have to rent out the whole movie theater just to take your family to the movies, something is wrong. I mean, that's not living. To be that famous where I can't have an intimate moment with my wife or girlfriend or kids, that's not cool to me. Tom lives in that world."

He had started 127 consecutive games and his career record was 100-27, a winning percentage of .790. All the winning had given him tremendous clout, with the public and in the locker room, although he wasn't wired the way some thought he would be. Or, more accurate, who *they* would be if they had his power and influence. He was sensitive to the locker room messages he could potentially send by politicking management. On one hand, it would ensure that things got done. On the other, he's not really one of the guys, is he, if he's orchestrating deals in a way that no one else can? It was better for him and the team to be a strong player, a quarterback, a captain, and leave the coaching and front-office decisions to those who are paid to do those jobs.

With that said, he was ecstatic at the beginning of March when there was no drama with Randy Moss. The record-setting receiver had redefined the concept of a make-good contract in 2007. The team had taken a chance on him, he had in turn taken a chance on himself by reducing his deal to one year, and both parties were rewarded with twenty-three touchdown receptions. That led to a new, three-year $27 million contract.

Moss caught the Patriots' final touchdown in the Super Bowl, a catch that was oh-so-close to being the game winner. The game was going to nag the consciences of each player leading up to the start of the season and likely beyond. One of those players, cornerback Asante Samuel, would be doing his postgame analysis in another city. He signed a $57 million contract with the Eagles, so he could think about "his" plays in Philadelphia. After a loss like that, every player had plays that he considered his own. For Samuel, who had great hands for a corner, it was an Eli Manning pass that sailed high and just off the defender's fingertips. They would have won with that interception. There was also the miracle catch of the game, the one where David Tyree slapped the ball to his helmet and fell to the ground without allowing the ball to touch the turf. Rodney Harrison had been there, wrestling and pulling, but Tyree held on. It was a huge play in the game, a thirty-two-yarder over the middle, and it gave the Giants the life that they needed. The problem was that it really wasn't Harrison's assignment. It was Samuel's. But the Patriots freestyled on defense at times, and it had helped more than it had hurt over the years. This one stung.

The loss was hard enough, but no one could move on from it or the season because both were stuck in a Spygate holding pattern. There was that *Herald* report that the Patriots had taped the Rams' walk-through, and now there was a former New England employee, Matt Walsh, who was hinting that he had information that might put the Patriots on trial again for the videotaping scandal. Pennsylvania senator Arlen Specter wasn't letting go, either. He was convinced that Roger Goodell was lording over a cover-up, and he was determined to get to the root of it.

It was funny. Specter believed that the commissioner was helping the Patriots, and the Patriots believed that the commissioner was trying to demolish what they had built. April was not only Bill Belichick's birthday; it was when he was the NFL's version of homecoming king during the draft. He would trade only with two divisional opponents, the Bills and Dolphins, and he had cleaned them both out when they'd bartered with him. The Bills were on their fourth quarterback and third head coach since Belichick made the Drew Bledsoe trade with them six years ago. The Dolphins, who had gone 1-15 in 2007, had given the Patriots a second-rounder that became Corey Dillon, and sent them star receiver Wes Welker for draft picks that the Patriots didn't want.

The Patriots had been well positioned with two first-round picks in the 2008 draft. But part of Goodell's Spygate punishment was to snatch the Patriots' first, which was number thirty-one overall. That was the bad news. Fortunately the trade with the 49ers had worked out better than anyone expected. The traded twenty-eighth pick in 2007 had turned into the seventh overall pick in 2008. It was a rare chance for a team this good to select an impact player, and the Patriots knew exactly who they wanted. He was a heady linebacker from Tennessee named Jerod Mayo, and the scouts and defensive coaches loved to gather and watch his film. He played with the energy of someone who knew exactly where he was going, and when he met a ballcarrier, the player either stopped in his tracks or fell backward.

Mayo would be the bridge between Bruschi and the next generation of Patriots because the inevitable was beginning to happen. Bruschi knew he wasn't as fast as he used to be, and his bosses could see the same thing. It was a similar story for several popular players, Harrison, Vrabel, and Troy Brown among them.

Two and a half weeks after the draft, in mid-May, Brady did an interview on WEEI radio in Boston. The interview coincided with a Goodell press conference in which the commissioner announced, finally, that he'd heard everything he needed to from Matt Walsh. The dismissed employee did not have an explosive tape or any other information that would lead the Patriots to further punishment. Most important, there was no pre–Super Bowl taping of the Rams' walk-through. The press conference was carried live in Boston and nationally on ESPN. Afterward, ESPN commentator Mark Schlereth was among many who were unconvinced that the tapes were innocuous. This was going to be the immeasurable penalty for Spygate: constant doubt. Brady was asked about the nonstop videotape chatter.

"I think it's just kind of the environment right now," he told the radio station. "I think that's the way guys make it. They say the craziest things. That's what ESPN has become. ESPN, to me, is like MTV without the videos. They just have highlights, instead."

ESPN and every other media outlet in the country, and world, had a statement from the Patriots and an apology from the *Herald*. Reporter John Tomase, who wrote the errant story about the Rams walk-through, apologized in print and on television. Yet Spygate, not even a year old, was embedded in the culture. There was no delineation between what the Patriots actually did, what they were accused of doing, and what analysts and writers imagined that they could be doing.

It led to the Patriots becoming the most reviled franchise in the league. At least that's why the out-of-towners said they didn't like New England and "Belicheat." New Englanders said it was the winning, from the Patriots and everyone else, and they had a case. In June, the Celtics completed a sixty-six-win regular season by beating their rivals, the Los Angeles Lakers, in the NBA Finals.

Belichick and Brady had arrived in town when all the championship stories were viewed on dated posters; now they were *told* by posters on the Internet, kids in their teens and early twenties, who all had shining trophies as their avatars.

The expectation, of course, was that the Patriots would be featured on the familiar parade route after the 2008 season.

The first game of the year was against Kansas City, a team that had decided to rebuild and go young. It was going to be a big passing day for Brady. At least it seemed that way seven and a half minutes into the first quarter with a twenty-eight-yard Brady-to-Moss completion. Except no one was paying attention to the completion. It was the hit in the backfield that jarred everyone in Gillette Stadium. Safety Bernard Pollard ran around running back Sammy Morris and hit Brady low. The quarterback was in an odd position, following through on a throw and getting hit low. His upper body was going forward, his left leg going too far back. His anterior cruciate and medial collateral ligaments snapped. He screamed; the crowd groaned. The coaching box was silent and, if it was possible, this felt worse than the Super Bowl loss to the Giants. As bad as that was, you knew Brady would be back for whenever the next game was. That was not going to happen in 2008. His season was over.

After raging about Pollard's hit, and the absence of Kevin Faulk for blitz pickup rather than leaving the job to Morris, it was time to plan for the new New England Patriots. Their starting quarterback was now Matt Cassel, a man who hadn't started a game since he was in high school, nine years earlier.

"We had been playing the role of favorite for so long," Tedy Bruschi says. "You hold yourself a certain way. It was consistent. It was a mentality. And then after that hit, a reset button was pushed. 'Okay, we're not that anymore. Let's just see what we can do.'"

They'd be able to beat teams like Kansas City, for sure, although the final was just 17–10. But how about other teams in the division? After five consecutive AFC East titles, all their divisional neighbors were on their level now. Would they be able to beat the Jets in week two? The Dolphins in week three?

Brady's injury made everyone feel older. It was the peek at the future that no one wanted to see. What if you have Belichick and no Brady? It might look and sound like this. Just one day after the injury, there, in Brady's usual six thirty a.m. radio slot, was Cassel.

"I'm not trying to be Tom Brady. I'm just trying to be Matt Cassel," he assured the audience. "I don't know where that's going to take us."

No one knew, but there were some educated guesses. If the starting quarterback hadn't started in college, hadn't started in the pros, and looked uncomfortable when he started in preseason games, what did that suggest?

The first real test was against Mangini and the Jets. That combination had given Brady trouble, so what could be expected from Cassel? Probably not the 19–10 win that pushed the Patriots to 2-0. Week three was strange. Brady was spotted with his year-old son, John, at a bookstore shortly before kickoff. He was probably seeking a self-help book about how to cope on NFL Sundays. He'd always been at the stadium. No one ever told you *how* to be injured, and he was a real rookie at it. When Deion Branch checked in on him from Seattle, he told his old receiver that he expected to be back to himself in four to five months. Branch told him to relax. No one, not even Tom Brady, was going to recover from ligament tears like his and be back in the NFL that quickly. The Dolphins, meanwhile, were happy not to face him and won big, 38–13.

It was the bye week and Brady was out temporarily. One of his former teammates, Troy Brown, decided to be out for good. He was thirty-seven and had been more of a spiritual than physical contributor to the 2007 team. His last game of consequence was the conference championship loss to the Colts. Now, in 2008, he didn't have a job and he determined that he couldn't play anymore. His retirement announcement was attended by Belichick, along with Brown's young sons, Sir'mon, ten, and SaanJay, eight. Brown thanked Belichick for believing in him and allowing him to become a starting receiver in the league. He also said he was proud that he could wear the same jersey for fifteen years and, although he had a chance to go to the Jets with Mangini, he couldn't imagine putting on green and white. There were questions from the media, but the best one came from Sir'mon, who cried throughout the press conference.

"If you love this game so much, why are you retiring?"

The room was quiet, and grown men and women clenched so they wouldn't tear up. It was an emotional moment. Brown, who didn't share much as a player during press conferences, showed that it was a new day as he stood there as a former Patriot, soon-to-be media member, and loving father.

"I would love to keep playing, but there comes a time when the man upstairs, called God, you can't outrun Him as much as you try to and want to. He just catches up to you and tells you that you're thirty-seven years old. It's a sad day for me, too. I saw you out there crying for me and I love you, and it's going to be okay."

It was one of those days when the typical Patriots fan was right there with Sir'mon. It was a reminder of the great plays, yes, like Brown on the final drive of the Super Bowl against the Rams. Or the Super Bowl against the Panthers when he broke his nose, kept playing, and then showed up at the parade saying, "Bingo! We got Bingo! We win again, baby!" But this season, one month in, was about football mortality. No Brady and now no Brown. They were among the players who had poured the foundation of what the organization had become. It was strange to see the games go on without them.

When the Patriots went to the West Coast in October to play the Chargers, Robert Kraft gave an update on Brady. He'd had surgery, was working hard, and, the owner added, "We hope to have him here for another ten years." Who could even think that way after a year like this? Brady was going to play until he was forty-one?

On cue, Harrison returned to San Diego, where he started his career. The next week, in a blowout win at home over the Broncos, he was carted off the field. Torn quadriceps. He shook hands and waved to the crowd as if he wouldn't be waving again wearing a uniform. He was thirty-five. He'd had three major injuries in the last four seasons. If Brown was looking for a media partner, Harrison would be a good fit.

After eight games, the Patriots were 5-3. They weren't great, but they weren't embarrassing, either. Which was also a good scouting report on Cassel. He could no longer be described as a high school quarterback. He belonged in the NFL.

"Cassel was like everyone's little brother that you'd give shit to every time you saw him," Bruschi says. "He'd make you laugh. He'd be funny. He'd be self-deprecating. You could just mess with him. He was good friends with almost everybody. Were there points that he wasn't playing well? Yeah, but our reminder was, 'Who do you think it is?' It's not Tom. We had to have a different mentality. We didn't panic."

Cassel didn't panic, either, and he was playing well enough to get a starting job for someone in 2009. He had back-to-back games where he finished with four hundred or more passing yards. Josh McDaniels was at his creative best, deftly mixing a power running game with the passing abilities of Cassel. Most fans were similar to Bruschi: It's Cassel at quarterback; let's sit back and see where the ride goes. The present, actually, was much more pleasant than the future, for several reasons.

The big signee at linebacker, Adalius Thomas, broke his arm and was out for the season. He had been good for the Patriots, not special. For all his versatility, it didn't seem that he quite fit here. A man who did fit, in playing style and worldview, was Vrabel. His teammates loved his brain, which allowed him to spit out information as he made plays, like a pass-rushing Belichick. He was hilarious, too, and even Belichick tried to avoid eye contact with him when a serious point was being made because Vrabel had a way of turning anything into a comedy bit. A frequent target of his was Belichick, mostly for the coach's professed love for the old Giants that he coached. Vrabel would imitate Belichick and have his teammates, and head coach, laughing as he exaggerated the résumés of the tough players that Belichick often praised. What Vrabel and the others didn't realize was that one day Belichick would be talking about him and Willie McGinest, Tedy Bruschi, and Rodney Harrison in the same way that he flattered the Giants. No question, Vrabel was a three-time champion, with his initials in the foundation along with a handful of others.

Vrabel was opinionated, and he was also a player representative. He and others in the league knew what Goodell and the owners had in mind. They wanted a new collective bargaining agreement where they could significantly reduce the players' portion of revenue, which was at 60 percent. If that reduction didn't come, there would likely be a lockout following the 2010 season.

"They raise the ticket prices twenty-five percent, but the salaries don't go up twenty-five percent. Nobody gave Tom Brady a twenty-five-percent raise," he told Ron Borges, now of the *Herald*. "The fans are paying twenty-five percent more to see the entertainers, but the entertainers aren't being paid twenty-five percent more.

That needs to be talked about. You look around at what they've built here. Every bit of it is tied to the team, but none of that revenue is included. I'm curious about how that goes. How'd this get built? Where did the revenue come from? The financing's based on the value of the team and the ties to it, but they keep all that revenue."

The "here" he talked about was Patriot Place, an outdoor mall next to the stadium that included restaurants, a movie theater, a performance center, retail shops, and a hotel. His questions were valid, maybe valid enough to prepare the road for him out of town.

As the regular season came to a close, the Patriots found themselves in an unfamiliar and uncomfortable position. They needed help from a former friend, Mangini, to get into the play-offs. The problem was that they hadn't played well enough against potential play-off teams, and they didn't own the tiebreaker in the East. So they faced the possibility of finishing 11-5 and missing the postseason, unless the Jets could beat the Dolphins. The Jets had been unreliable down the stretch, losing three of four, and with their quarterback, the erratic Brett Favre, it became four out of five.

The Jets were out and so were the Patriots. The non-play-off seasons were viewed through completely different lenses. For Cassel and for Belichick, they were viewed optimistically. In New York, they were calamity. It had been two straight disappointing years for Mangini, who was fired.

With Romeo Crennel also fired in Cleveland, it meant that Belichick's two previous coordinators were out of work. He was still Belichick, though, and so two new names with Patriots connections became hot prospects on the job market. One was McDaniels, who had turned down interview chances after the 2007 season. He was ready now, and Cleveland and Denver were among those interested. The other name was Scott Pioli, the man who had slept on the couch in Belichick's dorm when the coach was coordinating the Giants defense. Pioli had wanted to learn, and Belichick had allowed him to crash on the pullout so he wouldn't have to make daily ninety-minute round-trip drives. Cleveland, where he started, wanted to talk. Kansas City wanted a sit-down as well.

The Pioli-Belichick relationship was a rare model. It was proof of all the things Belichick could be, as well as what he never could or would be again. He'd been gracious enough to mentor a kid he barely knew. He'd watched him grow from a Browns scouting assistant who was making airport runs in the early 1990s to a Patriots vice president who sat next to him on the plane, talking strategy, in 2008. It was an inimitable tale. He and Pioli, technically, were colleagues. But they'd vacationed together, done silly weight-loss competitions together, argued over players, shared holiday dinners, had been uncle and godfather figures to each other's children, confided in each other about the present and future, happily discussed football and family dreams.

The present-day Belichick could never be as casual and open as he had been in the old days, even if he'd wanted to. He was a Hall of Fame coach now, a national celebrity. There could never be an organic mentorship like the one with Pioli. Also, frankly, the souring of the relationship with Eric Mangini had made him think of the pitfalls of giving so much. He'd be much more guarded going forward, so Pioli had seen the best of him and the last of him like this.

Brady wasn't used to being injured like he was now, but he knew the drill with coordinators and front office executives getting new opportunities. He'd seen it play out, over and over. He'd stay in touch with everyone, no matter where they went. When he gave updates on the status of his knee, and all the reports about infections and setbacks, he'd likely give them to a new coordinator and new vice president of personnel. He'd even have a new backup in the quarterbacks' room.

Every year, a few more people from the Super Bowl days in New Orleans moved on. Brady saw some of them traded, some departed in free agency, and some retired. McDaniels and Pioli got new jobs, McDaniels in Denver and Pioli in Kansas City. Their initials were on the foundation walls, too. "JM" and "SP." Of course, some players from this team were leaving. You could always guess a few; the others, no matter how much you braced for it, were always a stinging surprise.

CHAPTER TWELVE

FRANCHISE SHIFTS

There is usually a pencil tucked behind one of Bill Belichick's ears, his constant reminder to be ready when an idea flutters and then suddenly drops. An insight about his franchise is always nearby. There is a coaching point for himself, an area of emphasis for an assistant, or an illustration for the players. The pencil is both symbolic and essential for what lies ahead in 2009. It's time to restructure, rethink, and ultimately rewrite the franchise. Fortunately for him, he's been a part of this process a couple of times already.

Nearly twenty years earlier, in Cleveland, he had insisted on vivid language throughout the organization. He was serious about it. Details mattered. Words mattered. He wanted everyone to be precise in their descriptions of who a player was and what he could do, so precise that you could practically feel, touch, and see that player coming to life off the page.

He and Mike Lombardi, his top personnel man at the time, had spent months on the writing of the new scouting manual. They were building something from scratch, so they were wise enough to be patient with the unknown. It was going to take a while to turn some core ideas into an articulated football world. They knew that intelligence, power, and versatility had to be part of their players' profile, but that still wasn't specific enough. By the time they started to figure it out, they got fired.

In 2000, in New England, Belichick's writing partners were Scott Pioli, Ernie Adams, and Bucko Kilroy. They wrote with clarity and power, accurately describing some of their championship players before they were even in the building. They wrote of their ideal defensive lineman: "He must be able to play with fast, strong hands. Two-gapping is not a passive catch and read technique. It involves knocking the offensive line back and establishing a new line of scrimmage. If the defensive tackle gets doubled, he can't get moved back. He must be able to hold his ground and work laterally. He must be able to disengage and make plays."

One year later, they got *that* guy, Richard Seymour. He went beyond the description, actually. He was faster, stronger, bigger, and smarter than the prototype. He was far and away the number one player on their draft board, even though many fans had swooned instead for Michigan receiver David Terrell. But when Terrell's career was ending four years later, Seymour was dominating through his third consecutive first team All-Pro season.

For the most important position in football, Belichick and his writing team coveted the same general concepts that other franchises did. Of course they wanted a quarterback who was a leader, good decision-maker, and accurate passer. But even those traits can be subjective to scouts who are trying to give the boss what he wants. So the specific instruction was that the quarterback must "throw accurate passes that can be caught by our team. Pretty spirals don't count if they land out of bounds, or even worse, if the defense can put their hands on the ball. The word 'accurate' means that if the ball is supposed to be thrown to the receiver's right number, that is where the ball gets thrown. It does not get thrown to his left number." As for his style around the team, their quarterback-on-paper would be held to a higher standard than everyone else. He'd be smart, a natural leader and tone-setter, a man who couldn't be out-worked or outstudied by anyone.

That was their guy, too. Good fortune allowed them to be in position to select Tom Brady; their good writing allowed them to quickly appreciate what they had in him. He was a mold-breaker as well, showing an ability to ascend in his personal life—cover shoots, commercials, movie cameos—while maintaining genuine connections with his boys.

It was no wonder that going into the 2009 season, the Patriots' decade had included six division titles, four conference champion-ships, and the three Super Bowl wins. They'd had two foundational players emerge from the pages of a football manual and leap firmly into the starting lineup. They were the capstones of the offense and defense, so any conversation about changes with them was naturally a conversation about changes with everyone. Many of the organiza-tion's parts were movable, but these two weren't.

Some type of planning session needed to happen. Brady was coming off major knee surgery, and there had been delays in rehab due to a postsurgery infection. It was premature to think about his career being in jeopardy, and it also seemed unfair to expect him to be the same quarterback he was in 2007. He'd be in the same offense with a different coordinator in Bill O'Brien. As for Seymour, he was still playing at peak level. He was in the final year of his con-tract, and the team needed to pay him and defensive tackle Vince Wilfork.

There was a lot to think and write about.

Belichick's insistence on writing what he wanted to see shouldn't have been a surprise to anyone. He and his father had combined their collection of football literature and put it on dis-play at the Naval Academy. You spend that much time collecting and reading books, and a love for language and ideas is inevitable. In fact, Belichick's habit of writing things down longhand and then later putting the information into a Word document was the same approach David Halberstam used throughout his career. The author conducted interviews with pen/pencil and paper and then made the transfer to the computer. It was as if it wasn't real until it was first on a page.

After Halberstam died in a car accident in the spring of 2007, several of his friends shared remembrances. Paul Simon said he didn't have a "Ted Williams song" for Red Sox fan Halberstam, so he dedicated a tender version of "Mrs. Robinson." John Lewis, the Georgia congressman and civil rights leader, talked about Halberstam's compassion. Anna Quindlen marveled at his fearlessness and journalistic vision. In Boston, Belichick went on WEEI radio and spoke of him reverentially. He rattled off the names of a half-dozen Halberstam books and, in some cases, offered plot summaries.

"He was a very vibrant man; a brilliant guy," Belichick told the radio audience. "He had a great background in just about every area. It wasn't just sports. It was politics. Religion. World affairs. People. You name it. He was a very interesting man who pulled a lot of different people together. He could carry on a conversation with pretty much anybody."

Only on the surface was it ironic that Belichick, usually a man of few public words, would find the appropriate ones in that situation. Pulling a lot of different people together and finding common strands was the essence of coaching; investigation, discovery, and problem-solving were staples of writing. Belichick literally was the writing coach as he set things in order for the upcoming season.

He had to formalize his good-byes to Pioli and Josh McDaniels. Pioli had been at his right hand for nine years. He'd been next to him on the duck boats in downtown Boston, in the draft room when Seymour and Brady were selected, even on Nantucket in the summer.

McDaniels, for eight years, had been the student who had accepted the professor's critical red pens and cross-outs. He'd come a long way from the coaching assistant who was instructed to write out the play, of course, so he'd know the game better. His submitted work to Belichick used to be returned with dozens of sticky notes, pointing out misidentifications and other errors. Labels. Details. Specifics. He'd driven the importance of those to McDaniels, and the sticky notes became fewer and fewer. The young assistant not only learned to label better; he became a better thinker.

Now they were off to Kansas City and Denver, and it wasn't real until it was on paper.

"To sum up in words everything Scott Pioli has meant to this organization and to me personally would be difficult, if not impossible," Belichick wrote in a statement. "From the day I met him, he has demonstrated a passion for football and respect for the game that is second to none. It has been extremely gratifying for me to follow Scott's career ascension from the bottom of the totem pole in Cleveland to his place as a pillar of championship teams in New England. Now, with the opportunity to steer his own ship and a vision of building a winner, there is no more capable, hardworking, loyal, team-oriented person than Scott Pioli."

For McDaniels, Belichick had authored a booklet of things to expect as a head coach. No first-time head coach, no matter his age, could grasp the breadth and scrutiny of the job. McDaniels, thirty-two, was no different. The book was private; the statement was for all to see and hear.

"Josh McDaniels is one of the finest people and brightest, most talented coaches I have ever worked with. Since joining us eight years ago, Josh performed a variety of roles and excelled in every one of them. Between his work on defense, in scouting, player evaluation and coordinating the offense, Josh is a very well-rounded coach whose outstanding body of work speaks for itself."

It was now Bill O'Brien's turn to shape the offense that McDaniels had inherited from Charlie Weis. He had refined and updated it so it reflected the evolution of Brady and the league. O'Brien's mission was to keep adjusting the offense while finding out who the postinjury Brady was. It was Nick Caserio's turn to help Belichick find the next seventh-round gem like Matt Cassel. Caserio would be the one supervising the search for the next free agent, like Mike Vrabel. The linebacker had fit so perfectly that it was hard to believe that he'd begun his career outside of New England.

Late in the 2008 season, he had shared his disbelief of the owners' claims that the collective bargaining agreement wasn't a good deal for them. He specifically mentioned Robert Kraft and his outdoor mall, Patriot Place. He didn't think it would have been possible without the performance of the players. Could Kraft have disagreed with Vrabel and still kept him on the team? Sure. But that was just a theory, because in March, Vrabel and Cassel were traded to Pioli's Chiefs. Belichick gave the move the writing treatment that it deserved.

"When Mike arrived in 2001, we knew we were adding a solid outside linebacker. But where Mike took it from there exceeded our highest hopes. Mike Vrabel epitomizes everything a coach could seek in a professional football player: toughness, intelligence, playmaking, leadership, versatility, and consistency at the highest level. Behind the scenes, Mike's wit and personality is one of the things we have all enjoyed about coming to work every day. The toughest aspect of my job is the day I stop coaching people like Mike, who did everything in his power to contribute to team success.

"Of all the players I have coached in my career, there is nobody

I enjoyed working with more than Mike. In the same way people recognize guys like Troy Brown, we appreciate and thank Mike Vrabel. He is one of the very special Patriots champions."

It wasn't a rebuild, not with Seymour and Brady still on the roster, but why did it feel that way? Why did it feel different? The Patriots had dealt with this drain before, several times. It was the parade after the parade, the exodus of various personnel off to see if they could make it away from home.

The Patriots received a second-round pick, number thirty-four overall, in the Cassel-Vrabel trade. The selection was a reminder that although the Patriots were in transition, they weren't too far away from their draft roots. As they had done several times in the past nine years, they took an asset and maximized it far beyond its original value. In a sense, they were draft flippers. Cassel had been the 230th overall pick in 2005. By 2009, the Patriots had moved pick 230 for pick 34, and it was all based on the 2008 performance of the twenty-seven-year-old quarterback. It was a great financial move for him as well because he had entered 2008 making $520,000. As soon as he got to Kansas City, he signed a $63 million contract with $28 million guaranteed.

At fifty-seven years old, Belichick was as energized and focused on the job as he had ever been. He wasn't thinking of retirement, although the league was starting to look like the head table of a Belichick reunion dinner. His lieutenants were stationed all over the country. Thomas Dimitroff was the general manager in Atlanta. Pioli and McDaniels represented Kansas City and Denver. Mangini had replaced Crennel in Cleveland. Jason Licht had left for Philadelphia and Arizona, but was now back in New England. And there were a handful of college coaches he leaned on for insight on players and collegiate trends: Chip Kelly and Pat Hill on the West Coast, Kirk Ferentz in the Midwest, Nick Saban and Urban Meyer in the Southeast, and Greg Schiano in the Northeast.

During the April draft, some clues about the 2009 season began to reveal themselves. The 2007 and 2008 drafts had been headlined by a safety and a linebacker. In 2009, Belichick traded out of the first round in exchange for extra picks now and next year. He wound up with four second-rounders: Oregon safety Patrick Chung, Boston College defensive tackle Ron Brace, Connecticut cornerback Darius Butler, and Houston offensive lineman Sebastian Vollmer. It was obvious that something was stirring on defense, and what it was became tangible in the summer.

Before that, though, there was good news. Brady was back. He wore a huge, black brace on his left leg, and there were times when he seemed a step off during the early days of team activities. He had a rebuilt body and workout routine, courtesy of a trainer named Alex Guerrero. The two of them reworked Brady's throwing program as well as his diet. Brady returned to the office, so to speak, and it was similar to when he left. Randy Moss and Wes Welker remained the primary receivers, and the Patriots had signed a potential third option in thirty-seven-year-old veteran Joey Galloway. He looked lost most of the time in the scheme, and it even seemed that a rookie seventh-rounder, Julian Edelman, was getting it quicker than he was.

Edelman was one of those players, like Vrabel and Troy Brown, that Belichick dreamed up during his free-verse writing sessions. They were players that had primary positions, but they could theoretically be plugged in anywhere. He was a prospect worth watching.

Yet it seemed for every player who arose like Edelman, there was another valued one saying good-bye. In June, there was the expected announcement from Rodney Harrison. He was retiring. He had missed time with significant injuries in three of the previous four years, and he was now better at describing his time away than fighting to get back. He admitted to losing his all-consuming hunger to play football, and he had already been hired to bring his verbal punch and candor to NBC's football studio show.

As Belichick prepared to write again, the endeavor seemed tenuous. There was a lot of institutional knowledge and instincts leaving; what was actually coming? Was the established culture *that* secure where it could remain stable despite the changes?

"In the biggest games, in any situation and on a weekly basis, his production was phenomenal," Belichick wrote. "Rodney embodies all the attributes coaches seek and appreciate: toughness, competitiveness, leadership, selflessness, hard work, intensity, professionalism— and coming from Rodney, they are contagious."

After all, there were many "normal" things in the locker room that weren't necessarily normal in other places. Harrison was among those who were there for the installation of things that were now taken for granted. The players, for example, were coachable, maybe because some of their toughest coaches were their peers. All of their competitions were based around improving team performance.

They gave out that mental error belt to prevent mistakes in the game. They challenged one another to get to work early and interrogated players who tried to leave early. They took the punitive nature of being late for meetings away from the coaches and handled it themselves; if you were the last one sitting down, no matter what time it was, you were late. In fact, Harrison learned that lesson when he first arrived from San Diego. He and others became enforcers of that rule and many more. They checked one another's plates for fatty foods.

Fried chicken again today, huh? No wonder you're making so many mistakes in the game.

They joked. They easily crossed racial lines while socializing. They crossed spiritual lines in the cafeteria; there were times when

Heath Evans, a Christian, would have debates with Robert Kraft, who is Jewish, about the Old and New Testaments. That was the culture and it had led to the creation of the atmosphere, yet it wasn't *consciously* created. It came to be spontaneously, and now many of its custodians and caretakers were moving out.

The changes weren't glaring at the beginning of training camp. Some of the scenes there appeared to be normal. Belichick's friend, musician Jon Bon Jovi, was asking about the new coach of the Jets, Rex Ryan. He was the Jets' fourth head coach since Belichick arrived in New England. In June, Ryan had targeted Belichick and said he hadn't taken the job to "kiss his rings." Belichick had certainly heard his share of hyperbole over the years, so he barely reacted when he answered Bon Jovi, "I think they'll play hard for him."

Kraft, meanwhile, approached his friend Seymour. He asked the giant standing next to him, "Is this the best group of players on paper?" Seymour hesitated. He respected the owner and had taken one of the most significant trips of his life with him. He and his wife, Tanya, had gone to Israel with Kraft and his wife, Myra. The Seymours had been baptized in the Jordan River, an incredible experience for both of them. He knew he could have given Kraft a better answer than his "It's up there…" But there was so much uncertainty. His contract situation was unclear. Some of his teammates, who were under contract, were unproven. It was hard to tell how, or if, this team would come together.

Once again, goodness, it was coming apart. It felt like corporate America with its sweeping buyouts of senior employees. Seymour was a key part of the franchise's stonework, but there was chipping and shifting in the mortar. And dramatic breakaways. Maybe some careful observers could see it coming, with the way they watched Tedy Bruschi limp around the field. He'd had surgery on a knee in

2008, and when you're thirty-six years old, an injury from 2008 still throbs and pokes and taunts in 2009.

Bruschi knew he wasn't the same player. He and Roman Phifer had a lot in common, including their love for watching film. They'd sit in the meeting rooms and pick up tells and insights that other players didn't always see. Bruschi was such a student that he would instruct his linebacker coaches to double-check what they were teaching him. "Is this what was covered in the meeting?" he'd say as they wrote on the board. He wanted to be sure he was practicing the proper technique because "I know what happens around here when you get it wrong."

But there were other problems in August 2009. He didn't like the way he looked on film. He thought he was slow and stiff. Phifer had said the same thing about himself four years earlier when he decided it was time to stop playing. Phifer was with McDaniels as a member of the Broncos coaching staff, watching films and making them as well. A couple of years into retirement, he had attended a meeting of retired players and was startled at the debilitating issues they'd had as a result of playing in the league. Hip and knee replacements. Depression. Dementia. He was determined to do something and raise awareness. He helped produce a documentary called *Blood Equity*.

Beyond the medical issues, walking away from football created another void. "We've been a part of a team all of our lives," Phifer says. "If we don't find another pack, we struggle. We're like wolves. Football and everything it provides, it's a tough act to follow. You can get bits and pieces of it in other places, but you can't replicate it."

Bruschi's new pack was going to be on TV. After thirteen years as a football player, he was walking away. Only his teammates and coaches knew just what a creative and instinctive player he was.

It didn't translate to Pro Bowls. No, it was much more impressive than that. He created a playing style at middle linebacker that the coaches accepted but did not teach; he taught himself.

He once overheard a conversation that teammate Ted Johnson was having with their old defensive coordinator, Al Groh. Johnson was taller and heavier than Bruschi, and he had once hit a Dolphins guard with such ferocity that the player's helmet split in two. He was a big, physical thumper. After one of those thumping games, Groh said to Johnson, "That's the way we want it done." Bruschi mentally shook his head. He couldn't play that way. He was too small. He'd use athleticism and mind games instead. He'd take a lineman on early, but slip him later on in the game.

He was a poet with his teammates, putting his hand on their shoulder pads before games and looking into their eyes. "You good? Family is good? Bills are paid? All right, let's play ball." He negotiated his own contracts. He saw his parents file for bankruptcy when he was a kid, so he was preoccupied with buying a home and immediately paying it off, with no mortgage. Bill Parcells once told him after practice, "I've lost some players to drugs, but I've lost more to the IRS. I think you're going to be in this game a long time; do you have an accountant?" Bruschi went back to his apartment that night and called a lawyer he knew in Arizona. "We need to get an accountant."

An original, through and through. It's why Belichick took his words about Bruschi to the cameras. Television stations in New England carried the announcement live, and everyone was stunned when Belichick became emotional as he honored the linebacker.

"If you ask me to sum up how I feel about Tedy Bruschi in five seconds," the coach said, pausing and holding back tears, "he's the perfect player." He paused again, trying to pin the tears down. His voice shook. He repeated the compliment and more: "He's the perfect player. He has helped create a tradition here that we're all proud of. The torch has been passed, and we'll try to carry it on."

It was going to be hard to carry it on. By all measures, the team wasn't as smart as it had been in previous years. It wasn't as tough. It wasn't as respectful. It wasn't the Patriots.

The biggest blow of the season came one week before the games actually began. It was a Sunday morning, September 6, and Seymour was at home. He was away from his phone for a while, and when he finally got to it he saw that he had five missed calls and a text from Berj Najarian at the office. Belichick wanted to speak with him. He suspected nothing. What he heard on the phone was puzzling.

"Al Davis made a trade for you," Belichick said. "And you're now a member of the Oakland Raiders."

"I was like, 'Huh?'" Seymour says now. "I talked to my wife, my mom, my agent. And that was really it. There had been no speculation of that happening, no hint of it, so it felt really abrupt. The kids had just started school. We had a new house. We were entrenched in the community. Honestly, it took a minute to process it. I just couldn't jump up and leave like that.

"For a couple of days, I didn't talk to the Raiders or the Patriots. I saw a lot of wordplay about 'whose property' I was and who 'owned my rights.' I didn't like the way it felt, and I didn't like the way it sounded. From a personal standpoint there for a couple of days, I had to do what was best for my family."

Seymour was a month away from his thirtieth birthday, and he was still recognized as a dominant player. The Patriots had acquired Oakland's 2011 first-round pick for him. So in terms of locker-room accounting in 2009, the Patriots had traded away Seymour's dominance and smarts and in turn received a promissory note for 2011. As brilliant as the Belichick-Brady tandem was, there was no way to overcome the losses of the Seymour trade immediately. The NFL didn't work that way, not even for Belichick and Brady. Seymour was a rare talent, and everyone around the league knew it. The Patriots had good reasons for trading him when they did, planning, as always, for future cap flexibility. Yet they might have known, looking at their own internal writings, that they'd never again have a defensive lineman like him.

When he finally reported to Oakland, he viewed things differently.

"It was a lot deeper than football," he says. "I went to a team that personally needed me. There were a lot of young guys out there who had money, but no guidance. I was out there to lead men. I personally felt a lot of satisfaction. And as a defensive lineman, there's no better place to be nasty and tough than the Raiders and Al Davis."

Seymour was surprised when the eighty-year-old Davis approached him and started describing plays he'd watched the lineman make at the University of Georgia. "He was such a football guy," Seymour says.

That simple phrase said it all because, back in New England, the Patriots didn't have enough of them. Football guys. You knew them when you saw them, when you heard them, or in the case of Belichick, when you coached them.

Brady was the same as he had always been. He stayed in the pocket more, and that brace may have been the only thing he'd ever worn that didn't look stylish on him. He still had the mind of an engineer, deconstructing how a defense functioned and then coming up with a plan of attack with Belichick and O'Brien. He was comfortable enough to go into Belichick's office, notebook in hand, and share his observations from his film study once a week. These were one-on-one business meetings, with one careful observer,

Brady, reporting what he saw to a man, Belichick, who is just as careful if not more so. There weren't a lot of surprises revealed. In many cases, they were confirming what they already knew.

The trend for the Patriots was disturbing. They were a good team at home; they couldn't close out games on the road. They lost their first matchup to Ryan's Jets, with the new coach playing up the rivalry by leaving a voice mail for season ticket holders. The message: Be loud. The Patriots scored just 9 points in that game. In their first trip to Denver against McDaniels and the Broncos, they had a 10-point lead early and a 17–10 lead in the fourth quarter. A fumble, a missed field goal, and a taunting penalty later, they lost in overtime. They won big at home over the Titans, but Adalius Thomas was inactive for it. One of the team leaders, Thomas had missed practices in the previous week and Belichick wasn't happy about it. He also wasn't happy with the way Thomas was playing. He was making no impact plays, so he sat. Belichick and Thomas were headed for a confrontation.

Conflict was the New Patriot Way. Even Belichick didn't seem like himself at times. In Indianapolis, the Patriots lost a game when they had a lead late and the head coach decided to go for it on fourth-and-two from the Patriots' own twenty-eight. The theory was that he was trying to end the game so Peyton Manning wouldn't have a chance to, but a couple of TV commentators suggested that it showed a lack of faith in the New England defense. Those commentators were named Rodney Harrison and Tedy Bruschi. He loved them, obviously, but when they were on TV he'd use what they said to inspire his current team.

"I've heard it said that I don't have confidence in you, which is a bunch of bullshit," he told the team the next day. "If you guys don't think I have confidence in you, I don't know what you're doing every day…ignore the noise."

When the Patriots played the Saints in November, New England was 7-3. New Orleans was 10-0. It wasn't even close. The road-weary Patriots barely competed, which led to Belichick's admission to Brady on the sideline, "I just can't get this team to play the way it needs to."

It was a bold confession from Belichick because his teams had routinely played well in December. But going into this December, the Patriots had won only a single road game in the United States. They got a win over Tampa, but that was in London. And they weren't always great at home, which Thomas could attest to when he was nine minutes late for a team meeting and Belichick sent him home. The linebacker protested the move and Belichick shelved him for the rest of the season. Amazingly, he'd never play in the league again.

Belichick had come into the season believing that some adjustments were what the team needed. But it was a lot more problematic than that. Too many players were trying to win on *their* terms, which didn't always include an attentiveness to winning football. The Patriots needed to get back to those players. Thomas and his supporters were going to be cut loose; Belichick was going back to his football roots.

CHAPTER THIRTEEN

TIGHTROPE

When Alge Crumpler got the phone call in March 2010, he was sitting on a couch in his suburban Atlanta home. He'd spent the previous season in Tennessee, primarily as a blocking tight end. As he told the caller, Bill Belichick, he considered himself "damn near retired" at thirty-two years old. He'd sat on that couch a lot lately, so his listed playing weight of 262 was no longer accurate.

Belichick told Crumpler that he wanted him in New England because he didn't have a tight end on his roster; Crumpler told Belichick that he was 320 pounds and that he'd love to give it a shot in New England. He needed to stop first in New Orleans, the home of Mackie Shilstone, trainer for tennis star Serena Williams and many others.

"Coach," Crumpler said, "I can't walk into that building until I'm in shape."

Belichick thanked him for being honest, welcomed him to the Patriots, and hung up the phone assured that at the very least he'd added a conscientious professional to his 2010 team. The 2009 Patriots won the division, the seventh time in nine years that New England could say that. But it was a counterfeit Belichick team. It wasn't good on the road, it wasn't infused with a passion for self-correction, and it became the first Belichick squad to lose a play-off game at home.

"We have no mental toughness," the coach said to Tom Brady as the two of them stood on the sideline during that embarrassing November defeat in New Orleans. It was an immense admission, not only because it was early in the fourth quarter of a game, but also because he said it to a player. There was no mind trick involved here. He said what he said to his quarterback because he trusted him and knew he could relate. "We can't play the way we need to play it…I just can't get this team to play the way we need to play."

There had to be major changes to the Patriots, aesthetically and spiritually, and part of it entailed signing dependable players. Belichick also offered a key to what he was thinking with that phone call to Crumpler. He had long been fascinated with the tight end position, and the upcoming draft was one of the best ever for tight end depth. He was at a critical turn in his coaching career, a turn that most coaches don't have the luxury of getting to. He was entering his eleventh season with the same franchise, which meant that he had held his plot of land while the world around him changed. In 2000, the league was full of Mikes (Riley and Sherman), Jims (Haslett and Fassel), and Daves (Campo and McGinnis). Now Belichick was just one of three coaches—Andy Reid and Jeff Fisher were the others—who remained in the same place they were at the beginning of the century. That was twenty-nine different head coaching names and places from when he first started rebuilding the Patriots—90 percent of the profession had turned over.

There was an advantage to the continuity, obviously, but it also carried the trap of complacency. The league didn't pause for anyone, not even coaches on their way to the Hall of Fame. Belichick had suggested to his staff that the Patriots were predictable and thus easy to defend offensively. It took him less than thirty seconds, with no film necessary, to explain how to stop them: Take away Moss over the top, bracket slot receiver Wes Welker underneath, and they were done. In Belichick's view of things, a real offense was one that could prominently feature a hybrid tight end. Big. Fast. Intimidating. The problem was that he didn't have one.

It had been his football mission for years, the ideal that kept wriggling away. He thought he had it in 1995, when he was prepared to take Penn State's Kyle Brady, six feet seven inches and 280 pounds, with Cleveland's first-round pick, number ten overall. But the tight end went off the board, unexpectedly, one pick ahead of them to the Jets, and Belichick was upset enough to indignantly trade out of the top ten in exchange for a future first. There wasn't anyone in that spot that he'd wanted more than Kyle Brady. That draft became even more miserable when he saw a player he liked in the third round, Curtis Martin, but Bill Parcells got to him first— ironically when the Tuna coached New England.

Seven years later, he came back to the concept. He moved up in the 2002 draft for six-foot-four-inch, 260-pound Daniel Graham. He thought he was getting a multifaceted catching and blocking weapon who could be utilized in several formations. But Graham wasn't as effective with all the formation roaming, preferring instead to occupy a traditional tight end's spot. And although Graham was an otherworldly blocker, one who quietly dominated during the Patriots' Super Bowl win over the Panthers, Belichick didn't move up eleven spots in the first round for superior blocking to be the primary payoff.

Two years later, in 2004, it was Benjamin Watson's turn. He was fast, strong, and exceptionally bright. He was six foot three, 255 pounds, and he could be paired with Graham to create middle-of-the-field mismatches with linebackers and safeties. He was good and the idea was good, but that's all it was. Good, whispered. He was looking for that guy, someone who could walk into the franchise description of what a tight end should be and perhaps redefine the position.

Fifteen years after Kyle Brady was taken away from him, he was still seeking the hybrid difference-maker. It became such a fixation that when Kyle Brady was a thirty-five-year-old free agent in 2007, Belichick leapt at the opportunity to sign him. Graham was in Denver now, Watson was off to join Eric Mangini with the Browns, and Chris Baker, who had been on the team in 2009, wasn't asked to return. That left a hole that Belichick was going to begin to fill with someone like Crumpler, a blocker who wouldn't demand the ball and someone who could mentor the rookies.

"A tight end for the New England Patriots must have good functional Football Intelligence," Belichick's writing team stated in 2000. "He must learn the run offense like a lineman and he must learn the pass offense like a receiver. He must have the toughness to block a DE 1 on 1 (this is a common matchup). He must have good quickness. Most of his game is played against LBs in a short area. He must play with suddenness, getting off the line—getting in and out of cuts—getting open quickly and getting into blocks to secure the edge."

One month away from the draft, with the Patriots holding the twenty-second pick in the first round, the consensus top tight end in the draft was Jermaine Gresham from Oklahoma. In one season as a starter, the six-foot-five-inch Gresham set a school record with fourteen touchdown receptions. He was told at the scouting combine in Indianapolis that he was the best tight end in the draft, to which he replied, "I don't think I'm the best. I've got room for improvement."

Gresham sounded nothing like the number two tight end, a six-foot-six, 265-pound entertainer from Arizona named Rob

Gronkowski. He had become known as a touchdown-maker in his brief college career, accumulating sixteen in eighteen games. He missed his entire junior year with surgery to repair a herniated disc and nerve damage. That did nothing to quell his energy, confidence, and humor. He had been draped with nicknames since high school, where he used to be called "Dangerous" due to his tendency to accept all dares, including riding his bicycle off ramps. In Tucson, he was "Drago," "Robby," "Big Rob," and finally "Gronk." He was forced to run laps once in practice when, after he and a teammate talked trash the entire time, Gronk ended it with a big catch and a spike... off his teammate's helmet.

"I believe I have great hands," Gronk said at the combine. "I'll catch anything in my path. I would say I'm the top tight end in the draft because I bring the whole package. I'm ready to take on the big D-ends. I'm ready to go out there and catch some passes."

This appeared to be Belichick's year. Besides Gresham and Gronk, there were a half-dozen tight ends worthy of being drafted in the early rounds, including Jimmy Graham, a basketball player who was new to football; Dennis Pitta; Ed Dickson; Clay Harbor; Tony Moeaki; and Aaron Hernandez, a University of Florida junior who grew up in Connecticut wearing Drew Bledsoe jerseys and rooting for the Patriots.

Belichick was a draft junkie, probably because it combined so many of his skills into a singular event. The draft rewarded you for homework, strategy, bargain shopping, interviewing techniques, and player evaluation. The hard work began months before the actual event with the scouts and their all-day, cross-checking shifts in conference rooms. There were also the trial balloons that many teams sent out, trying to throw the rest of the league off the scent of the players they truly wanted.

The selling for Belichick began at the owners' meetings in late March when he raved about Hernandez's quarterback, Tim Tebow. He said the quarterback was probably capable of doing anything asked of him, such as "playing nose tackle if you asked him to play nose." Belichick already had a quarterback and, for that matter, a newly signed nose tackle. That didn't stop the speculation of how he could possibly use Tebow on the Patriots. He had commented on the quarterback's overhauled throwing motion, and how improved that motion appeared to be when Tebow and his teammates worked out for scouts at the Florida campus in Gainesville.

Selling became trolling the next week when the notoriously private Belichick ventured to the North End, one of the busiest neighborhoods in Boston, to have dinner with Tebow and Nick Caserio. For those who weren't certain it was Tebow, the quarterback took away all the mystery when he stood outside the restaurant on Hanover Street, the main drag in the North End, holding a football. Belichick could sense that there was rising interest in two players, Tebow and Oklahoma State receiver Dez Bryant, and the Patriots met with both of them.

The truth was that the Patriots were interested in a few Florida players who were not named Tebow, and Hernandez was among them. At twenty, he was one of the youngest players in the draft. His 4.6-second forty-yard dash, on a soggy field at Florida's pro day, made him intriguing as well. He had been the nation's top-rated tight end in high school in Bristol, Connecticut.

It was four years later, but people in Connecticut still excitedly talked about the incredible game in which Aaron had 376 receiving yards on just nine catches. He ran beautifully, a former running back who moved to tight end because he could, not because he had to. He was good enough to play anywhere, and when he had the ball in the open field, trying to tackle him was like chasing down a blur.

It was the same story at Florida, particularly his final season, when he won the John Mackey Award as the nation's top tight end. Question was, if he was that good, if he ran that well, if he was the top tight end in high school and college, why was no one mentioning him as a first-rounder? Or even a second?

There were some euphemisms used, such as "immature," "character issue," and "something's not quite right," but for most teams the character issue was the private information that they had: He had been suspended one game for marijuana use and, early in his college career, he had been the aggressor in a bar fight. For roughly one-quarter of the league, Hernandez was enough of a concern that he was taken off their draft boards. Everyone else looked at the talent and age, remained hopeful that sliding in the draft would humble him, and weighed whether a team with strong leadership could redirect an undeniably skilled pass-catcher.

He didn't seem to be a match for the Patriots, and it wasn't just because collective immaturity had been a problem for them in 2009. The bigger obstacle was their scouting manual, under the category of Major Factors. Most Patriots fans had bachelor's degrees in Team-Building By Belichick after studying the team for a decade, so the region was trained to cringe when it heard about a talented player with behavioral concerns. There were always exceptions, such as Corey Dillon and Randy Moss, but they were rare.

"Major Factors are behavioral, physical and mental aspects of a player that we, the New England Patriots, put at a premium. These factors will be included in every report, at every position and remain static regardless of position."

The first item under Major Factors was "Personal/Behavior." According to the description, scouts were to consider, "What is the player's core character, work habits, and level of integrity? We must press hard for the answers to these questions. *We cannot let up easily on this line of questioning.* We need accuracy and truthfulness." What followed were nine questions:

- Has he been in any trouble on the field or off the field?
- Is he ready to act like an adult?
- Are we going to need to keep an eye on this player?
- Would you let this player spend time with your family (children)?
- Can he handle tough coaching?
- How does he respond to pressure situations?
- Does he love football?
- How important is football to him?
- Can he handle coming to football as a job every day?

The Patriots had spent a lot of time at Florida over the years, and Belichick had become friendly with Gators coach Urban Meyer. If there were questions about a player's game and/or character, the Patriots believed they could get valuable insight from the Florida staff. Hernandez and his agents were tipped that New England had questions about him, so his agents drafted a letter that he signed. Typical of pre-draft savvy and spin, Hernandez began his letter to Caserio acknowledging an issue while never admitting to having it:

Dear Mr. Caserio,

I am writing in regards to some of the feedback I am receiving from my agents, Florida coaches, and other personnel. These sources have indicated that NFL teams have questions about my alleged use of marijuana. I personally answered these questions during the pre-draft process, but understand that NFL teams want to conduct thorough due diligence before making the significant financial investment inherent in a high draft pick. I have no issue with these questions being asked, but thought that it made the most sense to communicate with you directly regarding this issue so you would not have to rely upon second-hand information.

While not admitting to marijuana use, Hernandez went on to mention a solution:

I thought that the best way to answer your questions and your concerns was to make a very simple proposition. If you draft me as a member of the New England Patriots, I will willfully submit to a bi-weekly drug test throughout my rookie season (8 drug tests during the 2010 regular season). In addition, I will tie any guaranteed portion of my 2010 compensation to these drug tests and reimburse the team a pro-rata amount for any failed drug test...My point is simple—if I fail a drug test, I do not deserve that portion of the money.

I realize that this offer is somewhat unorthodox, but it is also the only way I could think of to let you know how serious I am about reaching my potential in the NFL. My coaches have told you that nobody on our Florida team worked harder than me in terms of workouts, practices or games. You have your own evaluation as to the type of impact I can have on your offense. The only X-factor, according to the reports I have heard, is concerns about my use of recreational drugs. To address that concern, I am literally putting my money where my mouth is and taking the financial risk away from the team and putting it directly on my back where it belongs.

In closing, I ask you to trust me when I say you have absolutely nothing to worry about when it comes to me and the use of recreational drugs. I have set very high goals for myself in the NFL and am focused 100% on achieving those goals.

On the first day of the draft, Belichick and Caserio had things set up perfectly at number twenty-two. Tebow and Bryant were mystery players, and if some team was inclined to make a move on them, it was likely going to happen in the early twenties where the Patriots were positioned. The player Belichick and Caserio wanted in the first round was Devin McCourty of Rutgers, whom some teams had graded as a second-rounder. The Patriots had not, which was explained six weeks earlier by Belichick friend and draft expert Mike Mayock: "He might be the best special-teams player in the whole draft. From a return perspective, gunner, jammer, making tackles. You get quite a package if you draft Devin McCourty."

There was no doubt the Patriots were going to draft him. The way they interpreted the board, he'd be available to them anywhere in round one. So when their pick approached, they received a phone call from Josh McDaniels and Denver. The Broncos wanted to come up two spots to select wide receiver Demaryius Thomas. The Patriots were happy to move back and acquire a fourth-round pick for their shuffle. And just as they settled into number twenty-four, the Cowboys called for the pick. They wanted Bryant and were offering the Patriots a third-rounder to move down three slots. Not a problem. Two trades, a third- and fourth-rounder acquired, five draft slots lost, and still in position to draft the player they had wanted all along.

The first round had just a couple of surprises. Gresham went in the first round, slightly higher than projected, to Cincinnati at twenty-one. McDaniels drafted Tebow at twenty-five, a controversial choice for a player whom some viewed as a sufficiently hyped college quarterback and nothing else.

Gronkowski and Hernandez were available on day two, and the Patriots wanted both of them. They owned overall pick number forty-four, and no tight end had been selected since Gresham at twenty-one. As the selections got into the high thirties, the Patriots had a bit of a draft panic attack. They feared that the Ravens, holding the pick in front of them and in need of a tight end, would swoop in and take Gronk. Belichick and Caserio made a deal with the Raiders, forty-four for forty-two, so they could block Baltimore. It was a case of overanalysis because Baltimore wasn't planning to draft its tight end in the second round. Belichick and Caserio had gone two for two in targeted players.

"I think the kid's a first-round tight end that the New England Patriots just stole at pick number forty-two," Mayock told his NFL Network audience.

As Mayock spoke, the big kid in the gray pin-striped suit hugged his friends and family and bounded toward the stage and enveloped commissioner Roger Goodell in a hug. He wore a white Patriots baseball cap and curiously had the team's helmet in his hand. After he had shaken hands and posed with Goodell, Gronkowski huddled with his family and everyone chanted, "Gronk, Gronk, Gronk..." He put the helmet on then and started doing a dance. He took the helmet off. He high-fived, half hugged, and mussed up hair. He said it was the happiest day of his life, even though anyone could see that without any words or explanation.

Two rounds later, the Patriots were in position for more stealing with the fourth-rounder they had acquired from the Broncos. Graham, the power-forward-turned-tight-end, had gone at number ninety-five to New Orleans. Eighteen picks later, the Patriots had the choice of either bringing Hernandez back to New England or going with combine warrior Dennis Pitta of Brigham Young University. Pitta had bench-pressed 225 pounds more times, twenty-seven, than any other tight end in Indianapolis. He'd also aced shuttle runs and cone drills. The ceiling for Hernandez was considerably higher, because if he could just settle down, he and Gronk would be one of the best tight end duos in the league.

The Patriots went with Hernandez, believing that his issues were not dissimilar to other wayward young men in their late teens and early twenties. It was an ambitious projection, colored by Hernandez's supreme talent. He was fully capable of charming them in draft interviews, especially if they weren't diligent about their reminder to press hard for questions. There was something much deeper than the familiar college-kid-just-experimenting tale. But on the Saturday afternoon that Hernandez was drafted, those issues weren't top of mind for anyone. The Patriots had acquired a first-team All-American and prestigious award winner in the fourth round.

Shortly after the completion of the draft, *Boston Globe* reporter Albert Breer broke a story that didn't win him many friends in the Patriots offices or among New England fans. Yet the story began to get closer to the problem, and it was truer than anyone, especially Hernandez, wanted to admit.

"According to sources with three NFL teams," Breer wrote, "the Florida product's precipitous fall was because of multiple failed drug tests for marijuana as a collegian." Breer quoted a team executive who said of Hernandez, "He had multiple positive tests, so he either had issues or he's dumb. One or two tests? Fine. But four, five, six? Come on, now you've got an addiction. He's not a bad kid. He just has an issue."

Based on Hernandez's adaptation to the Patriots' offense in

training camp, the executive's either/or was answered. He was not dumb. He picked up the offense quickly, and he refused to be pushed around.

"Both he and Gronk had an incredible work ethic," says Crumpler, who had kept his word from March 2010 and dropped forty pounds. "Aaron Hernandez understood the offense as well as anyone in that room. And he never turned down a rep in practice. I remember one time Aaron tried to block down on [330-pound] Vince Wilfork. He liked a challenge."

Crumpler had been around too long to confuse ease on the field with ease in life. He was a dozen years older than Hernandez, so the two didn't have much in common besides knowing how to get open as tight ends. Crumpler was at the end of his career, and Hernandez was at the beginning of his, one where he hoped to match and exceed the four Pro Bowls that Crumpler had.

While the veteran didn't sense that anything illegal was going on with the rookie, he constantly went up to him and offered, "If you need help with anything, and I mean anything, just let me know."

But there was nothing. Hernandez would be the silly face in the background waving and smiling to Crumpler's three daughters, whom he saw daily because their father Skyped from the locker room. Crumpler's oldest daughter called Hernandez "Mister Aaron." He became angry with Crumpler just once in camp and the preseason, and it had to do with hair. Crumpler was the barber for the rookie haircut tradition, and Hernandez didn't like the thought of being buzzed. He became amenable to it when Crumpler decided to shave cornrows into his hair; he loved *that* look.

These rookies appeared to be the jolt that the offense needed. Gronk was all business in practice and backed up his remarks from the combine: He really did look like the best tight end from his draft class. Brady found that if a pass was in the area of Gronk, it was a ball that would be vacuumed by the tight end and his reliable hands. He was a force in the running game as well. With Gronk and Hernandez added to an offense with Wes Welker and Randy Moss, the days of being easily disassembled were over.

The abilities of the top two draft choices, McCourty and Gronk, were a reminder of how far the Patriots had come in their drafts of the past four years. The 2006 first-rounder, Laurence Maroney, had spent several one-on-one sessions in Belichick's office the previous year, watching film and being tutored on the art of hard, inside running. Actually, that was the way a less-talented runner, Ben-Jarvus Green-Ellis, naturally attacked opponents. Green-Ellis was undrafted and worked his way up from the practice squad. Each time he carried the ball it was as if he were fighting for his job. He pushed Maroney so much that it eventually made him expendable.

It's how a former first-rounder, number twenty-one overall, was traded to the Broncos for a fourth-round pick. Add that to the release of Maroney's draft classmate, Chad Jackson, and the Patriots' ability to accurately gauge their own Personal/Behavior questions had become a concern over a two-year period. Maroney and Jackson, class of 2006, didn't succeed in part due to immaturity and less-than-strong work ethic. And although Brandon Meriweather, class of 2007, had been selected to the 2009 Pro Bowl, the Patriots were already planning to replace him after 2010. Belichick and his staff weren't risk-averse overall, but they usually didn't tread there in the first round.

With Maroney traded, it seemed likely that another deal was on the way. Mankins, the pickup-driving, straight-talking, lineman-crushing guard, was upset and said he wanted to leave. He had skipped minicamp and training camp, and none of his public comments sounded conciliatory. As the Patriots were a few days away from their first game of the season, September 12 against the Bengals, Mankins wasn't there like usual to protect Brady.

The quarterback did seem to have a protector, the heavenly kind, close to his home on September 9. It was 6:34 a.m. and he was driving his Audi S8 near the intersection of Commonwealth and Gloucester in the Back Bay section of Boston. Brady had a green light and was starting to drive through it when his sedan was struck by a Mercury Villager minivan. The driver, twenty-one, had failed to stop for a red light. There were several witnesses on the scene, and many of them called 911 because of the severity of the crash. No one knew then that the most famous athlete in the city was involved.

"There was just a huge crash!" a frantic 911 caller reported. She was asked if anyone was hurt. "I think so," she replied. "There's someone in the back of the car screaming and crying."

She was right. It was the minivan driver's father, forty-nine, who was in the passenger seat and had been on his way to a doctor's appointment. The collision caused fractures to his nose and ribs and had cracked some teeth. He was also feeling sharp pain in his back. Boston firefighters needed to use the Jaws of Life to remove the man from the minivan. Brady was not injured. He declined medical attention, went to practice a few hours later, and, as fate would have it, signed a new four-year $72 million contract that temporarily made him the highest paid player in football. What a day.

He was thirty-three, and the terms of the contract ensured that he would be a Patriot until he was thirty-seven. It certainly seemed that he would play his entire career with the Patriots. That fact, along with the events at the corner of Commonwealth and Gloucester, made him appreciative of what he had.

"I was looking in the other car to make sure they were okay," Brady said as he recapped that day on WEEI radio in Boston. "I was kind of sitting there in the car, looking around, trying to get my bearings. I was just thinking, 'How am I going to—I've got to call Coach Belichick. I'm going to be late for practice.' And then once I got home, then it really hits you."

Helicopters and serious reporters had flocked to the stadium to see how Brady moved and practiced after the crash, but he and the rest of the team waved off all the attention.

He was more excited about the game against the Bengals, eager to see the debut of his new offense. It couldn't have begun better, with the rookie Hernandez catching a pass, getting into the open field, and cleverly weaving for a forty-five-yard pass play. The kid was an artist with the ball, and he wasn't the only one. Brady threw for three touchdowns, two to Welker and one, of course, to a six-foot-six tight end who was playing his first football game in two years. It was Gronk, for the score. That's all he did in college, and apparently that was going to continue in the pros.

There was nothing to complain about after the game, a 38–24 win over a good Bengals team. Welker was scheduled to talk with the media about his quick return from a January ACL injury and his two touchdowns against Cincinnati. Unfortunately for him, Moss got to the podium before he did. What followed was a season-altering press conference.

Moss had begun talking about his contract in February at a softball game hosted by former teammate Heath Evans. He tried to get clarity on his status in June. In August, agitated and offended now, he isolated himself at the team's Kickoff Gala, a charity event in which donors sit and interact with players. Not Moss. He put on his headphones and wouldn't talk with anyone. After game one, he sounded like the Moss that his teammates had only read about but had never seen in person.

"I love being here, but from a business standpoint, this will probably be my last year as a Patriot and I'm not retiring. I'm still gonna play some football. I just wanted to get that off my chest and let you all understand that this is business."

He had a lot more on his mind.

"I think in the New England area, I don't want to say here in the organization, but a lot of people don't want to see me do good," he said. "And the reason why, I don't know and I really don't care."

What his teammates in New England had come to love and understand about him is that he really did care. He had been portrayed as many things, but rarely the one that stood out to them: sensitive. In a good way. "He's one of the best, most caring human beings I've ever met in my life," Evans says now. Although Moss said he wasn't talking about people in the organization, he couldn't shake what he perceived as dismissiveness. Brady, Vince Wilfork, and even kicker Stephen Gostkowski had new contracts that gave them security. He wanted what they had.

"Sometimes, you want your boss to tell you that you are doing a good job," he said. "If you do a good job and think you are doing a good job, you want to be appreciated. I really don't think that, me personally, that I'm appreciated."

He talked for nearly twenty minutes, with Welker going in and out of the room, checking to see if he was finished yet. The first win of the season wasn't even an hour old, and this was already the story. This wasn't going to be sustainable. Belichick was going to have to make an in-season assessment of what to do with Moss, and it wasn't going to be a simple fix. Telling some players to forget about the contract until after the season worked. For Moss, he had locked in on the contractual issue at the beginning of the year and, nine months in, he was still with it. Telling him to move on from it at this point didn't seem realistic. Besides, this year was different; a player couldn't think, *I'll wait until 2011 free agency* because, players had been warned, a lockout was coming.

With the contract on his mind, he might even start to misinterpret what offensive coordinator Bill O'Brien was doing with the offense. On orders from the boss, O'Brien had diversified the scheme, and now there would be significant involvement from the rookie tight ends in addition to Moss and Welker. There was also the fledgling talent of Julian Edelman and Green-Ellis's ability to provide a power running game when necessary. This was not going to be like 2009, when Moss was targeted roughly nine times per game.

Things got worse the next week on the road against the Jets. Moss did get those targets, ten of them in fact. He even caught one of the most memorable touchdowns of his career, a one-handed grab over New York's Darrelle Revis. But the Patriots lost the game by two touchdowns, and Brady's focus on Moss was not the spirit of the offense that Belichick and O'Brien had in mind. It seemed as if catering to Moss came at the expense of every other offensive resource that they had. The team got a win the next week in Buffalo, with three targets and two scores from Moss. And then, at the one-quarter mark of the season, it was time for a change.

The Patriots had scored 40-plus points seventeen times since Belichick became their head coach, so seeing routs like those were not unique. But the eighteenth 40-plus game of his Patriots career, on October 4 in Miami, would qualify as his favorite. No head coach in the league loved special teams as much as Belichick, and he backed it up with capital. His top draft choices in 2009 and 2010, Patrick Chung and Devin McCourty, rose on New England's draft boards because of their value on teams. That was on display in south Florida when the Patriots turned a 7–6 halftime deficit into a 41–14 win over the Dolphins on *Monday Night Football*. The obvious game standout was Chung, who blocked a punt, blocked a field goal, and had a fifty-one-yard interception return for a touchdown.

There were other notables as well. It was the one hundredth regular-season win of Brady's career, and one hundred fourteenth overall. He won those hundred games faster than any quarterback in league history, getting there eight games faster than Joe Montana had. Brady's career winning percentage stood at .760. It was a statistical head trip: Since Brady had been in the NFL, the rest of the league was successful against him less than 25 percent of the time.

"I've played on a great team for my entire career, the same organization that's committed to winning," he said after the game. "I'm privileged to be a quarterback for this team. I hope I'm here forever."

The contrast to that was Moss. Even with the big win, he'd had a tough night. He'd screamed at O'Brien at halftime, pushing him to make offensive adjustments. There were wrinkles in the second half, but they didn't include Moss. He left the game with one target and no receptions, the first time in four years that he'd left a game without catching a ball. He didn't say much after the game, but he was angry. He had done everything he could to get their attention, to let them know that while he wanted to be in New England, he wanted them to want him here. And to prove it with that contract. It wasn't going to happen, now or ever. After his press conference in week one, he'd talked with his agent and asked him to explore a trade. The agent was dutiful and so were the Patriots. When Belichick approached Moss on the plane ride home from Miami and found an unresponsive player, he knew it was time to put the plan in motion.

The Patriots landed in Providence early Tuesday morning, October 5. Less than forty-eight hours later, on October 7, Moss's career in New England was over. He was traded, along with a seventh-round pick, to Minnesota, the franchise that drafted him in

1998. The Patriots received a third-round pick in return. It closed off a fascinating room in Brady's career, a forty-game exhibit that would forever answer the question, "What do you think Brady could do with a truly elite number one receiver?" In their forty games together, Brady and Moss combined for thirty-nine touchdowns. It really was iron sharpening iron, an unspoken athletic-mental understanding that was reserved for the greats. If it were strictly about football, Brady and Moss would have been teammates for a lifetime. They got each other. But pro football is a game of hyper-evolution and cap slots, so it was time for Moss to leave.

"Randy really knows how I feel about him," Brady said. "I love him as a guy, as a person, as a player. He did a lot of great things for this team."

While Moss was going back to where his career began, so was his replacement.

As tough as the Patriots' offense was for some to learn, there weren't many players capable of joining their season in progress and actually contributing. One of them, probably the perfect one, was Deion Branch. He had been traded to Seattle as a twenty-six-year-old rising star. A few knee, groin, and foot injuries later, he was now viewed as a thirty-one-year-old solid professional. The Seahawks had a completely different offense than the Patriots', yet he had mastered both of them. In Seattle, the quarterback was throwing to a spot in the West Coast offense; in New England, Brady was throwing to the actual receiver. The Seattle offensive verbiage was all numbers and words; New England's was strictly words.

Branch retained everything he had learned his first time in New England. When the Patriots gave up one of their extra fourth-round picks to bring him back, he was thrilled. The faces had changed, no question, as he had played with just eleven of the players on the fifty-three-man roster, but the offense was in him. Everything was positive about his return, even the potential negative: Two months before the trade, he had finally sold the condo that he'd had the first time around with the Patriots.

As soon as he played his first game, Branch made an impact. He got the most targets, twelve, of anyone on the team, scored a touchdown, and made two big catches in overtime for a 23–20 win over the Ravens.

The points, and wins, without Moss continued to rapidly stack:

Thirty-nine points in Pittsburgh, with the rookie touchdown-maker, Gronk, scoring three times.

Thirty-one points at home against the Colts, with solid performances from rookie costars: a touchdown reception from Hernandez and an interception from McCourty.

Forty-five points on the road in Detroit, featuring a trio of twos: two more interceptions for McCourty, two touchdowns for Branch, and two for Welker.

They were 9-2 after their Thanksgiving win over the Lions. Nine wins by Thanksgiving usually means it's time to wrap up the division. This year was different. They were tied for the divisional lead with the Jets, and the teams were scheduled for an early December matchup in Foxboro on *Monday Night Football*. Rex Ryan's style was working in New York. He had a *Let's go for beers* persona, a guy who could have the headset on one second and be calling in to WFAN, Rex from East Rutherford, the next. He was more of a friend than a boss with his players, and they loved him for it. He also had an outstanding defense, led by cornerback Darrelle Revis.

In week two, Revis had to leave the Jets' 28–14 win early because he pulled his hamstring. He missed a couple of games after that, but he was healthy and willing to meet any challenge. He usually trailed a team's number one receiver and silenced him for an entire afternoon and/or evening. The Patriots' offense was completely different from that first meeting, when they were lukewarmly buying into having a traditional number one like Moss. It was hard to say who that was now, as the Patriots were spreading teams out and generally doing whatever they wanted.

It was more of the same on that December night. The windchill was fifteen degrees, although fifteen seemed to be a misreading; that number was too high. Jets quarterback Mark Sanchez, a second-year player from Southern Cal, trotted to the field for some practice throws and sprinted back to the locker room a short time later. "It's too cold for football," he said as he left the field. Maybe he was joking. His play indicated that he wasn't.

It was 17–0, Patriots, after the first quarter, with a short touchdown run from Green-Ellis and a twenty-five-yard scoring pass from Brady to Branch. At halftime, when it was 24–3, Tedy Bruschi was honored. He engaged the crowd with a call-and-response technique: He called out the names of his Super Bowl–winning teammates and they responded with delirium.

Everyone had the same idea after three quarters, when it was 31–3: This team is going to hang yet another of those banners that Bruschi referred to. Who was going to beat them? No one in the entire conference appeared to be capable.

Brady, as he had been all season, was dazzling. He saw mismatches all over the field, negating the brilliance of Revis. He threw four touchdown passes in a 45–3 wipeout, and the productive evening helped him bring his season totals to twenty-seven touchdown passes and four interceptions. He hadn't thrown an interception since the Baltimore game, in week four, or 228 passes ago.

The Jets, with a three-interception night from Sanchez, filled hearts and notebooks with doubt. THE FOXBORO FLOP declared a headline in the *Bergen County Record*. More than twenty-two thousand fans responded to a *New York Post* poll asking, "Does this loss convince you that the Jets are pretenders?" Nearly 68 percent of the respondents said yes.

"I came here to kick Belichick's ass," Ryan said after the game, "and he kicked mine."

That wasn't unusual for the Patriots. They reached the thirties in points per game for the remainder of the regular season, pausing at the end of it for some intimidating totals:

Brady was certainly going to be the league MVP with thirty-six touchdowns and, still, those four interceptions. His streak of passes without an interception had reached 335; Gronkowski and Hernandez combined for sixteen touchdowns, which doubled the production of last year's duo, Ben Watson and Chris Baker; Green-Ellis rushed for thirteen touchdowns, many of them behind Logan Mankins, who settled his differences with Kraft. Mankins played just half a season, yet that was still good enough to make him one of six Patriots Pro Bowlers; one of the rookies, McCourty, also made the Pro Bowl; the Patriots led the league in scoring, averaging 32 points per game. And with a league-best 14-2 record, they didn't have to leave the comfort of home during the postseason.

The Jets began to struggle after their loss to the Patriots, with the 9-2 start turning into a 2-3 finish. Ryan had talked about winning the Super Bowl at the beginning of the season, but for that to happen the Jets had to begin the play-offs on the road against Peyton Manning and the Colts.

In getting his team prepared for the wild-card game in Indianapolis, Ryan was deftly able to compliment Manning while also sneaking in an uppercut on Brady and the Patriots. He said nobody in the league studies like Manning and added, "I know Brady thinks he does. I think there's a little more help from Belichick with Brady than there is with Peyton Manning."

He knew what he was doing.

If there was a team the Patriots and their fans hated more than the Jets, it was the Colts. And if there was anything that annoyed a Patriots fan as much as a reference to Spygate, it was the notion that Manning was better than Brady. Ryan wasn't concerned about that. He was already revealing part of his New England game plan, if the Jets made it that far: Hit them in an area where they are trained not to hit back…in the public, pregame arena.

It turned out that Ryan was onto something. Jets-Colts turned into a bruising, low-scoring game, and that's not the way the Colts were built. Trailing 16–14 with a few seconds left in the game, the Jets lined up for a thirty-two-yard field goal.

"You watching this, bruh?" Deion Branch said to teammate Vince Wilfork.

"Yes sir," Wilfork replied. "If the Jets win this, we've got our work cut out for us."

And they did. The Jets, 17–16 winners over the Colts, were headed to Foxboro for a divisional play-off game.

"This is about Bill Belichick versus Rex Ryan," Ryan said at the beginning of the play-off week. "There's no question. It's personal. It's about him against myself, and that's what it's going to come down to. I recognize that he's the best and all that, but I'm just trying to be the best on Sunday, and I plan on being the best coach on Sunday. That's what it is. I recognize that my level has to come up, and he's going to get my best shot. He's going to get everything I have on Sunday, and if he slips at all, we're going to beat him."

Ryan got the first step in the Talking Game, and he and his players continued with the comments daily. The Patriots were strongly encouraged, and flat-out instructed at times, to do their talking on the field. Over the years, they had dealt with a pregame talker or two, but not a chat room. Some of the comments were personal, yet the Patriots were told to keep their mouths closed. Someone told Ryan that Brady had been at a Broadway show, *Lombardi*, instead of watching Jets-Colts and he cracked, "Peyton Manning would have been watching our game." Cornerback Antonio Cromartie gave an interview in which he profanely said he hated Brady. Ryan returned again, saying that Brady had taken a shot at him by pointing to the Jets' sideline. The talking had become so commonplace that three days before the game, one of the brashest and most outrageous talkers ever, Reggie Jackson, went on a New York radio show and told the Jets to "shut up and play football."

That wasn't going to happen. Since the Patriots were barred from speaking directly, Welker had a subtly subversive idea. He was friendly with Ryan, and he frequently included the Jets coach on a group text with Mike Smith, Welker's college roommate. Smith was interested in coaching and was in his first year as a Jets intern. The trio teased one another throughout the season, sending playful texts about defenders who were going to cover Welker (Ryan wrote that he'd use a nose tackle) and how unstoppable the Patriots' offense was. There had been an online video circulating about Ryan, apparently role-playing with his wife and focusing on her feet. The usually talkative Ryan didn't offer much when he was asked about it by New York media members.

Welker, though, used the incident to talk about the play-off game. He never smiled, winked, or changed his tone of voice when he answered several questions with increasingly out-of-place foot references.

Reporter: What is Tom Brady's postseason value?

Welker: It goes without saying, the guy is who he is and he does a great job of making sure everyone is on the same page and putting their best foot forward...

Reporter: How do you convey a sense of urgency to younger players for the postseason?

Welker: It's a play-off atmosphere and you can't just stick your toe in the water...

Reporter: What makes Revis so good?

Welker: I think he is very patient. He has good feet...

It went on for nine minutes, and Welker didn't break character once. Not even when he gave the biggest clue that he was just going to find any way possible to mention feet.

Reporter: How is the team handling the play-off atmosphere at practice?

Welker: We're really moving forward and we're going out there being good little foot soldiers...

Many of Welker's teammates loved it. But it didn't matter what the players thought of it. One man, Belichick, wasn't even slightly amused. On Twitter, Jets center Nick Mangold answered Welker by using the receiver's rhetorical device:

"Wes Welker is a great player. He's really taken advantage of watching film. If we don't keep a Spy on him, he could really open the Gate."

On game day, the humor was gone from everyone. The league had notified both teams to stop talking, probably spurred by Bart Scott's statement that Welker's "days are numbered." It was a play-off game trapped in the middle of a cultural war. No matter what happened after this game, the winning team here, on January 16, 2011, was going to refer to the result constantly. It's just what happened between Boston and New York.

Minutes before game time, a rumor started to circulate on the field: Welker was going to miss the first series as a disciplinary move for his comments about Ryan. Crumpler was among those who didn't agree with the move.

"I still can't figure out the Wes Welker not starting thing," he says. "I felt that when Wes made his comments, it was kind of the icebreaker that we needed. The first play of the game I was always next to Wes. A lot of people were trying to figure it out."

The Patriots were trying to figure out the Jets. New York was holding down the number one offense in the league, and Brady's interception streak was snapped in the first quarter. The Patriots looked bad. It didn't help that Crumpler dropped a touchdown pass in the first quarter. "Still can't believe I didn't catch it," he says. They didn't get the touchdown, but they got a field goal, and those were their only points of the half. They trailed 14–3.

Crumpler got a touchdown in the third quarter, and the Patriots were successful on the 2-point conversion to make it 14–11. It was becoming that kind of day, though, and New Englanders knew the feeling. The devastating upset. The opponent who was thought to be overmatched but refused to play the part. The young quarterback, Mark Sanchez, who is supposed to be overwhelmed by Belichick. Instead, he was beating man coverage with poised and precise throws. They answered everything the Patriots did, and 14–11 suddenly became 21–11. After a Patriots field goal made it 21–14, it quickly became 28–14.

They were running out of time. The Patriots, 14-2 and dominant, were at home and staying there.

"That was a weird game, man," Branch says. "Clearly, this was a team that shouldn't have been able to hold our jocks. We lost that game. We had so many mental errors throughout the course of it. And then there was the stuff with Wes...who knows what we could have done if we had won it?"

They lost it. And losses to New York teams in the postseason are always scarring, always some New Yorker's retort to settle an argument.

"This was not your garden variety postseason elimination. Losing to the Jets is worse than losing to the Lakers," Dan Shaughnessy wrote in the *Boston Globe*. "It might even be worse than losing to the Yankees and that is because of the lack of class demonstrated by the Jets in the days and months leading up to yesterday's epic showdown. The Jets are all about smack talk. They hurled insults at New England for a week. Then they came to Foxboro and backed it up."

All the awards didn't matter now. Brady was going to be the unanimous MVP and Belichick the Coach of the Year. It was a better team than last year's. More talented. More professional. Less needy. And the same play-off result: one game and out.

Who knew what next year was going to bring? The commissioner, Roger Goodell, had sent out warnings for years now concerning the lockout. It was finally time for it in 2011. As disheartening as that was, more pressing matters of the heart were around the corner.

CHAPTER FOURTEEN

CONSCIENCE AND CONFLICT

The scenes of victory were tough to take, and therefore it was time to get out of Gillette Stadium quickly on January 16, 2011. A lot of Patriots felt that way, and it had everything to do with expectation. This was all their fault. They had helped raise a generation of New England sports fans who had a hard time accepting that some team could actually enter the building for a play-off game and exit with a win. The fans and players didn't think they'd ever watch a Jets linebacker, Bart Scott, actually pretend to be a jet plane after a win: arms extended, gliding in for an interview landing, and then touching down on the ground.

Once Scott got there, he addressed a message "to all the nonbelievers." He was critical of ESPN analysts and former players Tom Jackson and Keyshawn Johnson, who had both picked the Patriots to win convincingly. He pointed out that the Jets were the third-best defense in football and the Patriots "can't stop a nosebleed."

That wasn't supposed to happen here in the postseason. This was the place where opposing players, even the MVPs, seemed to get stage fright. Peyton Manning came here in back-to-back years and totaled one touchdown and five interceptions in two losses. LaDainian Tomlinson came here with the Chargers, carried the ball twice in the cold, and then called it a day. The Jacksonville Jaguars, a twelve-win team, came here and suddenly couldn't block. They gave up four and a half sacks...to one player, Willie McGinest.

But last year, the Ravens had visited in January and left with an easy play-off win. Now the Jets, the chirpy little brother, had finally won a fight that mattered. They were going to the conference championship game after their 28–21 win and the Patriots had another game to debate during meals in the cafeteria. That really was a part of the culture that they had created, and most of the NFL would have thought them crazy if they'd been able to listen to some of their breakfast and lunch conversations. They had multiple rings, yet they'd sometimes wonder about the ones that got away.

Richard Seymour was on the other side of the country, in Oakland, and he still did it. He thought about the Mannings, how the Patriots had Peyton down by fifteen in the conference title one year and how he had Eli in the grasp in a devastating Super Bowl loss the next. "I feel like we could have won six," he says. Team president Jonathan Kraft did it. The veteran tight end, Alge Crumpler, was amazed when he sat with Kraft eating breakfast and heard him mention the "four or five" Super Bowls that they could have won. Imagine hearing that when you've never won a Super Bowl or even played in one. Deion Branch had gone away for four years, and when he got back he slid right back into the habitat that he'd left. He knew it was going to be a tough game against the physical and talkative Jets, but it took a while for reality to settle in.

"Not to be a spoiled brat," he says now, "but I couldn't have been happier the next week when they went to Pittsburgh and got their butts beat."

It was appropriate that a startling loss to the Jets happened at the beginning of the year. It was a reminder of the suddenness of things. The Patriots were used to the traditional interruptions of their football culture: trades, holdouts, free agent departures, coaching changes, retirements. But no player in the league knew what to expect from a lockout, not even the ten- and fifteen-year veterans. The last time the NFL had a strike, in 1987, Tom Brady was ten years old. Since then, whether the commissioner was Pete Rozelle, Paul Tagliabue, or Roger Goodell, the league had figured out a way to at least give the appearance that everyone was satisfied with a robust revenue pool.

That wasn't the case this time. Goodell became the commissioner in 2006, and he and the owners quickly made it obvious that they wanted to renegotiate a deal that they had just agreed to with the players. They had been preparing for this fight for five years, which most coaches and players didn't have the luxury of doing. The lockout was happening as scheduled, and it meant that everything would be frozen except for the draft. There would be no contact between players and coaches; players would not be allowed to work out at team facilities; there would be no signings, of free agents or draft picks; franchises would not pay for their players' health insurance; and, the ultimate leverage of ownership, players would miss sizable game checks if the lockout extended into the season.

Any player who considered himself naïve was about to get a baptism. This was going to be a slog. Really, from a player's perspective, it was going to be a fight against giants, seen and unseen. The players knew that the owners were wealthy because common sense and public information told them so. But when they asked owners to provide years' worth of detailed financial information, the owners refused. Yet as early as 2009, the small-market and publicly owned Green Bay Packers provided a glance of what the players were up against.

The Packers reported that their revenues were just over $20 million, which was a loss from the previous season. But their annual report also showed a "Preservation Fund" of $128 million, to be used in case of a lockout. In everyday terms, it was a piggy bank. Green Bay, the smallest market in the league, had $128 million plus the split revenue of a $1 billion DirecTV deal. If the Packers had that much, what was being stored away in New York, Chicago, Dallas, and New England?

Tom Brady's celebrity had earned him many things in his dozen-year career, but this was new. Along with fellow quarterbacks Drew Brees and Peyton Manning, he was the lead plaintiff in the players' fight to stop the lockout. The antitrust suit was called *Tom Brady, et al. v. National Football League, et al.* It was good for the players to have Brady as the face of their cause. He was the reigning MVP and the most successful winner in the league. He wasn't likely to speak much with the media during the dispute, if at all, but if he did, he certainly wouldn't say anything that would be interpreted as a gaffe. Even if his name happened to be in the lead for symbolic purposes, it was proof of his evolution in the past three years.

He had returned from his knee injury in 2009 with greater purpose. That was the positive part. His receivers, backs, and tight ends also learned how impatient he could be if they weren't doing what was expected. He had urgency. The game had been taken away from him for a year, and for the first time since his early days as a Patriot, he was a watcher. When it was time to come back and play, he wasn't tolerant of silly mistakes. Careers are short. Take advantage of what you can, when you can.

Maybe it was just a coincidence, but 2009 was also when he became more involved in the Players Association. Winning the Comeback Player of the Year award that season wasn't his biggest accomplishment. It was managing to be close to Kraft while planning to oppose him in court; it was being a passionate and informed union guy, but also being perfectly aligned with Belichick in team policy; it was being adored by millions, being paid millions, and sometimes getting special treatment by the coaching staff (he rarely practiced on Wednesdays during the entire 2010 season), and yet remaining grounded, tremendously respected by the rank and file.

He may have held his own and looked the part when he was plotting against the league's suits, but that really wasn't his game. A month and a half into the lockout, he wanted motion. The real kind, on the field, not the legal kind, to be filed.

Brady and his coach were identical in that way. They could be physically thousands of miles away from the stadium and football, but it was always in them. They weren't the folks who would say, "This is what I do; it's not who I am..." Yes, it was precisely who they were. Brady was a perpetually curious A-plus student. Belichick was a tireless teacher, always thinking ahead of a lesson or an illustration that would keep the star student, and others, engaged.

Belichick and Brady craved action. The lockout was a slow death for both of them. And, per NFL rules, they weren't allowed to talk with each other about it. One thing Belichick could do was get ready for a favorite event that was still happening—the draft. The coach's birthday was officially April 16, but it should have been the first day of the draft. He looked more at ease in the war room than he did on a golf course.

"It's a team-builder's league," says Louis Riddick, an ESPN analyst who played for Belichick in Cleveland. "Bill understands the profiles that he wants each player to have. He's got a specific profile of how he wants everything done, and there aren't many guys like that. He knows how he wants film corrected. How treatment, rehab, and weight training should go. How he's going to run practices and the practice squad. The profile of players by position, physical build, and mental makeup."

On his unofficial fifty-ninth birthday, April 28, it was once again time to see what he had learned from his draft homework. It was also time to get the payoff from that 2009 trade of Richard Seymour to the Raiders. Oakland finished 8-8 in 2010, so that middle-of-the-pack record left the Patriots with a corresponding first-round pick, number seventeen overall in the spring. They also had their own pick, number twenty-eight, but they were willing to trade it.

Belichick had no idea when he'd be able to coach a new left tackle, but he knew he needed one. Matt Light had been protecting Brady for a decade, and Light was getting close to retirement. There were two tackles the Patriots loved, Tyron Smith of Southern Cal and Nate Solder of Colorado, and they knew they wouldn't get Smith. He went ninth overall to Dallas, and Solder was scooped by the Patriots at seventeen. After that, it was the type of waiting that Belichick could appreciate: waiting for the phone to ring. The Patriots got what they were looking for shortly after, when New Orleans asked about twenty-eight. The Saints were willing to give up next year's first as well as this year's second. The extra second-round pick became running back Shane Vereen. An extra second for next year was created when the Patriots called Al Davis and got him to accept a 2011 third-rounder for a 2012 second.

But as much fun as it was for Belichick to make deals, the joy came from seeing those players and coaching them. Technically, the league's entire draft pool was pending. No one could do a thing until the lockout was settled.

In June, there was something familiar for New Englanders to celebrate. It was another championship, the seventh in ten years for a Boston sports team. The Bruins, who hadn't won a Stanley Cup since 1972, finally captured one. This time the rolling rally was in the summer, and fans were encouraged to take public transportation to avoid the hassle of closed streets. It sounded reasonable enough, but local officials weren't prepared for the number of people willing to take their advice: A crowd of 1.2 million, twice as much as the normal commute, filled inbound train stations to Boston. It was too many people and not enough trains, so many of the fans were stranded and missed the parade. Scathing blogs and letters to the editor followed, understandably so. But it was fascinating to compare the source of local anger in 2000 (no parades to plan) to the source of it in 2011 (no ride to the parade).

The celebration was in contrast to what Robert Kraft was experiencing in his professional and personal life. If he could have, he would have accepted every professional setback possible if it meant receiving a miracle at home. The business stuff, the lockout, was predictable enough. It had reached the one-hundred-day mark, and the public was far angrier than those T riders without a train to catch. Pro football was their favorite sport, and they didn't have the temperament nor the resources to understand the impasse. Why couldn't smart people figure out a way to divide over $9 billion? Even if they were smart and greedy, they still should have been able to solve that one.

What wasn't so easy was real, authentic life. Myra Kraft was in a fight for hers. By day, her husband would make phone calls and try to figure out a way to save the game. By night, he would rub his wife's feet and try to give her comfort against the ravages of cancer.

She was a brilliant woman, perhaps the smartest Kraft, and that was saying something with all the accomplishments and credentials in the family. It was her intellect that allowed her to make smart decisions as she either chaired or sat on several boards. Their range told part of the story of her personality: Combined Jewish Philanthropies of Greater Boston, the Boys & Girls Clubs of Boston, American Repertory Theater, Facing History and Ourselves. Another part of the story was her conscience, her demands for herself and those around her. This was her core, and since the Patriots were part of the family business, she pushed to make it a part of their core, too.

She got resistance on that sometimes, but she kept pushing. She had reservations about being involved in the NFL at all in 1994, and not because she thought it was bad business. She just wanted to be assured that the family's mission—calling, really—to be charitable wouldn't slow down. It didn't. Two years later, she called out Bill Parcells, on the record, when he thought he was being funny by calling a slow-recovering receiver "she" in 1996. "Disgraceful," Myra said, when describing the slight. "I hope he's chastised for that. It was the wrong thing for anyone to say."

A sense of social justice had been ingrained, as far back as kindergarten. Her father had escaped the Holocaust in the 1930s, but his parents and siblings had died in concentration camps. She was not one to stand by and wait for change. Jonathan Kraft recalled a time in apartheid South Africa where she saw black men being arrested by police. She asked the police what they had done wrong and was told that they didn't have the proper documents to be in the city at that hour. She told them that she didn't, either. "So arrest me, too!" Jonathan had to pick her up and carry her away from the scene.

She learned to love football, thanks to her husband and four sons. She loved the cerebral aspects of the game, so she not only watched it; she read about it as well. Michael Lewis's *The Blind Side* became one of her favorite books. Maybe it just wasn't possible to bring the world of pro football closer to some of the many philanthropic causes that she supported, but she was going to try. It probably never crossed her mind, nor those of the football operations staff, but she read people so well in interview situations that she probably could have picked up things about players, nonfootball things of course, that they couldn't.

A young Bill Belichick tried to change the way the Cleveland Browns viewed and described players, but there were certain messages that ownership and the fans didn't want to hear.

Going into his final season at Michigan, team captain Tom Brady (right) wasn't guaranteed to start. Three days before the season opener, he was in the same uncertain category as Drew Henson (left) and Jason Kapsner.

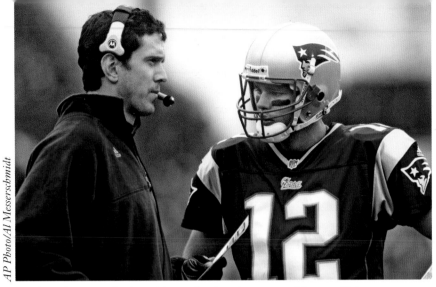

Brady, a few months into his professional career, told one of his roommates, "I'm going to beat out Bledsoe. You watch."

In 2000, Belichick and others rewrote the Patriots' scouting manual. In Richard Seymour, they found a defensive lineman who actually exceeded every category in their written ideal.

AP Photo/Tony Gutierrez

Ty Law (24) and Lawyer Milloy represented the new Patriots: There were many reasons to dance in big games, like this Law touchdown in Super Bowl XXXVI. But the business side of things was nothing to celebrate.

AP Photo/Charles Krupa

The most familiar quarterback meeting of the century was the annual one between Tom Brady and Peyton Manning. They never had to debate who was better; that ongoing conversation happened—and continues to happen—constantly.

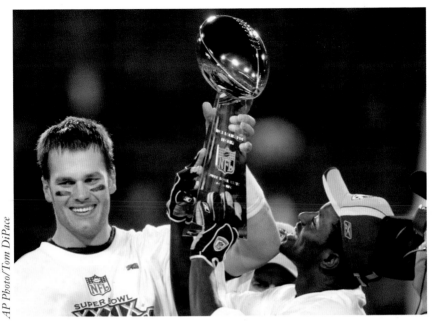

There was instant chemistry between Brady and Deion Branch, and it was on display in two Super Bowls. In this one, Super Bowl XXXIX, Brady completed twenty-three passes. Nearly half of them went to Branch, the game's MVP.

Initially, Roman Phifer told his agent that he didn't want to play in New England. A few years later, he had a different statement for teammate Tedy Bruschi: "Man, if we win this thing…we'll be a dynasty."

AP Photo/David Drapkin

Robert Kraft and eldest son Jonathan were early and frequent advocates of Roger Goodell, who became NFL commissioner in 2006. They supported Goodell's iron-fisted rule…until it crushed them in 2015.

AP Photo/G. Newman Lowrance

When the Patriots refreshed their offense in 2007 by adding the supernatural Randy Moss, it got the league's attention. "Everyone else was pros," a teammate said, "but he was like a Greek god."

AP Photo/Patrick Semansky

The 2009 season frustrated Belichick, and it culminated with his stunning admission to Brady on the sideline in New Orleans: "I just can't get this team to play the way it needs to."

AP Photo/Elise Amendola

Belichick coveted game-breaking tight ends for fifteen years. At first glance in 2010, it appeared that he finally found what he was looking for in the Rob Gronkowski–Aaron Hernandez rookie duo.

Brady's life away from football often includes galas, such as this one at the Metropolitan Museum of Art in New York. He and wife Gisele Bündchen are an international power couple, yet teammates insist "Tom just wants to be one of the guys."

One might think that it's just an ordinary football that Colts linebacker D'Qwell Jackson is holding on to in the 2014 conference championship against the Patriots. But that ball, and ten others, became the focus of the most disputed and expensive conflict in NFL history.

AP Photo/Mary Altaffer

Since being accused by the league, Brady has needed a team built for white-collar combat, guys with "JD" and "Esq." after their names.

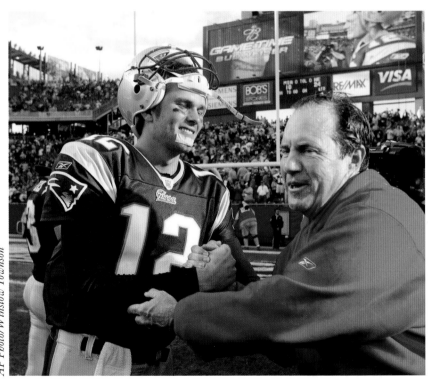

AP Photo/Winslow Townson

Belichick's surprise forty-eighth birthday present—drafting Tom Brady in the sixth round—has led to the most successful head coach–quarterback combination in NFL history.

A lot of people didn't know that she was as sick as she was in the summer of 2011. She still cooked, still checked in on her eight grandchildren, and still told Robert to go off and end that lockout. She was among the first to know when the lockout was ending, in the third week of July. That was also the time she died. She was sixty-eight.

On July 22, one of the hottest days in the history of Newton, Massachusetts, the NFL came to Temple Emanuel to honor and celebrate the life of Myra Kraft. Roger Goodell sat close to DeMaurice Smith, the executive director of the Players Association. Tom Brady and Drew Bledsoe shared a hug. Richard Seymour returned to the area for the first time since being traded, and sat near Belichick, the man who traded him. Conservatives such as Donald Trump and Rush Limbaugh were there, along with many liberal Massachusetts politicians such as Senator John Kerry and Governor Deval Patrick.

"Who else but Myra could bring such an eclectic bunch together?" Rabbi Wes Gardenswartz said. "Only one person on the planet. Only Myra could."

Elton John's version of Henry Mancini's "Moon River," the Krafts' favorite song, played softly in the temple. Three of Kraft's sons gave eulogies, but he did not speak. There would be football this year, and it was going to be incongruous to look above the field, in the owners' seats, and see Jonathan on Kraft's right but no Myra on his left.

Three days after the funeral service, Kraft and his sons were sitting shiva at the family estate. The prayers were over, and there were still visitors in the home. Robert asked his four sons and two of the visitors, Kerry and Patrick, if he should attend the press conference announcing the good football news. The vote was unanimous, 6–0, and that's how an unforgettable image became possible: Kraft and Colts center Jeff Saturday sharing a hug. The lineman said he wanted to thank Kraft for helping to "save football." The owners had preserved the power of the commissioner, given the players a less physically demanding workweek, but taken a bigger share of the revenue cut, 53 percent to 47 percent.

It was one of the strongest national moments for Kraft, and it allowed the rest of the country to see what New Englanders had experienced for decades. Kraft was a relatable and clever deal-maker. His strength was going to the essence of what the issue was and then figuratively getting the lawyers away from it. That was his way of emphasizing that common ground could be reached as long as both sides could unemotionally focus on their similarities and minimize their differences. That's how the NFL and Players Association closed a deal that would carry the sides until 2020.

"You can't solve a problem until you understand what the problem is," Kraft told the *Boston Globe*. "There were some very difficult, complicated issues, but there was a give and take. I hope the same happens in Washington. The NFL is not Washington, but culturally it is very important that we bridge our differences."

As the league opened its doors for a late start to free agency and training camp, the question of conscience tugged for the Patriots. They signed plenty of solid individuals, such as Shaun Ellis, Andre Carter, and Nate Solder, their first-round pick. But in a stunner, the team traded a fifth-round pick for a player who seemed to be the antithesis of every written rule of their organizational manual. Football was not Albert Haynesworth's top priority and everyone in the league knew it. He had the potential to be dominant, but he wasn't often enough, and the worst of his inconsistency had a birth date. It was February 2009, when he signed a seven-year $100 million contract with Washington, including $41 million guaranteed.

Worse than his being in it strictly for the money, though, were a myriad of character questions. He was arriving in New England with a misdemeanor sexual assault charge pending. A waitress at a Washington hotel said that she was fondled by the athlete as he paid the bill. While in camp with the Patriots, Haynesworth agreed to an exchange with prosecutors, who allowed him to enter a no-contest plea to one count of simple assault. Belichick and the Patriots often had foresight when they made a deal, but this was a bad fit.

Proving to be ever unpredictable, Belichick also traded late-round picks for a wide receiver who was a buddy of his but didn't seem to be his kind of player. Chad Ochocinco, who'd legally changed his name from Chad Johnson to match his uniform number—85—was brought in from Cincinnati. He had been a talented receiver, but his current skill seemed to be in self-promotion. He was a social media sensation, often regaling his millions of Twitter followers with homespun wisdom, humor, and his adventures with reality TV star Evelyn Lozada.

For those who were trying to articulate what was different about the league in general and these Patriots in particular, Tedy Bruschi beat them to it. The Patriots began their season in Miami, where Tom Brady somehow looked better than he had in 2010. He was able to help four different receivers accumulate at least six catches and 85 yards: Wes Welker, Deion Branch, Aaron Hernandez, and Rob Gronkowski. Welker's performance, eight catches for 160 yards and two touchdowns, topped them all. Brady finished with 517 yards and four touchdowns; Ochocinco caught one ball for 14 yards.

The next day, Bruschi was a guest on a radio show in Boston. He was happily talking about football until a producer put a tweet from Ochocinco in front of him. "Just waking up after a late arrival, I've never seen a machine operate like that n person, to see video game numbers put up n person was WOW." Maybe it was the fact that it was already past three o'clock in the afternoon and Ochocinco said he was just waking up. It could have been the awe, or just Twitter itself. Whatever the cause, Bruschi went on the air and told the receiver to snap out of it.

"Stop tweeting and get in your playbook," he said with passion. It was almost as if fans in drive time got to briefly feel what it was like for a wandering newcomer to be pulled back into shape by legendary Patriots like Bruschi, Rodney Harrison, and Willie McGinest. Bruschi's media instincts were as impressive as his football ones, so he was onto something. Ochocinco came from a numbering system with the Bengals, which meant that he didn't have to do any sight adjustments. He just ran a play. He wasn't going to be able to do that with the Patriots, and it was going to be a season-long problem.

But with so many of their former players in the media, the Patriots had to play the game: defend the current teammate and wave off the ex one, who can now be painted with a media brush. Tom Brady confidently did that when he commented on Bruschi's criticism of Ochocinco.

"I will say this about all those guys, whether it's Tedy making a comment—and I love Tedy, he's one of my great friends—and all those guys that have played for us, but honestly, none of those guys have any clue what they're talking about. They're outside of the locker room. They don't know what we're trying to accomplish. So, with all due respect to all of them and what they've accomplished... they don't know."

It was a good sentiment, especially since the media couldn't see practice. There, it was obvious just how lost Ochocinco was. He had played his entire career with the Bengals and it seemed that he couldn't get that offense out of his system. Near the midway point of the season, with the Patriots 5-2, Ochocinco had nine catches.

He hadn't scored. But if he wanted to revisit that WOW tweet, he had good subjects with the second-year tight ends, Gronkowski and Hernandez. Individually, they were at Pro Bowl levels. As a duo, they were unstoppable. Through seven games, they had combined for a good tight end's season: sixty-five catches, 793 yards, nine touchdowns.

Going into the season's eighth game, against the Giants, the scouting report on the Patriots was set. They were wonderful to watch on offense, but they gave up generous chunks of yardage defensively.

No one imagined that this defensive bunch had the ability to come up with a goal-line stand to win a game, or to even carry the offense on a low-scoring day. For the Patriots to get where they wanted, the offense had to take them there.

That was never more obvious than on November 6, Albert Haynesworth's last game as a Patriot. It was bad enough that the Patriots had lost the game in the final minute, when they seemed to have it under control. Haynesworth made it tough for anyone to excuse the way he played against New York, especially in the third quarter. He was pushed aside by Giants guard David Diehl, and he made no effort to recover. It allowed Giants running back Brandon Jacobs to run ten yards into the end zone. Twenty-four minutes were left in the game at that point, and Haynesworth sat out all of them.

On Monday, Belichick was asked about the benching of Haynesworth and he said the team was trying to utilize all of its defensive linemen. Not exactly. On Tuesday, Haynesworth was cut. With the release of Haynesworth, who finished his New England career with just three tackles, and the relative shelving of Ochocinco, the team seemed to be freer.

It started with the thirty-four-year-old Brady. He'd had more to worry about than anyone during the lockout, with his face and his name attached to it. The dispute had lasted more than one-third of a calendar year, 138 days, so it wasn't like he'd had much casual time to consider quarterbacking or vacations for that matter. Still, he was on pace to set a career high in passing yardage. He and offensive coordinator Bill O'Brien had a good relationship. They'd yell at each other, clear the air, and then proceed as if nothing had happened. They did that on national TV, during a game in Washington, and the exchange became a social media vine.

The wins and yards kept coming. They beat Washington on that screaming day, 34–27. That was their fifth consecutive win, a game in which Gronk had six catches for 160 yards and two touchdowns. The next week they were in Denver, and Hernandez got a chance to see his college quarterback. Tim Tebow had become one of the most popular players of the season because of his unusual quarterbacking. Brady had Hernandez on his team now, and it was his turn to dominate in a 41–23 win. He had nine catches, 129 yards, and a score.

The regular season closed with wins over the Dolphins and Bills, good for a 13-3 record and the ninth division title in the past eleven years. In their season-ending eight-game winning streak, the Patriots averaged 36 points per game. Brady had indeed finished with the most passing yards of his career, 5,235. His leading receiver, technically, was Wes Welker. But Gronk and Hernandez had tilted the field in such a way that the Patriots always had an advantage when they sent their tight ends into a route. Gronk caught ninety balls and scored a record seventeen receiving touchdowns, and added another rushing. Hernandez had seventy-nine catches and seven scores. Just like Brady and Seymour had previously, Gronk and Hernandez far exceeded the best-case standard, physically, for their positions.

As they entered the play-offs, even the potential disappointments worked out in the Patriots' favor. O'Brien wanted to be a head coach, and that opportunity was realized one week before the divisional play-off game against the Broncos.

Penn State had come off the worst year in its history with revelations about former assistant coach Jerry Sandusky and numerous allegations of sexual molestation of young boys. There was national outrage that officials at Penn State were aware of the accusations and didn't do more to help with the prosecution of Sandusky. The school's president resigned and legendary coach Joe Paterno was fired in November. On January 7, 2012, the school announced the hiring of O'Brien. He was going to stay with the Patriots until the postseason was over. Fortunately, he was going to have a postseason assistant to help him. Josh McDaniels, after being fired the previous year as head coach of the Broncos, had landed in St. Louis as offensive coordinator with the Rams. When their season ended with no play-offs, he was free to go anywhere he wanted. He went "home" to New England. Once O'Brien left, it was no secret that McDaniels would replace him.

In the play-offs, against McDaniels's old team, Patriots fans could see the effects of Hernandez's versatility. McDaniels floated the idea of featuring him as a runner and receiver, which is what he had always been. This would be like being back at Bristol Central High. He gained sixty-one yards on the ground, and another fifty-five in the air with a touchdown. The struggle to locate him further cleared the field for Gronk, who scored three times. It was on to the conference championship against the Ravens, the first team to win in the play-offs at Gillette.

On the surface, it looked like a game that would be decided by a field goal, which it was. But that wasn't the most significant development of the day. Nor was it receiver–kick returner Julian Edelman spending time at cornerback, getting two tackles and forcing a fumble; nor Brady, knee brace and all, diving *above* the pile on fourth-and-goal for the winning touchdown; nor, as dramatic as it was, a rookie free agent named Sterling Moore batting away a ball from Lee Evans that should have been the winning catch.

The topic that kept the Super Bowl preparation party tempered was Gronk. He caught a pass late in the third quarter and the defender, Bernard Pollard, held on any way he could. He started to wrap up around Gronk's waist, but that wasn't working for the safety, four inches shorter than Gronk. He slid down to his left ankle and hung on there. When Gronk fell to the ground, his ankle buckled under the 225 pounds of Pollard. He limped off the field. He was seen after the game in a walking boot.

Gronk was definitely going to play in the Super Bowl against, once again, the New York Giants. The only question was health and effectiveness. That was something they could worry about later. After a 23–20 win, Brady could look at the team's lowest scoring total in two and a half months and say, happily, to CBS's Jim Nantz: "Well, I sucked pretty bad today. But our defense saved us."

For the Patriots, traveling to Indianapolis for the Super Bowl made sense. While the best Super Bowl scenery was in New Orleans and San Diego and Pasadena, the game's AFC participants were frequently Patriots or Colts. It was the fifth appearance for Brady and Belichick since 2001, and the host city's team, the Colts, had been there twice in that span.

Belichick was usually understated with Brady, publicly and privately. There was tremendous mutual respect between the two, but there were no long dinners and old stories over beers. They were partners at the office, recognizing each other as the best there is. Just before the Super Bowl began, they talked briefly on the field and there was a knowing wink of what was at stake. They slapped five, sideways, and Brady said, "Good luck. Let's go get this thing, huh?"

Brady and the rest of the team had "MHK" patches on their jerseys for Myra Hiatt Kraft. They all talked about how special it would be to win it in such a difficult year for the owner. But the game started poorly, with Brady getting a grounding penalty that led to a safety. The Giants added a touchdown to make it 9–0.

This was where championship experience helped. Defensive tackle Vince Wilfork, playing in his third Super Bowl, stood on the sideline smiling. "It ain't nothing but a football game," he said. "That's all it is: a football game."

It was 10–9 Patriots at the half, and they were getting the ball at the start of the third quarter. They had settled into their normal game, with one exception: Gronk. His left ankle was heavily taped, from the bottom of his shoe to high on the leg. He had to be out there because of the stakes, but this wasn't the player the league saw all year. Giants linebacker Michael Boley told his teammates that in the third quarter. "Eighty-seven is a fucking decoy," he told them. "He a decoy. You see how he tried to run that route? He's gonna be outta here soon."

Yes and no. He wasn't the same. But decoy or not, he was the best tight end in football and he'd help. Even on one leg. Four minutes into the third, it was Hernandez who put the Patriots in control. He scored on a twelve-yard pass from Brady, and the Patriots had reeled off 17 points for a 17–9 lead.

But Giants coach Tom Coughlin's teams always played Belichick's tough. The two of them had been on Bill Parcells's staff with the Giants in the late 1980s, and they were too wise to the other's thinking to allow things to get out of hand. Neither of them was going to be outsmarted. And since they were partial to mentally tough grinders on their rosters, their players weren't going to be overwhelmed by deficits.

Sure enough, the Giants chipped away with two third-quarter field goals to make it 17–15 at the beginning of the fourth quarter. What happened next will long be debated in the Gillette Stadium cafeteria, on planes, in the locker room, or on vacation. It was another one that got away, another championship that was almost won.

With just over four minutes to play and the Patriots still clinging to that 17–15 lead, they had the ball at the Giants' forty-four-yard line. This was why all the talk about Brady and his receivers seeing the same things was so important. Wes Welker was in the slot, and the Giants were so confused on defense that they weren't prepared to defend a huge passing window, right down the seam. If Welker saw it like Brady did, he'd have at least a huge first down that would help bleed the clock. He'd also have the Patriots in field goal range, for a 5-point lead, or a touchdown to put it away.

Welker did see it. He ran down that seam and Brady lofted the ball to the five-foot-nine receiver. The ball wasn't perfect, but it was soft and catchable. Besides, it was the Super Bowl. It's not just great receivers who make those plays in the final game of the year; all receivers, with their hands on it, are expected to bring it down. Welker got two hands on it, the pigskin right on his gloves, and then he dropped it. Wilfork and several defensive linemen had their heads up in anticipation when the ball was thrown. They dropped their heads when the ball was dropped. *It ain't nothing but a football game*...and the game could deliver one hell of a punch to the gut.

"Whoa, that was the game," referee John Parry said as he eyed the almost-winning catch.

No kidding.

The Patriots got no points out of their drive. When Eli Manning and the Giants got the ball, they were backed up at their own twelve-yard line. Welker's play was one that he could routinely make. Manning, though, had a low-percentage opening to guide a ball to receiver Mario Manningham. It was a pass through a narrow slot, and you got the sense that the area was so tight that the only way Manning could have gotten the ball there more securely is by a machine. Perfect throw, perfect catch, with a toe tap on the side-line. It was good for thirty-eight yards, and Bill Belichick threw his challenge flag because he had to. But he knew. It was a catch.

And a sick feeling. It was happening again, just as it had in November in the regular season against the Giants. Just as it had four years ago, in the desert, against the Giants. With one minute to play, it became official: The Giants had the lead, on a touchdown run by Ahmad Bradshaw, and they weren't giving it back.

They were Super Bowl champions again, over the Patriots.

When Gisele Bündchen walked out of the stadium, she was taunted by fans. Not one for holding her tongue, she responded, "My husband cannot fucking throw the ball and catch it at the same time!" This loss was going to sting forever. At least the Patriots still had championship talent, and with a healthy Gronk and Hernan-dez, their future was bright. Or so it seemed.

CHAPTER FIFTEEN

BROKEN TRUSTS

By now, everyone in New England had heard and practically memorized what Tom Brady said about Wes Welker. The quarterback had absolved the receiver for The Drop. He said Welker was a great person and teammate. He said he wanted to keep throwing footballs to him for as long as he could. He said he loved him. Gracious words all around, leaving no space for second-guessing or resentment.

But still. This was New England. The day after the Super Bowl, that play got hours and hours of nonstop, frothing analysis. The same thing happened the next day, and the day after that, too. Welker was from Oklahoma, but he had been in New England for five years. That was long enough to realize that there are errors in big games, and then there are errors in big games against teams from New York. Those are the worst of all. Even if New Englanders were wired to move on, which they weren't, the New Yorkers would be there with smug reminders. Their jeering "eighteen and one" chant after the Super Bowl in the almost-perfect season was bad enough. Now there was this drop in their 21–17 Super Bowl win, which they used to prop up Eli Manning as a big-game quarterback and Tom Coughlin—*He's 2-0 against Belichick, you know*—as a Hall of Fame coach.

It just so happened that Welker was the biggest practical joker on the Patriots. His drop, after a season in which he caught an incredible 122 passes, was the worst payback of all. It also coincided with negotiation time. His contract was up and, in March 2012, he was looking for an extension. Instead, the Patriots announced that they were placing their franchise tag on him. He suggested that he might not sign, nor show up for minicamp in June. He didn't get his commitment. What he received, on national TV, was a lesson in Patriots economics from Willie McGinest.

McGinest was one of many ex-Patriots in the media. It was startling to hear their thoughtful and unfiltered opinions, after years of being intentionally bland and guarded as players. These days, they went on TV and radio and more than made up for lost time.

"During my tenure in New England, no matter how big you were or who you were, nobody said that they weren't coming to a mandatory minicamp. If you know anything about New England, understand that you're expendable. Unless you're Bill Belichick or Tom Brady, you're expendable."

As strong as his words were, McGinest could have gone further. He could have mentioned that Welker was thirty-one, two years removed from a torn ACL, and on the same team as two tight ends, twenty-three and twenty-two years old, whom the Patriots wanted to sign to long contracts. As a player, McGinest didn't get too many challenges after he had spoken, but as a media member, he received a pointed tweet from Welker: "why did u ever leave the Pats and play for the Browns?" McGinest, who collected $12 million from Cleveland during the last contract of his football career, replied, "My point exactly. We're all expendable at Patriot Place."

A few weeks later, there was another tweet from Welker: "I signed my tender today. I love the game and I love my teammates! Hopefully doing the right things gets the right results. #leapoffaith."

There was a lot for Bill Belichick to think about, and Welker's contract was one of those things, but it wasn't the top item on his list. The Super Bowl loss had confirmed that the offense just wasn't the same without Rob Gronkowski. In postgame interviews, Gronk had claimed to be completely healthy and said he felt no pain from his high ankle sprain. That was obviously not true and, a week after the game, he'd undergone surgery on an ankle that had multiple ligament tears. He was expected to be completely healed by training camp, which would allow Josh McDaniels plenty of time to reimagine the Gronk–Aaron Hernandez offense.

McGinest was right: Going from major player to replaced player was the inevitable progression, and it rarely happened on the player's terms. One of those rare moments took place in May when left tackle Matt Light announced his retirement. It wasn't an unexpected move, and it was part of the reason Belichick and top personnel man Nick Caserio decided to use last season's first-round pick on left tackle Nate Solder. Light was going to be missed, not just for his ability to protect Brady's blind side, but for his energy and wit.

When Brady was part of a *GQ* magazine photo spread that included, remarkably, a picture of him holding a goat, Light and other linemen made copies. They taped it to their backs and made sure that Brady had to look at that outrageous picture of himself for each snap of practice. Once, Light was even bold enough to sneak into Belichick's office and replace his computer mouse with a gag one; each time it was touched, it provided an electric shock. Belichick recalled, at Light's retirement tribute, how that little stunt went horribly wrong and erased some notes that the coach had written.

Light's departure was significant for another reason: It meant that there was now one member of the team, Brady, with three Super Bowl rings. There were twenty-two of those three-ring guys, but they were scattered now. There was a better chance of seeing all those rings on TV than in Foxboro. McGinest could wear his on the NFL Network. Bruschi could wear his on ESPN. Troy Brown and Ty Law could display theirs locally since both were on Comcast SportsNet New England. Teammate Matt Chatham was across town with his at the New England Sports Network. The recruits who dreamed of playing in the Rose Bowl could see them on the fingers of Adrian Klemm, coaching at UCLA, and Mike Vrabel, coaching at Ohio State. Richard Seymour, the headliner of Light's draft class, had his in Oakland. But not for long. He was planning to make the upcoming season his last one as well.

Brady's former teammates understood that there were several keys to longevity, and the fact that he continued to possess them and profess his love for them was impressive. Ty Law said he knew it was time to leave when he started to get easily injured and the fun of football started to feel like a wearisome job. Rosevelt Colvin acknowledged that he was worn down near the end of his career as well, tired "of the games and, honestly, you get to the point where you tune Bill out. And I think he's a great guy. But he rides everyone, whether it's [running backs coach] Ivan Fears, Josh [McDaniels], Charlie Weis, me, Tom. Mentally, it's a lot to be out there."

Christian Fauria said it was Brady's "work behind the curtain" that amazed him. The extra stretching. The disciplined sleep schedule, which usually had Brady in bed before nine p.m. The concentrated study on the upcoming opponent, players and coaches alike, then wiping the slate clean at the beginning of the next week and doing it again. The careful diet. The weight work.

"Really, I just got sick of it all," Fauria says. "But Tom is amazing. He's religious about his routine."

For Seymour, it was a combination of several things, some of which Brady never had to be concerned about in New England.

"I was starting to get worn thin. I had a couple of different head coaches, and a new general manager. There are lots of small routines that you get into, and one coach would know how to take care of you and another one wouldn't. My wife and kids got tired of the travel, and I didn't want to be on anybody's schedule anymore. I didn't have to if I didn't want to.

"I think I'm the exception to the rule. I left the game on my own terms. I don't have regrets. Some guys have to keep playing and take deals that the teams say they have to take."

Brady was thirty-five years old and not even considering joining the retirement community on TV or in the stands. Part of the job was not just an ability to do it, but an infinite desire to do it. He had that, with an abundance in reserve. He didn't need to do anything that the Patriots demanded, and he was the only player Belichick ever had who could say that. He never had to worry about getting a contract, just crafting one. He felt great about his arm strength, his overall health, his diet, and the stewarding abilities of Belichick and his staff when it came to building the roster and coaching it. When he restructured his contract in the spring, creating more than $7 million of cap space, the corresponding move seemed to be obvious: Brady was making space so the team could sign his buddy Welker.

Right idea, wrong player. The new deal was going to Gronk and, like him, it made a statement. He was twenty-three, and his $55 million contract could keep him with the Patriots until age thirty-one. Brady often said that he wanted to keep playing football well into his forties, and if he was able to manage that, he'd still be throwing touchdown passes to Gronk.

At the rate Belichick was going, he would still be coaching both of them. He once said that he didn't plan to be the next Marv Levy, who coached Buffalo until he was seventy-two. But Belichick, who turned sixty in April 2012, sounded and looked energetic on the job.

Off it, with his girlfriend of five years, Linda Holliday, he always had a smile on his face. Holliday threw an elaborate, Moroccan-themed surprise party for him at a Boston hotel on his sixtieth birthday. It was game-planned thoughtfully; even the servers were banned from smartphones, so some of the celebrity guests, such as the Bon Jovis, didn't have to worry about unauthorized pictures. Bill Belichick at work could be intense, but socially, he knew how to have fun.

Since Gronk was signed through 2019, the focus naturally shifted to his dynamic twin, Hernandez. In 2010, he had written his letter to the Patriots, essentially promising them that they wouldn't find trouble with him. He challenged them to put language in his contract that would penalize him for failed drug tests, his way of telling them that they wouldn't have to worry about the issues that scared off some teams in the draft process. Some of those issues were superficial, such as the tattoos that covered his arms. Some of them were more serious, such as the habitual marijuana use or his association with a few suspicious characters from his hometown. Those characters seemed to pop up in Gainesville a lot, and a couple of them appeared to be significantly older than a kid who arrived on campus at seventeen. They weren't his relatives. Just older guys, ranging from their midtwenties to early thirties, who seemed to be hangers-on. At best, they were people who wanted to be around Hernandez when he made it big. At worst, well, they fulfilled the gangbanger stereotypes that many people didn't want to verbalize, for fear of being labeled out of touch, bigoted, or racist.

At a glance, Hernandez appeared to be doing everything he said he would. His signing bonus with the Patriots was $200,000, nearly $300,000 less than the player who was drafted in his slot the year before. The Patriots structured his contract so he would have to earn his money in workout and roster bonuses. Not a problem. He was there all the time, and he knew exactly where he was supposed to be on the field.

Even some of the real issues that other scouts mentioned, what they perceived as Hernandez's low self-esteem, moodiness, and sullenness, were being dealt with. After his rookie year, Hernandez spoke openly and passionately about the need for mental health professionals in Latino communities. Hernandez, whose late father, Dennis, was Puerto Rican, teamed up with the Massachusetts School of Professional Psychology to raise awareness and funds for mental health in underserved communities. He unashamedly talked about his reliance on therapy as a teenager after his father's death.

The contrast was astonishing. In April 2010, his character was being questioned and there were stories about his drug use. In April 2011, he was the celebrity being lauded for helping out in the community. On a Friday afternoon, he spoke with 120 kids and their parents at the predominantly Latino Gardner Pilot Academy in the Allston section of Boston. That night, along with the mayor of Boston and three state senators and representatives, he attended a fund-raiser in Newton, Massachusetts, for mental health services.

"There are a lot of young kids that don't have that guardian or role model to talk to or that person that they can go to and just lay everything out," he told the *Boston Globe*'s Greg Bedard. "Sometimes the psychologist, when you have no one around you, can be there for you and be that person you let your feelings out to, the person that you can talk to and can give you guidance in making the right decisions when you really don't have the right people there to help you with those big decisions in life."

He was still making trips back to Connecticut, but that could be easily explained. His older brother, DJ, was the head football coach at a high school near their hometown. As for some of the shady characters who would travel from Bristol to Gainesville, the Patriots didn't see much of them, although they were around.

As the Patriots were just over a week away from training camp in mid-July 2012, New Englanders began to get excited about the team's chances for the season.

There was a lot to look forward to and a few new names to learn. For that reason and others, many *Globe* readers probably glanced over a story on July 18. It was exactly the kind of article some sports fans skipped because they were using sports to escape the depressing tales of city life. It was sad, though: Two young men, twenty-nine and twenty-eight, from Boston's strong and proud Cape Verdean community, had been killed in a drive-by shooting on Shawmut Avenue, near downtown. The initial speculation was that it was a gang-related shooting.

But the young men, Safiro Furtado and Daniel de Abreu, had no gang ties and no criminal records. They were friends who worked together at a cleaning company in Dorchester. They had left a club around two a.m., got into a car with three other friends—de Abreu was driving and Furtado was in the front passenger seat—and began making their way home. They were waiting to turn left onto Herald Street when a silver Toyota 4Runner with Rhode Island plates pulled up beside their black BMW. The driver of the 4Runner was angry and yelled, "Yo, what's up now?" He then fired six gunshots into the car and sped off. The three friends in the backseat survived; Furtado and de Abreu were dead when police arrived at 2:32 a.m.

"They were my employees, but they were also very good friends of mine, like brothers," said their boss, Jose Centeio. "This is a mystery, why anyone would want to kill two people who never bothered anyone. They had no issues with anyone, and I'm sure of that, because I spent a lot of time with them."

No one in New England would have presumed that a player at Gillette Stadium might have known exactly what happened that night on Shawmut Avenue. Reporters wanted to talk about Gronk and his celebrity offseason. He and Matt Light had angered some fans by dancing, happy and shirtless, after the Super Bowl loss to the Giants. Next, Gronk was in a Dunkin' Donuts commercial; hung out at the ESPYs; had a nude photo shoot with *ESPN* magazine; and met with the Kardashians about the possibility of a Gronk family reality show.

Hernandez was asked about his summer, compared to Gronk's.

"I just chill," he answered. "I don't pay attention to all that stuff, but I'm sure he was having fun. I definitely get laughs when people tell me about some stuff, but I'm more laid back, chilled and relaxing."

One month later, with camp over and great anticipation for the season, the Patriots had an announcement: Hernandez had agreed to a new contract. It was for seven years and $41.1 million. He was assured of at least $16 million in guarantees and he received a $12.5 million signing bonus. In a single offseason, the Patriots had ensured that the Gronk-Hernandez combination would be together until at least 2018. One of the first things Hernandez did with his money was donate $50,000 to the Myra H. Kraft Giving Back Fund.

"Now, I'm able to basically have a good chance to be set for life and have a good life and I have a daughter on the way, and I have a family that I love," Hernandez said. He was emotional as he talked about the Patriot Way and how Robert Kraft had changed his life. He said he was moved by the contract because it was Kraft's way of saying that he trusted Hernandez's character and decision-making skills. He seemed amazed by the opportunities that the contract afforded him and his family.

"It's just knowing that they're going to be okay, because I was happy playing for $250,000, $400,000. But knowing that my kids and my family will be able to have a good life, go to college, it's just an honor that he did that for me. He gave me this opportunity. So the $50,000 to help his foundation, obviously it's basically saying thank you."

It didn't take long for Gronk and Hernandez to make the Patriots look wise for their investment. In the first game of the season, at Tennessee, both tight ends caught six balls and both had touchdowns. There had been chatter about Welker's role being reduced, and the Titans game seemed to suggest it was more than a rumor. Welker had just fourteen receiving yards in the game, on three receptions. Other than that, as well as a bloody nose from Brady and some questionable calls by the replacement officials (the regulars were being locked out), there wasn't a lot of negative news to report.

In less than a year, Wes Welker had watched the Patriots sign linebacker Jerod Mayo, Gronk, and Hernandez to significant contract extensions. As they were being extended, he was being reduced, on and off the field. Welker indicated that the team had initially made him a two-year offer worth $16 million and then changed it. Later, he backtracked from the story, but something wasn't adding up. He wasn't the biggest contract priority, and he was on his way to being a secondary on-field priority before an injury changed things.

Early in game two, an uncommon home loss to the Cardinals, receiver Julian Edelman caught a short pass from Brady, with Hernandez blocking to Edelman's left. When Edelman was tackled, his momentum carried him toward Hernandez's right ankle, and the receiver landed hard on it. Hernandez immediately grabbed the ankle as he rolled on the ground. This didn't look good. He was going to be out for a while. With Hernandez injured, Welker's importance increased again. He was able to accomplish a milestone, too, in the game. He caught five balls, which gave him 562 catches as a Patriot, the most in franchise history.

Three games later, with Hernandez still missing with the severe ankle sprain, the Patriots hosted the Broncos at Gillette. Denver's new quarterback was Peyton Manning, who had been cut by the Colts following his spinal fusion surgery and season away from football. Indianapolis was now led by rookie Andrew Luck, while the Broncos expected Manning's record-setting right arm to get them to the Super Bowl. Although the game was hyped as the thirteenth Brady-Manning matchup, the star of the afternoon was Welker.

He looked like the same Wes, grabbing thirteen balls for 104 yards and a touchdown in a 31–21 win. He stayed on the field after the game to do a "talkback" interview on Comcast SportsNet with host Michael Felger and a familiar analyst duo, Troy Brown and Ty Law. Asked about his big game, in light of his diminished role at the beginning of the season, Welker said it was enjoyable. "It's definitely nice to stick it in Bill's face once in a while, so this is a good one." All four of them laughed, and all four of them realized just how true the statement was. A couple of days later, predictably, Welker said, "I don't know what else to say about it; it was a joke. But Bill and I, whether y'all believe it or not, have a good relationship. It was a joke, and I'll make sure to keep that in-house going forward."

The lack of a contract, the reduced offer, and then the reduced role had led to the "joke," so it had history and heat attached to it. And Belichick didn't think it was funny. The next week, in Seattle, it was Brady's turn to be the object of someone's humor. Hernandez returned, for the first time in a month, and had a touchdown. But the Patriots couldn't hold a 13-point fourth quarter lead and wasted a 395-yard passing day from Brady. They lost 24–23. A second-year cornerback, Richard Sherman, intercepted Brady and then badgered the dejected quarterback as he walked off the field at the end of the game. Later, he posted the picture on Twitter with the caption "U Mad Bro!"

Brady was mad, and it had nothing to do with Sherman. The

Patriots were 3-3 and inconsistent. They were able to slip by the Jets the next week in overtime. The Gronk-Hernandez offense was back again, with the tight ends combining for eleven catches, 132 yards, and two touchdowns. It was back, and then it was gone. Hernandez played those two games against the Seahawks and Jets, but his ankle wasn't responding the way it should have. He was going to miss the next few games and, if all went well, he'd be back in a month.

The Patriots didn't need Hernandez on November 18 against their old rival, the Colts, and their new quarterback, Luck. A strong passer and runner, Luck was able to do some breathtaking things on the field. But he was mistake prone, throwing three interceptions in this game, and the Patriots took advantage. It seemed that they could score whenever they needed to, but they stopped just short of 60 in a huge 59–24 win. Although Gronk had one of those Gronk games, eleven catches and two touchdowns, that wasn't what drew postgame interest.

Late in the game, on the Patriots' final extra point, Gronk went to block his man, former teammate Sergio Brown. His left forearm seemed to collapse on the spot. Fluke injury. His arm was limp, and he went to talk with Dr. Thomas Gill, a man whose name was going to be in the news a lot in the next several weeks. The forearm was broken. The biggest question of all was for Belichick, who had a starter on special teams. The head coach always did that, and it wasn't often that it warranted attention. But Gronk had been hurt on a meaningless play in a meaningless point in a blowout. People wanted to know, why was he even there? On his weekly Boston radio segment on WEEI, Belichick tried to answer.

"You only have so many players. You only dress so many players. Somebody's got to play. I think you've got to be careful when you're trying to run a team, to go up to one guy and say, 'Michael, we're going to leave you in the game because we care about you, but Glenn, we're going to take you out because you're really important. You other guys go in there because if something happens to you, we don't really care'...I think football players play football. I don't know how...you tell me which guy is going to get hurt and I'll get him out of there. I don't know how you do that."

Fortunately for the Patriots, they had a few things in their favor. It was November, which still left time for Gronk to return, at least for the play-offs. They were losing Gronk, yes, but Hernandez was returning. Ten games into the season, the two tight ends had played together for just three full games. Most important, there was a clear path to a home play-off game, if not a first-round bye, because the division was more mediocre than usual. The Jets were without Darrelle Revis, who was out for the season with a torn ACL. After two seasons when it seemed that Rex Ryan and the Jets would be a difficult matchup for the Patriots, the Jets were average in 2011 and even worse in 2012.

The Patriots got a big win over the Jets in the first post-Gronk game, 49–19, and the American sports fan got a win, too. One of the silliest plays in football history occurred in the first quarter, with the Jets already trailing 14–0. Quarterback Mark Sanchez went to run on a busted play, and as he carried the ball, it popped free after hitting the backside of his own guard, Brandon Moore. In soccer, it would have been an own goal. In football, this was being called the butt fumble.

"I've never seen anything like it in my life!" Cris Collinsworth exclaimed on NBC.

The fumble was scooped by Patriots safety Steve Gregory and returned for a touchdown. The Patriots were 8-3 after the win and the Jets were 4-7. The next week, in Miami, New England won the division, the tenth division title for Belichick and Brady.

There was a win at home the next week, against Houston, and Hernandez looked like the player he had been last season. He caught eight passes and scored twice in an easy 42–14 win over the Texans. Other than his ankle issues, he didn't indicate that anything was bothering him. He had mentioned in the summer that he was expecting a daughter, and she had arrived in style one month earlier, on November 6, her father's twenty-third birthday. Hernandez and his fiancée, Shayanna Jenkins, named the child Avielle. When his teammates heard the news, they overwhelmed him with hugs, smiles, and slaps on the back. Brady talked about Hernandez during his press conference and said he thought the tight end would be a "great dad."

It was interesting that Hernandez always seemed to be on the verge of saying something else when he talked about the humbling moments in his life. Without prompting, he frequently talked about "bad decisions" and "having someone to talk to" and "doing the right thing." On first listen, they were just clichés. But he wasn't reciting them like many athletes do when they want to get out of an interview as quickly as possible. He was speaking from a deep place, yet with a filter. The word that stood out, distinctly, when he talked about his life now was "reckless."

"Best birthday gift you could have, having a daughter on your birthday and especially Daddy's little girl," he said a couple of days after Avielle's birth. "It's an honor, and I couldn't ask for my life to be better at this point. My life is pretty good, and thank God for that, and it's a blessing; I still feel blessed daily. It definitely changed my life and I'm going to look at things differently. I'm engaged now, I have a baby, and it's just going to make me think of life a lot differently and doing things the right way. I can't just be 'young and reckless Aaron' no more."

Before the Patriots' next game, December 16 against the 49ers, there was a moment of silence on the field. Many people watching the game on television missed a large part of it due to coverage of President Obama speaking at a memorial service in Newtown, Connecticut. There had been a mass shooting there two days earlier, and the nation was still trying to comprehend how and why it happened. "No single law, no set of laws, can eliminate evil from the world or prevent every senseless act of violence in our society," the president said. "But that can't be an excuse for inaction. Surely we can do better than this."

In addition to the moment of silence, the Patriots wore a decal on the back of their silver helmets. The Associated Press carried a powerful photograph of the Newtown logo on the back of Hernandez's helmet. To the left of the blue "81" was a black ribbon with "Newtown" written above it. The site of the tragedy was thirty miles from Hernandez's hometown. It was hard to think about football, and the 34–31 loss to the 49ers didn't elicit much criticism from anyone.

Heading into the new year, after a 12-4 close to the regular season, there was optimism with the Patriots. Gronk had played briefly in the regular-season finale to test his arm. A plate had been inserted, and he felt fine. He'd have two weeks to rest it before the first play-off game at home, against the Texans. Finally, there would be a chance for the young tight ends to play together, healthy, for the first time since September. As for Welker, for all the conversation about his evolving role, it settled into the same as it always was. He may have said he was joking about sticking it in Belichick's face, but he was going to have a chance to do that in free agency. He followed his 122-catch 2011 season with 118 catches in 2012. Someone was going to be willing to pay for that kind of production.

There wasn't a lot to worry about pregame with the Texans. The Patriots had handled them in December, without Gronk, and they were likely to crush them this time with him. Eight plays into the game, though, there was a problem. A season-ending and season-changing problem. Brady went deep for Gronk down the right sideline, and in the tight end's effort to catch the ball, he landed on his left arm. He had been positioned in such a way that when he fell, the point of impact was at the top of the surgically inserted plate. The arm was broken, again, in a different place.

The win over the Texans was secure, and the Patriots were headed to the conference championship game for the second year in a row. It was a great accomplishment, but everyone had seen enough of the Gronk-Hernandez program to understand how good things could be when those two were together, and how problematic the Patriots offense could be without them.

Belichick was asked about Gronk, the tight end's health, and the decision-making of the team's medical staff after the game. He wasn't in the mood for any of the questions.

Was Gronk 100 percent when he went out there or was there a chance he wasn't completely healed?

"I covered that yesterday," he replied. "He was cleared medically. I don't have anything to add to it."

He was asked if putting Gronk out there was riskier, given the presence of the plate.

"I have nothing to add to it," he said.

He knew he was being pushed for more, and the questioners knew it, too. He knew it was game-changing, and so did the reporters, but he wasn't going to give them what they were looking for. They would have continued to ask if he had wanted to play the game, but he reached the point where he didn't want to dance any longer. He became annoyed when a reporter tried to use the side door with the questioning, asking about the evaluation process, in general, when trying to discern if an injured player is ready. The head coach spoke slowly and condescendingly this time.

"I [pause] have [pause] nothing [pause] to [pause] add [pause] to [pause] it."

The conversation was finished, but the topic wasn't. The Ravens were coming back to town, but this time they believed they were on a mission. Ray Lewis, their Hall of Fame linebacker, had announced before the play-offs that this would be his final season.

After a competitive first half, which ended with the Patriots leading 13–7, the game fell apart on New England. It was still just 14–13 at the end of the third quarter. But one play into the fourth, Anquan Boldin caught a three-yard touchdown pass and yelled loud enough for the entire stadium to hear him. This was personal for Baltimore. It wasn't just because they wanted to win for Ray. They thought they had been the better team last season when the Patriots beat them by a field goal.

Following the Boldin score, the Patriots' villain, Bernard Pollard, struck again. The safety was flat-out bad luck for anyone in a Patriots jersey. When he was nearby, the doctors had to be on alert. Running back Stevan Ridley tried to make a move in the open field and lowered his helmet to take on Pollard. The safety lowered his helmet, too, and it resulted in a nasty collision and a Ridley fumble. It didn't take long for quarterback Joe Flacco to find Boldin, again, and it suddenly wasn't much of a game. The Ravens won 28–13. They were going to the Super Bowl in New Orleans. And if that wasn't obvious enough, they did their own broadcast after the game.

"Have fun at the Pro Bowl!" shouted linebacker Terrell Suggs. "These are the most arrogant pricks in the world, starting with Belichick on down. Tell them to have fun at the Pro Bowl. Arrogant pricks. That's funny. Ever since Spygate, they can't seem to get it done. I don't know what it is."

It got even more inflamed when Welker's wife, Anna Burns, posted to Facebook after the game, "Proud of my husband and the

Pats. By the way, if anyone is bored, please go to Ray Lewis' Wikipedia page. 6 kids 4 wives. Acquitted for murder. Paid a family off. Yay. What a hall of fame player! A true role model!"

Once the damage-control specialists and public-relations spin doctors were finished and the Facebook post had been deleted, the tone all around was respectful. But it was totally fraudulent, nothing close to the way it really was. The same was true of a few other things connected to the Patriots.

Fans in New England were worried about a tight end, but they were concerned with the wrong one. A video of Gronk had surfaced in Baton Rouge during Super Bowl week. He was again shirtless, dancing freely even as a black cast restricted his left forearm. There was yet another video in Vegas, another shirtless occasion, and this time there were wrestling moves along with the dancing. A few weeks after the Ravens beat the 49ers in the Super Bowl, Gronk had his third forearm surgery in three months. This was to clean up an infection that was caught early, and it wasn't expected to extend his recovery time. Gronk had accumulated thirty-nine touchdowns in thirty-eight regular-season games, but his prosperous social life always made news. He was frequently thought of and portrayed as a partying frat boy with no boundaries.

"His arm is OK. His behavior is not. Gronkowski didn't break any laws or any bones in Vegas. But his bare-chested shenanigans are growing old, even if he's not," Christopher Gasper wrote in the *Globe*. "He has a responsibility to the Patriots, to his teammates, and most importantly to himself to make sure he doesn't do anything that could hinder or jeopardize what looks to be a Hall of Fame career."

If people only knew.

Gronk was fine. It was the other tight end, Hernandez, who was unraveling. And it wasn't new; it just hadn't been revealed to the public yet. He'd likely been holding on to a heartbreaking secret for nearly eight months, and although it would remain hidden a few months longer, it would soon be exposed. He'd been socializing with several friends with criminal records and one of them, Alexander Bradley, had accused him of shooting him in the face after they argued in a car heading north of Miami. That was in February, when the cameras were on Gronk and his dancing. Gronk dancing topless was ice cream and cookies compared to this. Bradley lost his right eye, allegedly from the shooting, and filed a civil complaint specifying his multiple facial surgeries and current disabilities, due to the actions of Hernandez.

In the past few months, Hernandez had also been spending time with the boyfriend of his fiancée's sister. The man's name was Odin Lloyd, and he was a semiprofessional football player for the Boston Bandits. He lived on a tough street, Fayston, in a tough Dorchester neighborhood. Lloyd didn't have his own car, but he would sometimes drive ones either owned or rented by Hernandez. They'd hang out in Boston clubs and drive back to Hernandez's safe house, in Franklin, Massachusetts. Or they'd hang out in Hernandez's mansion, in the finished basement, where a long pool table with a Patriots logo on it sat. The reminder of his employer didn't stop Hernandez from smoking marijuana a few feet from that table. He was still doing that, and doing it daily. He knew how to smoke and not get caught by NFL testing. Anyone who really knew him understood that the "failed a single drug test" story he tried to sell the public was high fiction. He was doing what he had to do to keep his real life from his Patriots life, and it was still working in March 2013. It wouldn't be for long, though.

In March, Wes Welker found that the market for his services wasn't as strong as he expected it to be. The Patriots had once offered him $8 million per season, but he wasn't drawing that type of interest in free agency. His market had changed, and the Patriots had changed course. They signed Danny Amendola of the Rams to replace Welker. That left Welker in one place, Denver, for two years and $6 million per season. He'd be one of the few receivers who could say he caught a bunch of passes from Tom Brady one season and Peyton Manning the next.

Any type of criticism over Belichick's personnel decisions came to a stop on Marathon Monday in Boston. The April day had begun normally, with the Red Sox game being played in the morning as the road race took over the city. But soon there were reports of a bombing on Boylston Street, the same street where championship teams had rolled through town in duck boats. There were three fatalities and hundreds of injuries.

When it became clear that the terrorists were from Cambridge, two young men who had been described by some as prototypical "normal neighbors," there was shock. How could people just down the street lead such depraved double lives like that? It was the question of the year; blind trust was becoming increasingly problematic.

In May, incredibly, Gronk had his fifth surgery in fifteen months: four on his forearm and one on his ankle. He was scheduled for a sixth, in June, to repair a herniated disc. All of the procedures and rehab for them were going to lead to missed games at the start of the 2013 season. Yet with the definite absence of Welker and the possible absence of Gronk, Brady went on WEEI and tried to remain optimistic.

"He's dealing with his situation," he said of Gronk. "I want him out there helping the team win. He's been battling through a long time. His mental toughness and excitement and what he brings to the team are really unmatched. When he's healthy, I'll be excited to have him out there. It will be nice to see what our offense can be like when Aaron is out there, and Rob's out there, and all the other guys that have been injured are out there and can contribute fully to the team."

Hernandez would never be out there again because the life he was accused of living, a secret one, finally enveloped his football career. Brady had asked his receivers to work out with him in California in April. Hernandez was there, but when he wasn't catching passes, he was paying for guns. He went to a Bank of America in Hermosa Beach, California, and wired $15,000 to a man named Oscar Hernandez of Belle Glade, Florida. In turn, a few days later, the Florida man sent a rifle, a .22-caliber Jimenez pistol, and a Toyota Camry to Hernandez in Massachusetts. The car and guns would eventually become items of great interest for authorities who'd search Hernandez's house.

Bill Belichick allowed the Patriots to leave minicamp one day early, on June 13, a Thursday morning. Hernandez spoke with reporters about being ready for training camp and helping the team. But other things were on his mind for his long weekend. The night before and even earlier that morning, he had been texting with Ernest Wallace, a friend from Bristol who had a long criminal record, including numerous drug violations. Wallace was sixteen years older than Hernandez, but it was Hernandez who was giving orders.

And give orders is exactly what he did after spending a Friday night and early Saturday morning with Odin Lloyd at a Theater District club called Rumor. On Sunday, Father's Day, he urgently texted Wallace, who was in Connecticut. "Get ur ass up here." Wallace, driving a Nissan Altima that was rented for him by Hernandez, arrived at Hernandez's home a couple of hours later. He was joined by another friend from Bristol, Carlos Ortiz. Together they traveled to Dorchester to pick up Lloyd. He got in the Nissan after two a.m., and they headed back to North Attleboro.

After three a.m., the car turned into an industrial park, one mile from Hernandez's home. Lloyd texted his sister, Olivia. "U saw who I was with. NFL…Just so U know." Hernandez had allegedly been agitated. He said he was having a hard time trusting people. There was speculation that Lloyd had information about the secret on Shawmut Avenue. It was Hernandez who would eventually be accused of targeting those Cape Verdean immigrants after the night at the club. The reason? They had accidentally bumped into him, causing his drink to spill. He felt that they didn't apologize, and perhaps they were trying to test him.

So it was Aaron Hernandez, star football player, who allegedly decided to leave the club, get in his Toyota 4Runner, and wait until two unsuspecting men got into their BMW. He saw them, ran a red light to catch up to them, and fired six shots. A week and a half later he went to training camp. A month after that he signed a new contract. And less than a year later, he was in an industrial park, one mile away from a $1.3 million mansion. One mile away from his fiancée and eight-month-old daughter, the family that was going to keep him from being "young and reckless Aaron."

There were five shots, authorities believe, from a .45 Glock. Hernandez, Wallace, and Ortiz returned to the player's house, and Hernandez's elaborate video system even captured him on camera holding a gun that appeared to be a Glock. Lloyd's body was found by a teenage jogger later that evening. When Lloyd's pockets were searched, keys to a rental car were found. They were in Hernandez's name.

It was over. When police knocked on his door late on June 17, he talked for a while and then said, "What's with all the questions?" Unfortunately for him, they were just getting started.

CHAPTER SIXTEEN

SECOND-GUESSING

A tanned Bill Belichick, familiar pencil tucked behind his right ear, stepped to the podium for the most difficult press conference of his career. It was hot outside, with the late July temperatures in the upper eighties, and the activity inside the room at Gillette Stadium made it even hotter. There were more reporters than normal, more cameras, more bright lights. All the Boston television stations went to live coverage, as did ESPN.

Everyone was looking for the football coach to go beyond football. Everyone was looking for him to at least partially answer a question that tugged at millions of NFL fans and observers, but one that very few knew the answers to.

How did we get here?

How did it get to the point where, on July 24, 2013, the head coach of the New England Patriots was describing how an accused murderer was in this same building just over a month ago? According to the timeline put forth by prosecutors and investigators, Aaron Hernandez had killed two people and then gone to training camp a week and a half later. He had donated in the name of giving back to the community a month after that when, if the allegations were true, he had actually been a menace to the community.

He had spent an entire season meeting and practicing, playing and traveling with men who had no idea how much of a danger he might have been to all of them. Was there any hint, any small detail about Hernandez that didn't connect at the time, but now, with the benefit of hindsight, provided a clue of the types of things he did when he left the stadium?

All around this room, people wondered. They wondered about Belichick, who drafted him, coached him, texted with him, and was even hugged by him a few times. Had he ever met Alexander Bradley, the godfather of Hernandez's eight-month-old daughter? It was Bradley who said he could get Hernandez marijuana on demand; Bradley who, these days, considered himself a former Hernandez friend because, he alleged, Hernandez shot him in the face in February and then left him on the side of the road bleeding. There were many instances like that, when you put up a split screen and watched on one side the made-for-TV league fulfill the football calendar, preparing for the scouting combine, free agency, and the draft, while on the other side Hernandez allegedly orchestrated sociopathic actions in private.

Did anyone in Foxboro recognize the faces that were now frequent images online and on the news? Did Belichick, Robert Kraft, or even a teammate recall seeing or meeting Ernest Wallace or Carlos Ortiz? The last time Belichick spoke to the media here, on June 13, he was announcing a day off for the players so they could start their summer vacations early. Aaron Hernandez's mind wasn't at rest, though. He texted Wallace that same morning, June 13, and said things were getting crazy. He was frantic, telling him that he needed clips, perhaps for ammunition, and CDs from a car, as soon as possible. He was restricted in minicamp because he was recovering from shoulder surgery. But it turned out football wasn't preoccupying his life. There were no texts about the shoulder and taking it easy in his real life. He was on the go, to Boston clubs and Providence restaurants, to a Dorchester neighborhood to pick up Odin Lloyd and then to an industrial park in his own neighborhood to allegedly kill him.

How in God's name did we get here?

Belichick stood in front of the room, occasionally shifting to the side as he read from a prepared statement he had written himself. It was a lot different from the internal writings he had done for football players. Now he was writing for and speaking to a national audience that was hanging on and parsing every word and intonation. He and the organization were on trial in a sense, because there had been lengthy blogs and debates around the region and country about what the Patriots should have known and could have done.

"It's a sad day," he began. "It really is a sad day, on so many levels. Our thoughts and prayers are with the family of the victim, and I extend my sympathy to everyone who has been impacted. A young man lost his life, and his family has suffered a tragic loss. There's no way to understate that."

He looked down and sighed. It was quiet in the room.

"When I was out of the country, I learned about the ongoing criminal investigation that involved one of our players, and I and other members of the organization were shocked and disappointed at what we had learned. Having someone in your organization that's involved in a murder investigation is a terrible thing. After consultation with ownership, we acted swiftly and decisively."

He was referencing the release of Hernandez on June 27. He had certainly seen the footage by now, of Hernandez being led out of his house wearing black sneakers, red-and-black gym shorts, and a white T-shirt draped over his torso and his hands in cuffs. That morning, similar to others in the past week, there had been media members camped near Hernandez's house. His teammate Deion Branch lived across the street and there was such a scene that

Branch was advised not to come home. Just before nine a.m. on the twenty-seventh, two black sedans and a North Attleboro police car parked in Hernandez's driveway. The cars emptied, and seven men went to the front of the house: one knocking on the door, one ringing the doorbell, two standing on the stairs, two standing on the sidewalk, and one near the driveway. When the door opened, all of them went in. They returned minutes later with Hernandez and escorted him purposefully past the hydrangea and into the backseat of the police car.

Hours later, Hernandez was a former Patriot. One month after that, his former coach was in a room trying to explain, as appropriately as he could, that this was not normal for him, either. The Patriots had taken plenty of so-called character risks over the years in the draft and free agency, but no one ever thought they'd lose a gamble so spectacularly.

"Robert and his family and I, since I got here in 2000, have always emphasized the need for our team and our players and our organization to represent the community the right way, on and off the field. We've worked very hard together over the past fourteen years to put together a winning team that is a pillar in the community, and I agree one hundred percent with that...Our players are generally highly motivated and gifted athletes. They come from very different backgrounds. They've met many challenges along the way and have done things to get here. Sometimes they've made bad or immature decisions but we try to look at every single situation on a case-by-case basis and try to do what's best for the football team and what's best for the franchise.

"Most of those decisions have worked out, but some don't. Overall, I'm proud of the hundreds of players that have come through this program but I'm personally disappointed and hurt in a situation like this."

Belichick spoke for a while, trying to explain scouting, evalua-tion, and determining a player's football readiness. Not including Hernandez, he had drafted 123 players between the ages of twenty and twenty-three since taking over the Patriots, more choices with one team than any coach in the league. He thought he had a feel for them all, from the super high achievers to the fifty-fifty bor-derline types. Aaron Hernandez wasn't the first kid he'd drafted who smoked marijuana and messed around with guns. Some at-risk young men he'd come across had responded to his direct messaging: "You can't come here and do all that shit anymore, understand?" Others never got it and therefore didn't make it.

There were scores of others, he wanted the crowd to realize, who didn't need a push. He had drafted a cancer survivor one year; an author in another season; the son of a Hall of Fame offensive lineman (who became a Pro Bowler himself) in yet another; a player who passed up a $250,000 workout bonus so he could study in the summer and get his college degree; a rugby player who wanted to try football; a cowboy who was tougher than the ones in Westerns—a guy who had played an entire season on a torn ACL. Not to men-tion the players acquired via trades, free agency, and waivers.

But this room of media members was reflective of the viewing audience, which was representative of the society at large. There were many with a thirst for something else. They wanted to know why he didn't know. Why no private eyes? Why wasn't there more aggressive vetting of the buddies? Why didn't he see all the red flags in the blue body ink?

The real answer made everyone uncomfortable: Sometimes you never know. If it hadn't been for the death of Odin Lloyd, police officials may have never made the link between Hernandez and the double homicide in Boston's South End. Robert Kraft said the entire Patriots organization was duped by Hernandez; a lot of people were. In a football sense, getting rid of his history was easy. The Patriots cut him and they offered to buy back Hernandez jerseys from all fans who had them. That was simply transactional. But there was another side to it, from all the people who interacted with him and never suspected a thing, even after the death of Lloyd.

The day after the murder, Lloyd's girlfriend, Shaneah Jenkins, got a phone call in the middle of the night. It was a Massachusetts state trooper, informing her of the tragedy. She immediately left Connecticut for Massachusetts, where she first visited Lloyd's family in Dorchester. She then traveled to North Attleboro to see her sister, Shayanna. As she was grieving the loss, she began to pace from the living room to the dining room, where she saw Hernandez. He put his hand on her shoulder, rubbed it, and told her that he'd been through losing a loved one, too, and it gets better with time.

Nothing was as simple as it looked. There were emotional and psychological aspects that were going to take years, if not a lifetime, to untangle and grasp.

"My comments are certainly not in proportion to the unfortunate and sad situation that we have here," Belichick said as he attempted to conclude his press conference. "But I've been advised to address the situation once, and it's time for the New England Patriots to move forward. Moving forward consists of what it's always been here: to build a winning football team, be a strong pillar in the community, be a team that our fans can be proud of. That's what we're here for."

Belichick mentioned having a winning football team that the fans could be proud of. The fans had been proud, but now they were embarrassed and effectively speechless. And that was a bad place to be, because the performance of the Patriots did not speak for itself. Too often lately, the actions of the Patriots, or former Patriots, cried out for context and explanations.

When it came to actual football, Bill Walsh, the architect of the 49ers teams that Brady grew up watching, had been prophetic in many ways when describing the labor and even the psychology of winning. But he didn't have any writings that began to explain the mentality of the New England fan base. Simply, the Patriots had dominated their division so much that a hat and T-shirt that read AFC EAST CHAMPIONS elicited smirks around the stadium. What they had done going into the 2013 season, win ten of the previous twelve division titles, was hard. The feat was often brushed aside locally because the competition wasn't viewed as high quality. The irony is that the state of the division was part of the accomplishment; Belichick had helped *create* the badlands in the AFC East.

Not many people recalled the deficit that Belichick inherited in 2000. They didn't remember that the Jets had four first-rounders to the Patriots' zero, and that the Jets still had Bill Parcells as their team-builder while the Patriots had his frequently browbeaten assistant of twelve years. They also had the first quarterback selected in that draft, Chad Pennington. But in the summer of 2013, Pennington and the other three first-round picks in his Jets draft class were long gone from New York, and all but one, John Abraham, were retired. Belichick had competed against fifteen different full-time coaches in the division since 2000, and they had collectively entrusted their fortunes to twenty-three primary starting quarterbacks.

In August, the University of Michigan's football players weren't interested in the quarterbacks Belichick had competed against. They wanted to hear from the one he had drafted and stood by since 2000. Before a preseason game against the Lions, Tom Brady returned to his alma mater to speak with the current Wolverines. It was refreshing to be on the Ann Arbor campus without a struggle, to know that he wasn't sharing the stage with Drew Henson. Brady was the headliner at Schembechler Hall, and that was more than sufficient. He had stayed at Michigan and become a champion, and he had returned as one as well. He was the only NFL player who had come back to Schembechler Hall with an equal winning percentage to the man himself, Bo Schembechler, whose Michigan percentage was .796.

Brady stood in the front of the room, looking out at teenagers and young men in their early twenties. Eighteen years earlier he was one of them, just trying to prove himself and get his coach's attention. Now, at thirty-six, he was speaking as the best Wolverine the school had ever sent to the pros. He wore sneakers, jeans, and a blue short-sleeved polo with a maize "M" on the collar. He paced the room, often clasping his hands together for emphasis.

"Do you know what the greatest honor I've ever received as a player is?" he said. "In my fourth year and in my fifth year, I was named team captain. That, to this day, is the single greatest achievement I've had as a football player. Because the men in this room chose me to lead their team. And these were my best friends. These were the guys that knew that I liked to work, that knew that I loved football, that knew that I loved to play, that knew that I wanted to be the quarterback for Michigan.

"And all the lessons that I learned here on State Street and in the Big House, that's still what I bring to practice today. And after fourteen years, I love the game more than I've ever loved it. But where did I learn the love for the game? Where did I learn to practice? Where did I learn to compete? It was sitting in the same chairs that you guys are sitting in today."

The upcoming season was going to test him. He was going to have to love practice even when his top target, Gronk, was there but not available to play in the games. He would have to love the games even after a *You gotta be kidding me* season opener in Buffalo. The Patriots beat the Bills, 23–21, and the replacement for Wes Welker, Danny Amendola, had ten catches. He also sustained a groin injury that was going to sideline him for a month.

What made the situation worse was that Gronk was having trust issues. He'd had back surgery in June, and it felt fine in September. The problem was the left forearm, still, ten months after it was originally broken. Some of the people advising Gronk questioned the quality of the original surgery. Doctors had to repair it for breaks and rebreaks, and they'd had to clean it out a couple of times due to infections. It was too much, and it caused hesitancy in a player who was desperate to be on the field. Every week, reporters would see him in practice and then speculate that he was close to being on the field. But he wasn't. He was taking his time, wanting to be confident that he was healed.

He wasn't there for a 13–10 win over the Jets, when a frustrated Brady yelled at receivers for not seeing what he did. There were eighteen opportunities to convert third downs into firsts, and the Patriots did it just four times. They were 2-0, but it was shaky.

Two weeks later, the *Globe* reported that Gronk was taking the trip with the team to Atlanta. But he stayed at home as the Patriots won, 30–23, to move to 4-0. It wasn't the same offense without Gronk, and it wasn't going to be the same defense, either. Vince Wilfork, a defensive captain, tore his Achilles against the Falcons and was out for the season.

Reports were that Gronk looked great in practice the next week, before a game against the Bengals. But he didn't play in the game, the Patriots lost 13–6, and the defense lost Tommy Kelly, the defensive tackle who was going to help minimize the pressure put on Wilfork. This was the cruelest 4-1 season yet, and it was going to get worse after week six. Brady was at his late-game best against the Saints. The game had two familiar things: a winning touchdown pass from Brady with five seconds to play and a season-ending injury on defense, this one to captain Jerod Mayo.

Gronk was finally ready to return, but it wasn't even to the same team. It had been suggested a week earlier that he might not be the same Gronk. No matter what the personnel or obstacles, the Patriots were expected to be competing for the Super Bowl. It was an ethos that had been introduced by the Patriots and infused into other sports teams in the city. Fans and media were so used to seeing seemingly impossible things come to life that it was sometimes difficult to recognize a hardship. Belichick and Brady were great at football, not healing the sick.

When Gronk did return, in a 30–27 loss to the Jets, Brady couldn't hide how excited he was. He targeted the big tight end seventeen times in his first game of the season. For all the talk about Belichick's secrecy, there was nothing mysterious about what he and Brady wanted to do on Sundays. They wanted to utilize Gronk. It was okay if other teams knew it. The beauty of Gronk, an available and healthy Gronk, was that no one could stop him.

The region felt the same way about the surprising Red Sox on October 30. They had finished last in the division in 2012, but they had ridden a Belichickian shopping spree (short contracts, midrange dollars) to yet another World Series title in 2013. It was the eighth Boston championship since 2000, but this one truly did belong to the region. The marathon bombing in April had pierced the soul of the city, and the healing had been symbolized by the words and actions of the Sox. David Ortiz had inspired millions when he held a microphone at Fenway Park a day after the city had been told to "shelter in place" as there was a manhunt for a terrorist. "This is our fucking city," he said to applause, "and nobody is going to dictate our freedom. Stay strong!"

On the day of the parade, November 2, everyone stopped on Boylston Street, at the marathon finish line, and sang "God Bless America" with Irish tenor Ronan Tynan. It was a powerful moment, and a reminder of just how connected the region is to all of its professional sports teams. As a further tribute, there were no fights nor arrests among the million-plus gathered downtown.

The next day, at Gillette, there was an enjoyable Patriots party. Brady and the offense had their best day of the year, as they totaled 610 yards and 55 points against Pittsburgh. They had entered the game in the bottom half of the league in total offense, eighteenth, but on a 432-yard passing day, Brady managed to spring Gronk for 143 yards and a touchdown, as well as get 100-yard passing days for rookie Aaron Dobson and Danny Amendola.

Brady had his team positioned at 6-2, and he didn't complain when he looked to Denver and saw what Broncos management had given Peyton Manning. They had signed Welker and added him to an offense that already had Demaryius Thomas, Eric Decker, and Julius Thomas. They were 7-1 and averaging 43 points per game. Manning already had twenty-nine touchdown passes. Pro football was not easy, but it was easier with that personnel.

Brady seemed to accept the challenge, both from the Broncos and the limitations of his roster. In week eleven, the Patriots beat the Broncos at Gillette in the biggest outlier game of the season. It was Brady-Manning, version fourteen, and it began with twenty-four consecutive Denver points. But the Broncos were having their success via the run and the strength of their defense; Manning had nothing to do with it. In the second half, the Broncos continued to run while the Patriots were passed along by Brady. He threw for

344 yards and three touchdowns; Manning threw for 150 yards and two scores. The Patriots won, 34–31.

With Houston and Cleveland on the schedule the next two weeks, a 10-3 record in December had them well positioned for the play-offs. The AFC East was theirs again, for the eleventh time in thirteen seasons, but as always the goal was much greater than the divisional attaboy. However, there was a problem against the Browns, and it wasn't that the game was harder than it should have been. The problem was that the season unofficially ended on a play at the Cleveland thirty-four-yard line.

Brady had dropped back to pass and found Gronk, open as usual, down the seam. A linebacker had struggled to cover him, and now Gronk had the ball in the middle of the field. A safety named T. J. Ward went low to tackle him and put his helmet directly on Gronk's right knee. Gronk fell to the turf, and it was obvious that it was bad. He didn't even grab the knee. Instead he lay there, his left forearm already heavily covered by a pad and brace, and now the same thing was going to happen with his right knee. He looked up through his red face mask and saw the guy he seemingly spent more time with than Brady, Dr. Gill.

What a year. The Year of the Tight End, New England style, was a show no one wanted to see. For the second year in a row, Brady was without Gronk and Hernandez together for the most important stretch of the year. It was going to be tough to win with a healthy Gronk. Now, with his ACL torn, the burden was on another area of the team to deliver. But guys on defense had the same issues. They had lost their ability to push the line of scrimmage with no Wilfork, Kelly, and Mayo.

In January, in a divisional play-off game against the Colts, it looked like the Patriots found the answer. Run. They believed they could always run on the Colts, who didn't have the size or toughness to stop them. Running back LeGarrette Blount had success on short runs, intermediate ones, and those that required a three-quarter sprint of the field. He scored four times and ran for 166 yards. It couldn't be this easy, could it? Could the Patriots possibly have another play-off game like this one, where they won 43–22 and Brady didn't throw a single touchdown pass?

The questions were going to be answered the next week in Denver, Tom versus Peyton, fifteenth round. It was the third consecutive conference championship game appearance for the Patriots, so theoretically they had a shot to win it. But they didn't have enough anywhere to compete like they needed to, and the win over the Broncos in November was largely irrelevant now. That first game had been played in the wind, as high as twenty-five miles per hour, and it made an already cold night feel like it was six degrees. Typical New England chill. On the afternoon of the conference title, though, the sun kissed those bright orange Broncos jerseys, and people in the stands stood comfortably in the low-sixties warmth.

It was all good news for Manning, who was going to thrive in these conditions against the competition. He was efficient and patient, and he wasn't touched once. Not a single time. The white 18 on the back of his jersey was immaculate. He wasn't pressured, sacked, or even breathed on heavily. He made it look easy as he threw for exactly four hundred yards. The Broncos led 13–3 at halftime, 20–3 after three quarters, and 26–16 at the end. Welker, the trickster, had stuck it to Bill again. This time he had collided with Aqib Talib, and the cornerback couldn't finish the game (Belichick thought it was a dirty hit and called it "one of the worst plays" he'd seen in four decades of coaching). And after a contract dispute with the Patriots, Welker was going to the Super Bowl with a team that had broken all of New England's offensive records from 2007.

The NFL was going to get all that it wanted from this postseason. There had already been another Brady-Manning game, and next up was a matchup of number ones. The Broncos had scored a league-record 606 points, and their opponent, the Seahawks, had given up the fewest points in the league two years in a row. If that wasn't enough hype, the location of the game would surely put it over the threshold. For the first time in the forty-eight-year history of the game, the Super Bowl was being held in the sizable shadows of New York City.

Although the Patriots were two hundred miles from the site of the game, they were still a part of the story. Their celebrity/popularity, their actions, and sometimes even their words ensured that they would be at the center of conversations. Belichick had gotten mostly negative pushback for his comments about Welker's play on Talib, and that was enough to trigger former *Globe* columnist Bob Ryan. Now semiretired, the excitable Ryan, a regular contributor on national TV and radio shows, had long suggested that New England had no idea how much America hated the Patriots. He used Belichick's comments on Welker to reintroduce his point.

"When Belichick stupidly acts out in public the way he did last Monday it reminds America about Spygate, something he has never owned up to and something that has never been forgotten in the outside world. Patriots losses are greeted warmly across America, and many people love to remind us that it is an undeniable fact that the Patriots have not won another Super Bowl, post-Spygate, a circumstance viewed by many as a form of cosmic retribution. Analysts less spiritually-minded think it has more to do with the lack of a championship-caliber defense all these years, but in any case, this failure to add another Lombardi Trophy to Belichick's collection makes millions of American football fans happy."

As if he had edited Ryan's column and was determined to live out every sentence of its truth, former Rams running back Marshall

Faulk agreed to do a Radio Row interview with Boston's WEEI. Officially, he was there to pitch a product, but he and hosts Lou Merloni and Mike Mutnansky understood that wasn't the case. He had a cause, and he had harped on it a year to the day earlier with another New England media personality, Tom E. Curran. Before that Super Bowl, between the Ravens and 49ers, Faulk told Curran, "I'll never be over being cheated out of the Super Bowl." He said he didn't understand why the commissioner had destroyed the Spygate tapes, why the Patriots appeared to be prepared for all their plays, and why Roger Goodell didn't punish Belichick more severely.

True to his word, Faulk wasn't over the loss from February 2002 when he talked with Merloni and Mutnansky in January 2014. Bob Ryan was right. He had company. Even Roger Goodell had mentioned, in a 2011 interview with Peter King, that he felt "deceived" by Belichick with his Spygate apology. Four years later, the league's leader said he'd expected Belichick to express his regret with more humanity, as opposed to releasing a statement. Spygate was almost seven years old now, but there was still first-day bitterness over it, in owners' suites, locker rooms, TV studios, and even league headquarters.

The Patriots and their fans were not paranoid; everyone was waiting for them to do anything small so they could retry Spygate and descend with a mightier punishment. There was a sense among the coaching staff as well as fans that the league was looking for anything, even if it was failing to signal on a right turn. If Faulk deserved credit for anything, it was his willingness to at least partially say what many in the league were thinking.

"I still consider Bill Belichick one of the greatest coaches. I still consider Tom Brady one of the greatest players. That team and what they did, and went on that run, it was great. The only thing that bothers me is there's something that exists that gives us doubt on why the game went the way it did. The question is, how did they become a championship team? Listen, I'm not going to be the only one to say this: Ever since they got fined and said, 'Okay, we're not doing that anymore,' they've won how many Super Bowls?"

He was told the correct answer. None. He was asked if they hadn't won because they weren't taping coaches anymore.

"I'm just telling you how I feel about it. If that's your perception of what I'm saying, then that's your perception. I'm not taking anything away from Bill Belichick and Tom Brady; they're great. I'm going to continue to tell you that…I'm just telling you it's just ironic that that's the case."

He was clearly saying what the hosts said he was. He just didn't want them to label it. But his words were not hard to comprehend.

"The only thing I know is ever since that happened and it got exposed, what we have is 0-2 in Super Bowls. That's all. I'm not saying they have anything to do with each other; I'm just telling you what the facts are."

Faulk was reminded that the Patriots had won the most games in football since Spygate, duplicating the success they had before the stick-to-their-ribs scandal.

"It's successful," he replied. "But we're talking about championships. There's a lot of teams that win a lot of games."

Belichick often told his players to ignore the noise. He had it written on the walls in football operations, clear enough and large enough for all players to see. But telling them to ignore the noise was akin to telling them to ignore the atmosphere. The sun. Day and night. The noise was everywhere, in and out of New England. There was that noise about their misfortune in championship games since Spygate. Noise about the system of Belichick, and how maybe he needed to load up the way former Patriots coach Pete Carroll had. His Seahawks had dominated the Broncos in the Super Bowl, winning 43–8. The Patriots couldn't touch Manning; the Seahawks couldn't keep their hands off him or his receivers.

Ignore the noise about the quarterback, too? There were always people talking about the lack of playmakers around him. Kenbrell Thompkins? Aaron Dobson? Even a magnificent talent like Gronk was no guarantee to be there at the beginning of the 2014 season. How do you ignore that? And although Brady didn't fear or hear the clock that reverberates in most aging athletes, he'd be thirty-seven in August. More than one person could hear that clock, and maybe even one of them was Belichick.

Chapter Seventeen

"WE ARE THE PATRIOTS. EVERYTHING IS A BIG DEAL"

Tom Brady has expressed the sentiment many times: There is nothing the Patriots can do to surprise him anymore. Nothing. He is the most grown of the grown men in the locker room these days, five months away from his thirty-seventh birthday. By March 2014, there isn't much he hasn't seen from the Patriots or even from the league itself.

He understands the nature of the game, from its brutality on the field to its corporate warriors in New York, always prepared for legal combat in the name of defending the shield. He's won more often than any player in football, and that isn't just about appearing in five Super Bowls and eight conference title games. At the genesis of winning is an understanding of how things and people work, and that is one of his overlooked skills.

He's learned a lot over the years. He, Matt Light, and Patrick Pass used to be the youngest of the twenty-two Patriots who were three-time champions. Now all but two, Brady and forty-one-year-old Adam Vinatieri in Indianapolis, are retired. If Brady is to win another Super Bowl, he'll do it with a bunch of players who will find it hilarious that there was no such thing as an iPhone or iPad the last time he palmed the Lombardi Trophy in February 2005. This game cycles through players and trends quickly. You've got to have two things ready at all times: an impromptu good-bye or a packed bag.

For Brady, it's always been the good-byes. He forced Drew Bledsoe's in 2002, was hurt by the abruptness of Lawyer Milloy's in 2003, and was angered over the negotiating that led to Deion Branch's in 2006. There is a story for all of them. Ty Law, fellow Wolverine, is the one who sold him the condo way back in the Cherrywood Lane days. Willie McGinest displayed unique leadership and introduced him to trusted friend and business partner Alex Guerrero. Mike Vrabel, chess player/coach on the field and comic in the meeting room, was the reminder that hard work could and should be fun. Randy Moss showed him how high the offense could go, specifically how far the quarterback could go, with a prodigy-in-residence. Light, who played with Crohn's disease and never made it public, was the consistent and loyal protector.

After listening to and watching Bill Belichick for fourteen seasons, Brady has heard the themes repeat. Be prepared. Ignore the noise. Do your job. Even for those like Brady, veterans knowledgeable in the departures and arrivals orchestrated by Belichick, the spring of 2014 still is full of twists.

The most shocking move was actually put in motion a year earlier. Darrelle Revis, the most talented player ever drafted by the New York Jets, tore his ACL in the third game of the 2012 season. The Jets' world changed in his absence: The general manager who drafted him, Mike Tannenbaum, was fired after the season. The new guy hired in 2013, John Idzik, traded him to Tampa for first- and fourth-round picks. Once there, Revis signed a $96 million contract with no guarantees and then *Tampa* got a new general manager, former Patriots scouting director Jason Licht. He had a vision for a young team, one that didn't include the high-salaried cornerback.

On March 12, 2014, the Bucs made it official. The best cornerback in the NFL was available for anyone to sign, although everyone could plainly see that one team made more sense than any other in the league.

The Patriots.

Sure.

Revis, twenty-eight years old and in his prime, in a Patriots uniform? The same player who seemed to enjoy every second of being on the New York side of the Jets-Patriots rivalry. The player who was angry because he said Brady prodded their sideline. He's the player who went on TV, twice, to deliver one-word putdowns of the Patriots. He called Randy Moss a "slouch" in 2010. Two years later, sitting next to Gronk in an ESPN studio, he was asked to share the first thing that came to mind about Belichick. "Jerk," he replied. The host was stunned, so Revis repeated it, clearer and louder.

Slights aside, Revis was a money player. He shut down top competition, and he expected to be paid well for it. Belichick and the Patriots hadn't been aggressive in free agency, at least not Revis-level aggressive, in seven years. The Jets, meanwhile, had history with him. And they needed him. But the Patriots knew someone who had a deeper history with Revis. That history went beyond Revis's draft day with the Jets in 2007, his national signing day with the University of Pittsburgh in 2004, and even his first day of high school in Aliquippa, Pennsylvania, in 2000.

"The house that I grew up in was the house that Darrelle's grandma [Aileen Gilbert] lived in," Ty Law says now. "I've known him since he was five or six years old. Let me tell you, he stood out even when he was a little kid. And that's saying something when you're from Aliquippa."

The small western Pennsylvania town, about twenty miles from Pittsburgh, is known for producing NFL talent. Law, eleven years older than Revis, grew up there watching Revis's uncle, Sean Gilbert, star for the Quips in high school basketball and football. Gilbert was a colossus, six feet five inches and three-hundred-plus pounds as a defensive tackle. He had his number, 71, retired in high school, alongside Mike Ditka's 80. He went to Pitt and was drafted third overall by the Rams in 1992. Law's cousin, Hall of Fame running back Tony Dorsett, also took the familiar Aliquippa-Pitt-NFL path. As had Ditka, a Hall of Fame tight end. When Revis became a free agent, many people knew how to contact him, but few knew exactly what to say. Law did.

He knew how every great athlete from Aliquippa was expected to be tougher and more competitive than most. They competed hard at everything, not just football. Law laughs as he remembers playing a game in which kids would get a twig, put it in a stream, and see whose twig was fastest, end to end. Anything and everything is turned into a competition when you're a Quip. Years ago, after Gilbert had been traded from St. Louis to Washington, the team made him its franchise player and offered a salary of $2.5 million. He told them in February of that year, 1997, that he'd never sign a deal that undervalued him like that. He said he was taking his family back to Aliquippa and that he'd sit out the season if he had to. That's exactly what he did, his firm stance closely observed by his sister's twelve-year-old son, Darrelle. The next year, he was traded to the Panthers and signed a then-record contract for a defensive lineman: a $10 million bonus and $45 million overall. It was about fairness, respect, and never, ever backing down.

Aliquippa no longer makes steel, and its unemployment and crime rates are high. But everyone in town follows the athletes who make it out, and they keep score.

Law made five Pro Bowls and was part of three Super Bowl champions. Like Gilbert, he wasn't afraid to talk about money and say how much of it he deserved. Like Revis, he'd let his emotions run high before and resorted to name-calling with Bill Belichick. He knew what it was like to have Belichick on your side in big games, and he'd experienced negotiating against him trying to get a big payday. He explained to Revis that Belichick isn't just the wooden guy from interviews and the sideline. The coach appreciates greatness, and he'd be willing to move Revis all over the field, allowing him to be as free and creative as he needed to be.

"I told him that it's about leaving a legacy," Law says. "He had all the numbers and awards over the years, but I told him that he doesn't want to be Champ Bailey. Great player, don't get me wrong, and I respect Champ. But he got all those Pro Bowls, and those are the only things hanging in the rafters. You want that championship banner.

"Darrelle had a lot of offers. There were teams that had just as much money as the Patriots, if not more. But this was a chance to play with Tom Brady and get a ring. I'm not saying he made his decision because of me, but I'd like to think I had something to do with it."

Revis signed a two-year, $32 million contract with the Patriots, officially. But the second year was a complex team option, and if the Patriots exercised it they'd have a cap charge of $25 million in 2015. That wasn't going to happen. So everyone understood up front exactly what this unusual Revis-Patriots union was. They'd likely be bound for just one year, and if everything worked out as planned, the marriage would dissolve yet all involved would leave with diamond rings.

Belichick's signing of Revis fooled some observers into thinking that the coach was changing the way he did business. The talent of

Revis, along with the anticipation of watching him play, obscured the fact that this was the same Belichick making yet another sensible signing. Revis for a year *was* good value, and not only did his presence improve team depth; it gave the defense its own Brady figure, a transformative player who emboldened ordinary play designs. It also deprived and frankly embarrassed the Jets. It's bad enough to have Revis return to the division, but even worse to see him with the Patriots. Missed opportunities like this would soon cost Idzik, the Jets general manager, his job.

Believing that the Patriots were "loading up," New England fans went into the second weekend of May, draft weekend, excited by the possibilities. The team's first two selections were twenty-ninth and sixty-second overall. For teams that consistently draft well, that translates into two immediate starters. There was a restless and vocal segment of the fan base that wasn't convinced that Belichick's economics worked for a late-career Brady. They wanted every move to be made with the quarterback's date of birth in mind.

After drafting Dominique Easley, a defensive tackle from the University of Florida who had bad knees and a reputation for having a bad attitude, they surprised everyone with their second-round pick.

When it was time to announce the sixty-second pick, former Patriot Willie McGinest took the Radio City Music Hall stage. He wore a red Patriots sweater under his tailored suit jacket, an outfit that led to resounding boos from the New Yorkers in the crowd. He teased the crowd, saying, "Your New England Patriots and my New England Patriots..." And then he gave the actual pick: Jimmy Garoppolo from Eastern Illinois. A quarterback.

"Wowww," said Rich Eisen, hosting the NFL Network's draft coverage.

It was an appropriate summary. With the first two choices, the

Patriots nearly guaranteed that they wouldn't get major contributions from their draft picks in 2014. Beyond that, the Garoppolo selection was significant. Belichick's Patriots had never drafted a quarterback this high.

When Belichick was asked to explain the pick on draft day, he managed to take a couple of shots at the Colts as he answered.

"Organizationally, I don't think we would put together a team the way Indianapolis did when they lost Manning, and they go 1-15 or whatever it was. I don't think that's really what we're looking for. Unfortunately, we lost Tom in 2008 and we had a player who stepped in and won 11 games. We want to be competitive even if something happens to a player at any position. I think depth is always important. You never know when you're going to need it. But I don't think we would be happy going 1-15, if we had an injury at one position. But other people have different philosophies."

The 2014 draft was spread over three days, Thursday through Saturday, and the selection of Garoppolo on day two, May 9, wasn't the only controversial event that day. Two Patriots employees, John Jastremski and Jim McNally, traded text messages that afternoon. There wasn't anything unusual about that in itself. McNally, a game-day operations part-timer, and Jastremski, a full-time assistant equipment manager, texted constantly. Their tone ranged from ordinary to burlesque. Their language reflected the culture they were in: direct, blunt, sarcastic, profane. That was never a problem in Foxboro. The issue was that their texts, in time, would be shared with the rest of America.

"You working," McNally asked Jastremski, about two and a half hours before the draft resumed with round two.

"Yup," Jastremski replied thirty seconds later.

"Nice dude…jimmy needs some kicks…lets make a deal… come on help the deflator."

When nearly ten minutes had passed without a reply from Jastremski, McNally sent a follow-up text: "Chill buddy im just fuckin with you…im not going to espn…yet."

That exchange, when eventually released to the public, would trigger debates and commentaries that would go far past the intensity of traditional rivalries played out on social media and talk radio. It would go past football and, really, all sports. It would go through owners' suites and across the mahogany desks of America's top lawyers. It would whistle through arbitration and district court. It would be the dividing line in a war that had text interpretation as one of its issues. No one was neutral on the texts, even though few were privy to the dozens of exchanges that happened before, exchanges that might have put the texts into context.

What a 2014 season it was going to be. At the end of it, no fan would be able to honestly say that he or she saw it coming. It's not every day that the league and one of the league's most valuable commodities line up across from each other and attack, blood on the shield be damned.

The beginning of the season, though, was conventional. The Seahawks were the favorites to defend their title, and the Broncos and Patriots were considered the best in the AFC. As usual, the expectation in New England was to get to the Super Bowl and win it.

The Patriots appeared to be a long way from contending on September 7, the opener in Miami. Brady had to feel worse than anyone, physically and psychologically. He threw a lot, fifty-six times. He got hit a lot, sacked four times and pounded on a half-dozen occasions just after he released the ball. He was responsible for three turnovers, two fumbles and an interception. Sam Monson, a preseason Brady doubter from Pro Football Focus, was onto something. Brady looked bad; his offensive line looked worse. There was a story there, too. A few weeks earlier, Belichick traded the team's nastiest and most experienced lineman, Logan Mankins, to Tampa for a backup tight end and a fourth-round pick. The deal was immediately panned, and there was nothing about *this* game that made it look smart. In addition to the battering of Brady, two rarities happened on the same day: The Patriots lost an opener and Darrelle Revis gave up a touchdown.

The team didn't look right, and that would have been the case even if they had pulled out a win against the Dolphins.

There was no insight about who they were the next week, in Minnesota. The Vikings were missing their offense, which is what running back Adrian Peterson was for them. Peterson was deactivated forty-eight hours before the game following news that he was indicted for negligent and reckless injury to a child. That child was Peterson's four-year-old son. The muscular running back, six foot two and 220 pounds, acknowledged that he struck his son repeatedly with a switch. He said it was the way he was raised growing up in Texas, and that this style of corporal punishment taught humility and manners.

The Peterson news capped a disastrous week for the league. The football talk was sandwiched between discussion of severe parenting and domestic violence. A video had emerged of one player, Ray Rice, punching his fiancée in a casino elevator in Atlantic City. Another player, Greg Hardy, was convicted of assaulting his ex-girlfriend and communicating threats. Roger Goodell said that he hadn't seen the elevator video when he suspended Rice for two games. Once TMZ got the footage and it went viral, the commissioner changed course and suspended Rice indefinitely. As for Hardy, who was convicted in July, Goodell never did suspend him. But with the attention on Rice, and now Peterson, Hardy was placed on the commissioner's exempt list. It meant that Hardy would continue to get paid, but he wasn't eligible to play in the games.

Criticism of Goodell and throat-clearing from corporate sponsors was beginning to compete with the games, so New England's 30–7 win over the Vikings didn't make much of a ripple. Much more instructive was the guest segment on *CBS This Morning*, five days before the game. Robert Kraft was scheduled to talk about the weekly *Thursday Night Football* package on CBS. But as he had done many times in the past, barely two minutes into his appearance, he volunteered his endorsement of Goodell.

"I know our commissioner has taken some heat," he said as he lounged comfortably in his chair, making eye contact with all three hosts. There were dozens of critics who wondered why the NFL was so slow to react appropriately to domestic violence. As for the graphic Ray Rice video, well, it essentially matched what was in the police report and what Rice and his fiancée, Janay, told Goodell when they met with him in New York. Kraft continued, "He had no knowledge of this video. The way he's handled this situation himself, coming out with the mea culpa in his statement ten days ago, and setting a very clear policy on how we conduct ourselves in the NFL, has been excellent. And anyone second-guessing that doesn't know him."

Kraft was comfortable enough to applaud Goodell, even when scores of fans and even players were pointing out some of the commissioner's obvious contradictions and conflicts of interest. Goodell swore by the letter of the NFL law when it was convenient, and when it wasn't he'd go with something else. His handling of Rice was a perfect example. He made his ruling with the original two-game suspension. It was light, by most accounts, but it was his binding decision. When the video was released, a video that the Associated Press reported someone in the NFL had seen prior to its TMZ release, Goodell deflected the heat by "retrying" Rice for a case the commissioner had heard months earlier.

Goodell was fond of saying that he would change his mind on penalties if he was given new information. In the Rice case, as disturbing as the video was, the information wasn't new; the overwhelmingly negative reaction was. Rice and Janay, who had married since the incident, talked openly about that night and how it was a test of their relationship. They'd gone to counseling. Rice was in a domestic violence diversion program. Obviously something happened to warrant that.

Even before the controversial fall of 2014, many players bristled at the inflexibility of Goodell. All any dissenting voice could do was lash out publicly because the seat of power was Goodell's.

"I have confidence in his judgment and whatever he decides is in the best interest of the game," Kraft told the *Globe*. "I have a lot of confidence that Roger Goodell is doing that all the time."

Kraft's early-season issue was public relations for the commissioner and the league. The on-field Patriots simply had an issue of execution. They were a raggedy 2-1 after beating the Raiders at Gillette, 16–9. Their next game, September 29, was a *Monday Night Football* special in Kansas City. America wasn't used to seeing the Patriots play like this. They were so bad in a 41–14 loss that with just over ten minutes to play, a familiar symbol of winning was out of the game, standing on the sideline with his arms folded. That was the nice way of describing Tom Brady's 159-yard passing day. In other words, Brady was benched.

No one expected young Jimmy Garoppolo to make his debut so soon, under these circumstances. He threw seven passes, completed six, and got his first touchdown pass when the touchdown-creator himself, Gronk, converted a 13-yard pass into a score. For the first time since the early days of Brady–Drew Bledsoe, Belichick was asked about his quarterback after the game. He had made a reference to evaluating everything, to which a local TV reporter, Mike

Giardi, followed up, "Do you consider evaluating the quarterback position?"

Belichick stared for a long time and smirked. It was his visual way of saying that he wasn't crazy enough to demote Brady. But the talk around his 2-2 team was imbalanced, and the combination of commentary and wild reporting had no limits. A few minutes after the game, former NFL quarterback Trent Dilfer stood on the field at red-clad Arrowhead Stadium and emphatically diagnosed the Patriots for his ESPN audience.

"When you're weak, when you're the weakest kid and you go into a bully's house, you get the snot beat out of you. We saw a weak team. The New England Patriots, let's face it: They're not good anymore."

There was more of that at the nearest media outlets, local and national. No one was spared. Three weeks earlier, during his weekly segment on WEEI, Brady had been asked a question about how long he wanted to play and he colorfully replied, "When I suck, I'll retire. I don't plan on sucking for a long time." There were numerous one-liners on sports-talk radio about Brady, leading the twenty-ninth ranked offense in the league, and when that retirement announcement was coming.

On and on it went, from former quarterback Boomer Esiason saying that "the Patriots have really big problems, and I don't see the answer on their roster" to ESPN reporter Chris Mortensen citing sources claiming that Brady had "uncomfortable tension" with the coaching staff and was unhappy due to his lack of involvement in game plans. Mortensen went on to say that Garoppolo would be the Patriots' quarterback "sooner rather than later," but not in 2014.

For players having a hard time ignoring the noise, the coach gave a primer in the middle of the chaotic week. At one point during his press conference, he was asked about problems in the Kansas City game. He answered, "We're on to Cincinnati," which was the next opponent. Again, a reporter asked about the offense. Again, Belichick responded, "We're on to Cincinnati." This time, a reporter wanted to know if Belichick felt that he'd given a thirty-seven-year-old Tom Brady enough support to be successful.

"We're on to Cincinnati..."

When the 3-0 Bengals finally arrived for a *Sunday Night Football* matchup, they met a team that hadn't been seen all year. Brady was well protected all night, was sacked just once, and threw for nearly three hundred yards along with three touchdown passes. Just to prove its versatility, the offensive line pushed the Bengals back all night and allowed Josh McDaniels to call a staggering forty-six running plays. Being on to Cincinnati was a good thing. The Patriots won 43–17.

They won again the next week, too, easily defeating Buffalo 37–22. Games against the Jets were tough, despite the talent level, so the next win was a much-closer-than-expected 27–25. Brady threw three touchdown passes, which gave him a total of ten in the past three games. No one mentioned retirement, tension on the coaching staff, or young Jimmy Garoppolo anymore. Yet Brady was agitated during the Jets game, and the texting Patriots employees, Jim McNally and John Jastremski, thought they knew why. Jastremski, whom Brady often referred to as "JJ" or "Jonny," was most responsible for preparing footballs so they had the proper feel for game day.

"Tom is acting crazy about balls," Jastremski texted to a friend about twenty-five minutes after the kickoff against the Jets. "Ready to vomit!" he added five seconds later.

The friend replied two minutes later. "He saying they're not good enough??"

"Tell later," Jastremski answered.

The next morning, Jastremski texted his fiancée about the previous night's footballs. "Ugh...Tom was right. I just measured some of the balls. They supposed to be 13lbs...They were like 16. Felt like bricks." Later, he and McNally got back into their texting routine regarding the overinflated footballs. League quarterbacks are allowed to treat the footballs as they please, with the intention of reducing the new-football slickness by game day. The only restriction is that the air pressure in the football has to fall within range of 12.5 and 13.5 pounds per square inch, or PSI. In October 2014, it was a topic that rarely, if ever, came up during football discussions. The talking heads on TV didn't mention it, nor did coaches, the commissioner, or the fantasy football crowd. It was the realm, presumably, of quarterbacks and officials.

"Tom sucks," McNally texted Jastremski. "im going to make that next ball a fuckin balloon."

"Talked to him last night," Jastremski replied. "He actually brought you up and said you must have a lot of stress trying to get them done. I told him it was. He was right though...I checked some of the balls this morn...The refs fucked us...a few of them were at almost 16. They didn't recheck them after they put air in them."

McNally responded, "Fuck tom...16 is nothing...wait till next sunday."

Twenty seconds later, Jastremski replied, "Omg! Spaz."

Since the Patriots played the Jets on a Thursday night, they had ten days before their next game, at home against the Bears. It was a stretch of games where Darrelle Revis and the entire defense would be challenged because it featured some of the most prolific quarterbacks in the game. In succession, the Patriots would face Jay Cutler, Peyton Manning, Andrew Luck, Matthew Stafford, Aaron Rodgers, and Philip Rivers.

Before any of that happened, leading up to the Bears game, McNally seemed to enjoy the text thread of screwing with Brady and the inflation of the footballs.

"Make sure you blow up the ball to look like a rugby ball so tom can get used to it before Sunday," he wrote to Jastremski five days before the game. Nine minutes later, Jastremski's reply was simply "Omg."

They resumed the conversation two days later, a full week after the Jets game. Jastremski picked up the thread this time with, "Can't wait to give you your needle this week," and included a smiling emoticon at the end. Seven minutes later, McNally wrote, "Fuck tom…make sure the pump is attached to the needle…fuckin watermelons coming."

"So angry," Jastremski answered.

"The only thing deflating sun. is his passing rating," McNally wrote for his walk-off line.

Once again, on Friday, two days before playing the Bears, there was more banter. Jastremski started it this time. "I have a big needle for you this week." McNally responded, "Better be surrounded by cash and newkicks…or its a rugby sunday." Thirteen minutes later he added, "Fuck tom."

Jastremski answered, "Maybe u will have some nice size 11s in ur locker." To which McNally wrote, "Tom must be working your balls hard this week."

Sunday, it turned out, wasn't as interesting as the exchange between the employees. The Patriots breezed through their first quarterback test. They had 38 points by halftime, and if McNally did anything sinister to Brady's footballs, the Patriots quarterback had no problems with it. He threw a season-high five touchdown passes, three of them to Gronk, and the Patriots prevailed, 51–23.

It had been just one month since the head coach was being asked about evaluating the quarterback; since many writers, fans, and former players suggested that Brady's best days were behind him; since that shrill statement from Trent Dilfer, above the postgame din of Arrowhead Stadium, that the Patriots were "not good anymore."

After a surprisingly easy 43–21 win over the Broncos, their fifth straight win since Kansas City, they really weren't good anymore. They were ascending past that, and they were unmistakably the best team in the conference. Before the Broncos' game, or Brady-Manning round sixteen, there was a lengthy ESPN story comparing the quarterbacks. One of Brady's friends, Kevin Brady (no relation), responded to the article in an e-mail to Tom, and part of the quarterback's reply provided a hint into his mind-set: "I've got another 7 or 8 years. He has 2. That's the final chapter. Game on."

Future aside, Brady and the Patriots had to go back in history to remember the last time they had seen a cornerback like Revis. In the ten-year space since Ty Law's departure and Revis's arrival, the Patriots had an assortment of corners with various quirks. Asante Samuel was a playmaker with good hands, but he wasn't physical and wasn't effective in all areas of the field. Devin McCourty had a great rookie season, but he lost confidence in year two, and by year three and now, he was a full-time free safety. A bunch of draft picks, from Darius Butler to Jonathan Wilhite to Terrence Wheatley, had track-star speed but struggled to track the football in the air. They'd all had frustrating episodes when they'd be facing the receiver, back to the ball, as the ball came zipping in past their earholes. The best corners had a quick clock in their heads, *one thousand one, one thousand two, one thou*—bam. Turn and look for that ball in about 2.6 seconds.

Revis was even better than that. He combined instincts and study, so he paid attention to receivers adjusting their gloves before a play (*This is his play, he's pulling his gloves*) and added that to his existing knowledge of the formation and the receiver's tendencies. The Patriots used to be bullied by the best receivers. But now they had an ace fighter at their fingertips, a guy who could get it done with toughness and smarts.

Going into Indianapolis on November 16, it wasn't a game for a skilled player like Revis. It wasn't even a game for Brady. When the Patriots played the Colts, it was elementary football, Big Kids versus Little Kids. Belichick was known for having different game plans for different opponents, and not being afraid to switch things up. It wasn't that deep against the Colts. The Patriots believed that they could line up and overpower them, and that's what they'd done since Chuck Pagano, a former Ravens assistant coach, took over Indianapolis in 2012.

The first time the Patriots played the Pagano-led Colts, in 2012, they scored 59 points and ran for 115 yards.

The second time they played, in 2013, they scored 43 points and ran for 234 yards and six rushing touchdowns.

This was going to be the third time, and the expectation from the offensive linemen was that they were going to be doing a lot of run-blocking for someone. On this night, that someone would be an undrafted muscle man named Jonas Gray. He was five-foot-nine and ripped, and he naturally ran low without much flourish. His running style was Man Runs through Wall. He was raw, basic, and he tapped into the Colts' biggest weakness. They were soft. They couldn't do a thing about it when good teams ran at them repeatedly. Gray finished the game with 201 rushing yards and four touchdowns in a 42–20 win. The Colts were the best team in their division, the AFC South, so they were headed to the play-offs. One team they didn't want to see in the postseason was the Patriots.

Before the next game, against the Lions at Gillette, Brady did an interview with one of his former teammates in the media, Randy Moss. Like many Patriots in their playing days, Moss was hesitant in interviews. But as an analyst for Fox, his natural personality was on display. All of his New England teammates enjoyed him, none more than Brady, whose locker had been next to Moss's.

The TV session began with Moss teasing the Fox crew, saying they were preparing rose petals for Brady the same way royal attendants did in the Eddie Murphy movie *Coming to America*.

"I heard that," Brady said as he walked on the set, drawing laughs from everyone.

The Brady-Moss interview captured the mutual respect between the men. Brady was extremely comfortable on camera, more comfortable than usual, and he gave Moss the most honest answer to date on the criticism he'd received earlier in the season.

"Really, for my pro career, I've never really had a lot of criticism. We won the first year that I played. And then we won two more shortly after that. Then we had some unbelievable years where we went undefeated. So this is really the first time that people have come down on me."

The understanding between the two, and all of America for that matter, was that Brady would be scrutinized for what he did on the field. And since he and the Patriots were on a seven-game winning streak, after a 34–9 win over Detroit, there wouldn't be much about which to complain.

In a boon for CBS, the network got to televise the game of the year, Patriots and Packers from Lambeau Field. With the way both teams were playing, 9-2 for the Patriots and 8-3 for the Packers, a Super Bowl meeting in Arizona was possible. As it was, the network was ecstatic over the ratings magnet of star quarterbacks Brady and Aaron Rodgers. During the game, which was as competitive as promised, play-by-play man Jim Nantz set up his partner, former Giants quarterback Phil Simms, to share a story about Rodgers's preparation of the footballs.

"He said something unique," Simms said, explaining that Rodgers told him, "I like to push the limit to how much air we can put in the football, even go over what they allow you to do, and see if the officials take air out of it." Simms said that Rodgers has unusually large hands, and that he finds large footballs easier to grip. Simms didn't name any other quarterbacks specifically, but he said most of them were the opposite of Rodgers in that they want the football "smaller and soft, so they can dig their fingers into it." Simms added one more nugget: "You know, the officials do check those footballs. Sometimes they can get lucky and put an extra half pound of air in there to help Aaron Rodgers out."

The Patriots lost to the Packers, 26–21, and air pressure was not the reason. The bigger problem was air space, as Rodgers was able to artfully complete a key third-down pass to receiver Randall Cobb, who was well covered by Patriot Logan Ryan. That play effectively won the game, preventing Brady from another opportunity against the Packers' defense.

The Patriots collected impressive wins in San Diego and at home against Miami before going to New York to take on Revis's old Jets.

The tone had changed considerably since Revis last played there. Head coach Rex Ryan used to be the loudest coach in the league, constantly bragging about the talent of his players and their abilities to frustrate anyone who challenged them. But he and John Idzik, the general manager, didn't view the talent the same way these days. Both men were most likely out after the season, which meant that the organization would have its fifth different head coach and fifth different GM since Belichick got to New England.

The Jets were 3-11, the opposite record of the Patriots. From a Jets perspective, there was something spiritually wrong about the best homegrown talent the organization ever produced going to New England and putting the Patriots in position to win another Super Bowl. When Ryan had arrived in New York promising to take down the Patriots, his words were backed up by the skills of

Revis. Now there was number 24, in red, white, and blue, helping to steamroll him. The game was close, 17–16, but the Patriots were back where they always were: division champs, preparing for the postseason, forcing another divisional rival to clear out a regime and start over.

As they began thinking about the play-offs, Robert Kraft and Bill Belichick also strategized on what to do about the words of Jets owner Woody Johnson. They believed Johnson was guilty of tampering when he answered a question about Revis at a press conference and said, "Darrelle is a great player. If I thought I could have gotten Darrelle, for [what the Patriots got him for], I probably would have taken him... I'd love Darrelle to come back."

It was one thing to say that about a player who was under contract for three or four years. It was just short of recruiting to say it about Revis, whom the league understood to be in a contract year. He also had history with the Jets and, in the NFL's dark world of back-channel dealing, it wasn't unrealistic to think that the Jets and Revis's representatives had been in contact about options after the 2014 season. As it was, the case seemed to be unambiguous when Johnson's comments were compared to the NFL's tampering policy: "Any public or private statement of interest, qualified or unqualified, in another club's player to that player's agent or representative, or to a member of the news media, is a violation of this Anti-Tampering Policy."

There was no question that there was a violation; the only question was what the NFL was going to do about it.

Maybe it was the nature of the litigious season, but there was definitely a *Gotcha* spirit as the play-offs unfolded.

When the Patriots and Ravens met in a divisional play-off game on January 10, 2015, it was almost guaranteed that something controversial was going to happen. The rivalry began with genuine mutual respect, but now it had devolved into one of those relationships in which both sides act like there's respect, for political reasons. Belichick recommended Baltimore coach John Harbaugh for the job in 2008, and there were many Baltimore connections, football and otherwise, for the Maryland native. But this is a competitive league, and this was the fourth time in five years that one of these teams was going to be ending the other's season.

Twice in the game, it looked as if the Ravens would be that team. They leapt to a 14–0 lead, and when the Patriots tied the score, the Ravens added two more touchdowns to make it 28–14 five minutes into the third quarter. It was a typical New England winter day, twenty degrees with a nasty windchill, but the Patriots offense was not equipped, at least not on this day, for the ground game associated with cold-weather football. They were one dimensional, and Ravens defensive coordinator Dean Pees was too smart to be fooled in those situations. If the Patriots were going to pass on every second-half play, they would have to be creative in their play-calling.

On their first touchdown drive of the third quarter, the Patriots confused the Ravens with their offensive formations. On one play, for example, running back Shane Vereen was lined up as a tackle. His number, 34, suggested that he was eligible to receive a pass, but on that particular play he wasn't. A Raven still accounted for him as if he were, and it sent the Baltimore sideline into some disarray. Harbaugh even got a penalty for complaining about it to the officials.

The Patriots were onto something. It didn't take a lot of creativity to find Gronk, who always seemed to be open. His score, on a five-yard pass from Brady, made it 28–21 in the third quarter. The fun began two minutes later, when Brady lateraled to Julian Edelman, who'd been a college quarterback at Kent State. With the defense drawn to him, Edelman lofted a perfect pass down the left sideline for Danny Amendola, who caught it and ran to the end zone for a fifty-one-yard scoring play.

Edelman may have had that pass, but Brady handled the rest of them. It was one of the best play-off games of his career, as he finished with 367 yards and three touchdowns. His final touchdown pass, to Brandon LaFell, was not only the game winner; it also moved him past Joe Montana for the top spot in career postseason touchdown passes.

After the game, a 35–31 Patriots win, Harbaugh was angry. He said the Patriots' clever declaration of eligible and ineligible receivers was "clearly deception" and said, "It's not something that anybody's ever done before. The league will look at that type of thing and I'm sure that they'll make some adjustments and things like that."

He was right and wrong in the same sentence. The tactic had been used several times in 2014, in the pro and college seasons. Despite that, the league wasn't always forward-thinking in these matters, so there was likely to be a change in the offseason.

For now, the Patriots were going to their fourth consecutive conference title game. They would face the Indianapolis Colts, the best possible opponent.

On the Saturday before the game, the Patriots were thinking of running on the Colts. The Colts were thinking of writing about the Patriots. Indianapolis equipment manager Sean Sullivan e-mailed Colts general manager Ryan Grigson, saying that he was concerned about the Patriots' footballs. He said that Colts coach Chuck Pagano had received a call from the Ravens' special-teams coordinator, and there had been some trouble with Baltimore's ability to use footballs that they had treated; instead, they were forced to use the slick, out-of-the-box ones.

"As far as the gameballs are concerned," Sullivan wrote, "it is well known around the league that after the Patriots gameballs are checked by the officials and brought out for game usage the ball-boys for the patriots will let out some air with a ball needle because their quarterback likes a smaller football so he can grip it better, it would be great if someone would be able to check the air in the game balls as the game goes on so that they don't get an illegal advantage."

Grigson received the e-mail and either forwarded it or referenced it in his own e-mail to the NFL: "Just another FYI below. Again, all the Indianapolis Colts want is a completely level playing field. Thank you for being vigilant stewards of that not only for us but for the shield and overall integrity of our game."

The league's senior vice president of game operations, David Gardi, replied that he would look into it and make the officials aware of the issue. At this rate, it seemed that the football was getting more attention than the actual football game. Which is exactly how it played out on Sunday evening.

Despite being warned about concerns over the footballs, referee Walt Anderson lost sight of the balls twenty-five minutes before the start of the game. He said it was the first time in nineteen years of officiating that something like that had happened to him. He lost the balls because a member of game operations, Jim McNally, had taken the balls to the field. But on his way there, he stopped in the bathroom and took the footballs in there with him.

All of these actions would be dissected and analyzed for the rest of the year, to a much greater degree than anyone realized on January 18. Was it a sting operation from the NFL? Did the Patriots tamper with the footballs? Did on-site league officials knowingly allow certain improprieties to happen, if indeed they did happen, just to prove a point?

Those questions and many more like them provided the only tension of the night. The game was similar to the first three Patriots-Colts matchups with Pagano as the head coach. It was a blowout, and it got there fast. The final was 45–7, and it led to a late-night party on the field at Gillette. Gronk danced, and so did Darrelle Revis's mom, Diana. Then there was a dance-off between Gronk and Diana. The fans stayed as late as they could, despite the cold and rain, because they wanted to enjoy the party as well. Bill Belichick looked at Jim Nantz and said, "We're on to Seattle..." That drew a stadium full of cheers because everyone got the reference, how "We're on to Cincinnati..." had turned around their season. The Patriots were returning to the Super Bowl for the sixth time under Belichick and Brady and, finally, this was an opportunity to shut everyone up about Spygate. If they could win this next game, against the Seahawks, it would force everyone to talk about football, and not scandal.

The problem was that in the eyes of the NFL, the football was the scandal.

As the on-field party was ending, a league investigation had already begun. In fact, the Patriots' twelve footballs had been measured at halftime and eleven of them were found to be below 12.5 PSI. Early on, at least, the league seemed unaware that all footballs, no matter what their inflation level, would lose air pressure in the cool January condition. The second half had been played with alternate, properly inflated footballs. Jim McNally had already been questioned for thirty minutes by NFL security at the stadium.

Now the chain had begun, in the middle of the night, and when it reached the Patriots and their fans, it was going to make them sick. McNally, just before midnight, spoke with equipment manager Dave Schoenfeld and told him that he'd been interviewed. With all the buzz on Twitter, Berj Najarian, one of Belichick's closest advisers, texted Schoenfeld at 1:45 a.m. The chain was rattling now, moving quickly. Najarian and Schoenfeld met in Najarian's office just before two a.m. Twenty minutes later, Pro Football Talk had a story about ball deflation. *Newsday* had a story at four a.m. The chain reached Brady and thousands of Patriots fans when three WEEI radio hosts, John Dennis, Gerry Callahan, and Kirk Minihane, interviewed him on air and asked what he knew about the story.

"I think I've heard it all at this point," he said with a laugh.

Minihane asked him directly if the Patriots deflated balls, and he said no.

The atmosphere was thick now, and no amount of mind-over-matter exercises would allow anyone, even Belichick, to ignore the noise. The noise was the norm. People wanted someone to blame. Same old Patriots, cheating again. That was the national refrain. Initially, the fingers pointed toward Belichick. But when he said, on January 22, that he had no idea about ball preparation and that Brady would know more, there was anticipation that Brady did it.

On the afternoon of the twenty-second, Brady stood before a press gathering that was clearly expecting some type of confession. That much was clear with their questions, their rising incredulity, and, at times, barely camouflaged anger when they weren't getting what they expected. Brady stood before them in a gray sweatshirt with a white T-shirt underneath it. He had on a Patriots winter hat with the team's original logo, the hiking minuteman, Pat Patriot, on the front. He was casual. The crowd was frenzied.

First question: "When and how did you supposedly alter the balls?"

The tone was set with that one, and it never ventured far from that register: Brady was expected to confess. The majority of these people believed that he did it. The majority of Americans, too. This session alone, with its fifty questions about air pressure and texture and grip, was going to more than make up for the first fourteen seasons of his career, when criticism was at a minimum.

"I didn't alter the ball in any way" was how Brady's response to the first question began.

Maybe Brady knew then that people didn't believe him. Or maybe it was that second question: "This has raised a lot of uncomfortable conversations for people around this country who view you as their idol. The question they're asking themselves is, 'What's up with our hero?' Can you answer right now, is Tom Brady a cheater?"

These were real journalists. But it was as if they were actors spoofing journalists. It was wild. It was still early in the process, so all the terms weren't known yet. Some of the questioners talked about actual pounds of air instead of air pressure. No one mentioned the ideal gas law—a scientific law not on the legal books. There weren't questions about the Colts' footballs or the process the officials went through to get those balls on the field.

This was all on Brady now.

"I feel like I've always played within the rules. I would never do anything to break the rules. I believe in fair play and I respect the league and everything they're doing to try to create a very competitive playing field for all the NFL teams. It's a very competitive league. Every team is trying to do the best they can to win every week. I believe in fair play and I'll always believe in that for as long as I'm playing."

The questions kept coming, some fair and most not, some neutral and most with a presumption of guilt. If they listened, Brady was telling them about the way he looked at the world, football and otherwise, but it was too much of a circus to consider the thoughtfulness that he'd put into moments like this. "I think part of being in this position and putting yourself under a spotlight like this and being open for criticism, I think that's very much a part of being a professional athlete," he said at one point. "We can only express to you what our side is and how we approach it. Then everyone is going to make their own conclusion."

He answered many questions that way, and he had no idea how long it would last. Just past the quarter pole was the sixteenth question: "How does it make you feel that they're calling your team cheaters?"

Answer: "I think a big part of playing here is trying to ignore the outside forces and influences and people that are maybe fans of our team or not fans of your team; or fans of yourself or not fans of yourself. Like I said, everybody is entitled to an opinion. Those opinions rest with those people. I think you can just go out and try to be the best you can be, deal with people with respect, with honesty, with integrity, have a high moral standard. I've always really tried to exemplify that as an athlete. I'll continue to try to do that."

Question twenty-seven: "Is this a moment to just say 'I'm sorry' to the fans?"

Question twenty-eight: "For the fans that are watching and looking into that camera, what do you say?"

Answer: "I'm not sure. What would you like me to say? I'm not quite sure."

No one in the NFL did press conferences like this, starting from the top. Roger Goodell had been the commissioner for nearly a decade, and he'd never stood like this and addressed a free-form session from journalists demanding answers about a scandal. Belichick certainly wasn't going to field fifty questions like this and answer them all patiently and expansively. Then again, perhaps the Belichick method was justified, because for all of Brady's direct eye contact and elaboration on answers, the room didn't believe him. He knew it. His friends knew it, too.

His business manager, former Patriots employee Will McDonough, received an e-mail from Assistant U.S. Attorney Eric Christofferson following the press conference: "The sanctimonious finger wagging over deflation might be the most absurd thing I have seen the media do, which is saying something. Some of the questions TB was asked today were more obnoxious than a congressional inquiry. Sucks that he had to go through that in the absence of any actual facts. In my business, those kind of questions get you sanctioned by a judge. He was amazingly calm. I'm sure he's relying on friends like you to keep him sane."

ESPN and other outlets carried the press conference live. When it was over, the ESPN crew of host Trey Wingo and analysts Mark Brunell, Jerome Bettis, and Brian Dawkins gave their opinions on what they had seen. None of them believed Brady. Brunell, a former quarterback, appeared to be emotional and on the verge of tears. "I just didn't believe what Tom Brady had to say," he said. Bettis said Brady missed an opportunity to take responsibility and admit a simple mistake. After a brief lecture he concluded, "I'm disappointed in you, Tom Brady." Dawkins lamented that this was a small deal that became a big one because "we have somebody who won't own up." Wingo made a reference to Richard Nixon and the Watergate scandal—the daddy of all "gates."

Everyone on the set fell into a pattern that was becoming common in the first week of the scandal. They often mixed commentary about the condition *of* the football with the air pressure *in* the football. Brady never said he wasn't aware of the footballs' condition, because he was in control of that. The final say on air pressure was at the discretion of the officials. The footballs that Brady approved had nothing to do with air pressure; he approved them based on how they felt. Ideally, he wanted them inflated to the lowest level permitted by the league, which was 12.5 PSI. It was up to the officials to do the inflating. Sometimes they got it right; sometimes they pumped it to the sixteen of the Jets game; sometimes they weren't exactly sure what they did because they couldn't remember which gauges they used and they didn't record relevant data.

The day before, with the conversation about footballs and air pressure reaching NPR, CNN, and all the morning news shows, in addition to the usual sports channels and sites, other Brady friends e-mailed. One, J. J. Dudum, was exasperated by the accusations, writing, "Will you tell these idiots to shut the 'F' up about these deflated balls!!! Give me a break!!! Maybe if it was close let's chat about it but 45–7 you kicked their Ass!! Don't they have something better to talk about?????"

Brady's reply was simple, yet it summarized the moment as well as New England football since 2007.

"We are the Patriots," he wrote. "Everything is a big deal."

They were going to Arizona to play in the Super Bowl, the ultimate goal for every team in the league. They would meet the Seahawks, the defending champion blessed with the number one defense in the league. It was going to be their toughest game of the season. And as difficult as the game was going to be for the Patriots, it felt like it wasn't even close to the toughest thing ahead of them.

Chapter Eighteen

DO YOUR JOB

It has been eight years since the New England Patriots first learned about branding. The powerful kind, the type that defies all reassurances and historical truths. Eight years ago, they were caught doing the wrong thing at the wrong time in sports history, and they were forever typecast as cheaters in all but six states.

They've found time does not heal all wounds. America is not always forgiving to those who admit mistakes. And while slates can be wiped clean, this is the Internet era; for better or worse, some people and some things are destined for permanence.

There is no question that Bill Belichick understands this as he stands before a surprised media crowd on January 24. Spygate has made the Patriots suspects for life. It's the reason Bob Kravitz, the Indianapolis columnist who broke the air-pressure story, wrote that Robert Kraft, "if he has an ounce of integrity," should fire Belichick. It's the reason influential TV host Michael Wilbon said the Patriots should lose their spot in the Super Bowl. Why else would former player Jerome Bettis, an analyst for ESPN, go on TV and call the Patriots "known felons"? Would the NFL leak to the media that it was "disappointed, angry and distraught" about the Patriots had it not been for 2007 and Spygate?

Two days earlier, Tom Brady stood at Gillette and told a boisterous crowd of reporters that he had no idea why the footballs were underinflated for the conference championship game. Based on the tone of their questions and the questioners' subsequent reports, most of them didn't take Brady at his word. It was a new experience for him, essentially being called a liar to his face, and it stung. Now Belichick was determined to share the information he'd learned after several days of performing science projects. He wasn't scheduled to meet with the media but alerted them at the last minute that he wanted to talk. He had simulated the treatment the Patriots give their footballs during the week. He simulated the whole process, as the team normally would, to figure out what happened. The Patriots beat the Colts on January 18, and nearly a week later the head coach is breaking many of the rules that he'd long established. He's looking back instead of forward to the Super Bowl. He's listening to and taking on the noise. He's doing someone else's job.

"I just want to share with you what I've learned over the past week," he says. "I'm embarrassed to talk about the amount of time that I put into this relative to the other important challenge in front of us. I'm not a scientist. I'm not an expert in footballs; I'm not an expert in football measurements. I'm just telling you what I know. I would not say that I'm Mona Lisa Vito of the football world, as she was in the car expertise area, all right?"

As appreciated as his *My Cousin Vinny* reference is, and as much sense as he makes with regard to plausible reasons for fluctuating football measurements, he has to know that the mistrusting public has one foot firmly planted in the Spygate archives. That's always the case with the Patriots, whether they are accused of a new scandal or not. That is the unwritten penalty of Spygate, the football spirit incapable of being exorcised.

"At no time was there any intent whatsoever to try to compromise the integrity of the game or to gain an advantage. Quite the opposite, we feel like we followed the rules of the game to the letter in our preparations, in our procedures, all right, and in the way that we handled every game that we competitively played in as it relates to this matter."

He has given hundreds of press conferences over the years. Maybe even he has developed that skill that journalists have, to recognize the moment when the conversation will change because something unexpected has been introduced. Belichick does exactly that, opening a gate for some reporter to walk on through when he says, "We try to do everything right. We err on the side of caution. It's been that way now for many years. Anything that's close, we stay as far away from the line as we can. In this case, I can say that we are, as far as I know and everything that I can do, we did everything as right as we could do it. We welcome the league's investigation into this matter. I think there are a number of things that need to be looked into on a number of levels, but that's not for this conversation. I'm sure it will be taken up at another point in time."

He was right. The league had a lot to explain with its timeline, its paper trail, and its protocol for measuring air pressure. But that was for later. He had just mentioned something that got everyone's attention. *We try to do everything right. We err on the side of caution.* The Patriots' reputation is one of envelope-pushing and line-stepping. It's why the league was leaving them unprotected in a sense, refusing to correct a three-day-old story by Chris Mortensen that it knew to be inaccurate. The veteran ESPN reporter was told that eleven of those twelve footballs were two pounds per square inch beneath the legal limit. It wasn't true. Nor was it ultimately true what David Gardi, the league operations director, wrote to the Patriots the morning after the conference title game, saying that one of their footballs measured as low as 10.1 PSI.

But... Spygate.

That had always been in the walls of any Patriots discussion. A conversation about Belichick or Brady, a conversation *by* Belichick or Brady, somehow circled back to that. It's the opposite of their early days together, when they were winning three Super Bowls in a four-year span. They'd never lost a play-off game, never been touched with a hint of real scandal, and their narrative then was valiant. They were capable of anything involving brainpower, ingenuity, composure. Ten years later, thousands of camera and hundreds of ball-deflation jokes later, they are the plausibly accused. They are capable of doing anything that's thrown against a wall or behind an anonymous source. The cameras happened; why wouldn't ball deflation? Why not bugging locker rooms? Screwing with opposing teams' headsets? Manipulating the game clock? They were forever saints or sinners.

Belichick tries to conclude his press conference in a conventional way. He has already stood up for Brady and everyone in the organization, including Jim McNally and John Jastremski.

"This is the end of this subject for me for a long time, okay? We have a huge game, a huge challenge for our football team and that's where that focus is going to go. I've spent more than enough time on this and I'm happy to share this information with you to try to tell you some of the things that I have learned over the last week, which I've learned way more than I ever thought I would learn. The process, the whole thing is much more complex— there are a lot of variables that I was unaware of. It sounds simple, and I'm not trying to say that we're trying to land a guy on the moon, but there are a lot of things here that are a little hard to get a handle on. Again, there's a variance in so many of these things, all right? So, I'll take a couple questions and then I'm moving on."

Does he think all the questions are going to be about the rubbing of the footballs, laces, stitching, tackiness, raised and lowered PSI? Some are, and a very obvious one is not.

"You said you always try to err on the side of caution and stay on the right side of the rules," the question begins, "but with the videotaping it was clear that you were pushing the envelope on that. Is that something that changed that?"

It's been eight years since Spygate and eight years since he'd said anything about it beyond the original sparse written statement. That has finally changed.

"I mean, look, that's a whole other discussion. The guy's giving signals out in front of eighty-thousand people, okay? So we filmed him taking signals out in front of eighty-thousand people, like there were a lot of other teams doing at that time, too. Forget about that. If we were wrong then we've been disciplined for that."

"But," the questioner challenges, "that's clearly not doing everything you can to stay on the side…"

Belichick, who came out to talk science and air pressure, is now replying to Spygate. He is annoyed by the questioning, but if he thought about it he'd see that this is the same thing the NFL does. The league connects anything his organization says to something that he has already done, whether the events are connected or not. The commissioner is talking about Spygate four years after he made his ruling on it. It isn't a leap to suggest that he and the people he represented, the owners, still have some resentment over Belichick's defiance. The head coach got caught, showed no remorse, and then his team reeled off eighteen consecutive wins. Were there New Yorkers, in the league office, rooting for him to fail then? Are there now? When it comes to Spygate, there is no statute of limitations. There always is the presumption of guilt. He animatedly interrupts the attempted follow-up.

"The guy's in front of eighty-thousand people. Eighty-thousand people saw it. Everybody on the sideline saw it. Everybody sees our guy in front of the eighty-thousand people. I mean, there he is. So, it was wrong, we were disciplined for it. That's it. We never did it again. We're never going to do it again and anything else that's close, we're not going to do either."

There are a few more questions about air pressure. He's clearly had enough. The NFL has already announced that its investigation into what happened with the footballs will be headed by prominent attorney Ted Wells and the league's executive vice president, Jeff Pash. Wells is known as a legal superstar, with a long list of wins for those whom victory seemed difficult. He got an acquittal for U.S. Secretary of Labor Raymond Donovan on grand larceny and fraud charges in 1987. A decade later, he got an acquittal for U.S. Secretary of Agriculture Mike Espy, accused of receiving improper gifts. He was even on the side of Exxon Mobil in criminal and civil disputes. Now he is on the side of a client, the NFL, that will pay him millions of dollars to produce a report on air pressure. His work has already begun on that. Meanwhile, Belichick and his staff can finally begin the work of focusing on Seattle.

In the time that Robert Kraft has owned the Patriots, the team has earned trips to seven Super Bowls. What Kraft doesn't realize, as he makes his way back to Glendale for title appearance number seven, is the appetite for conflict coming from NFL headquarters. It doesn't take much investigation to figure out that someone in the league office had tipped Chris Mortensen for his inaccurate air-pressure report. His story contained the same error, 10.1 PSI in one of the footballs, as David Gardi's letter to Kraft had. Earlier than that, there certainly was something that didn't add up about the communication between the Colts and the league before the game. It seemed like a concern that should have also involved the Patriots beforehand.

On January 27, Kraft and his son Jonathan were on the team plane to the desert as they learned that yet another leak had occurred in the supposedly confidential investigation. Jay Glazer of Fox reported that the league was focusing its investigation on a "person of interest" who was seen on camera taking the footballs into a Gillette Stadium bathroom. That person, still not known to the public, is Jim McNally. The Krafts finally caught on to what was happening, and it angered them. They could now see that the league had not been evenhanded in the early stages of the investigation. As the media awaited the arrival of the plane, the Krafts drafted a letter.

The plane's arrival in Arizona, the opening of the doors, and the greeters on the tarmac were all standard. All of that changed when the owner entered the sprawling resort hotel where the media awaited. He wasn't interested in the usual winking, backslapping, and niceties of Super Bowl week. He read from his letter.

"I want to make it clear that I believe, unconditionally, that the New England Patriots have done nothing inappropriate in this process or in violation of NFL rules. Tom, Bill and I have been together for fifteen years. They are my guys. They are part of my family. Bill, Tom and I have had many difficult discussions over the years. I've never known them to lie to me. That's why I'm confident in saying what I just said. It bothers me greatly that their reputations and integrity, and by association that of our team, has been called into question this week."

He and everyone else in the organization remembered what it was like the last time they were here. He remembered that endless session with the league in February 2008, hours before the Patriots were going to try to win one more game and thus win them all. The good news was that he had been to multiple Super Bowls. What annoyed him, and his fans, was that these things tended to avalanche.

"I am confident that this investigation will uncover whatever the facts were that took place last Sunday and the science of how game balls react to changes in the environment. This would be in direct contrast to the public discourse, which has been driven by media leaks as opposed to actual data and facts. Because of this, many jumped to conclusions and made scarring accusations against our coach, quarterback, and staff questioning the integrity of all involved.

"If the Wells investigation is not able to definitively determine that our organization tampered with the air pressure in the footballs, I would expect and hope the league would apologize to our entire team, and in particular to Coach Belichick and Tom Brady, for what they've had to endure this week. I'm disappointed in the way this entire matter has been handled and reported upon. We expect hard facts rather than circumstantial leaked evidence to drive the conclusion of this investigation."

Despite what NBC had planned on Sunday, this was the real pregame show. It was the power source of the Patriots, Kraft, taking on the NFL's representative of power, Roger Goodell. Kraft had been in the position of awkward dance partner, trying to support his coach and quarterback while also maintaining his status as one of the handful of owners who can move league mountains.

He had always supported Goodell, even when the commissioner made statements that seemed contradictory. The real lesson, the sounds of silence from his fellow owners, hadn't resonated yet. He would start to see those in the spring, the billion-dollar faces of self-preservation and the status quo. Soon enough he would learn that they would never dream of apologizing to him or the Patriots. Apologize? For something the commissioner had supported? No, no. Never that. Many of them were just like he used to be. Whenever they saw something that the commissioner had done, they either said nothing or cosigned on the dotted line.

The only meritocracy left for the Patriots was on the University of Phoenix Stadium field for Super Bowl XLIX.

There were just three Patriots players who were there in 2008 for one of the biggest upsets in NFL history: Brady, Vince Wilfork, and kicker Stephen Gostkowski. So at least there would be clear minds for this game against the Seahawks. Seattle annihilated the Broncos the year before, and there wasn't any drop-off from the 2014 version of the team.

"Two years in a row!" Seattle receiver Doug Baldwin screamed to teammate Ricardo Lockette before the game. "We proved that we belong! Let's do this." Baldwin's words were layered. He was talking about the team belonging, and he was talking about himself and Lockette. They were both undrafted players, and those players regularly fought to forge an identity and simply be remembered. What better place to achieve that than the Super Bowl?

Ball deflation and preparation had been on Brady's mind more than usual. He had been in constant contact with John Jastremski since the news from the Colts game broke. He was initially hurt by the torrent of criticism that "Deflategate" brought to his lap. But leading up to the game, he was able to block out the speculation and commentary and zero in on what the Seahawks did well. He, Josh McDaniels, and Belichick were all in agreement that they needed an even quicker, even shorter passing game to be successful against Seattle's speed and aggressiveness. He also knew, better than anyone on the team, how meaningful and personal a win would be for the team.

"It's our time," Brady told his teammates. "It started seven or eight months ago, right? All for this moment, all for this moment. It's about honor. It's about respect. We win this game, you're honored. Your kids are honored. Your families are honored."

In the first quarter, he played like a man who was happy, finally, to be facing a defensive line rather than a bank of microphones. One of his teammates, defensive end Chandler Jones, watched from the bench and said to Wilfork, "They can't stop the crossing routes." Although the opening quarter was scoreless, Brady knew there were points on the field to be had. "They haven't stopped us yet," he said to Edelman, bemoaning the missed chances.

The Patriots scored six minutes into the second quarter, Brady to Brandon LaFell for eleven yards. Just before the two-minute warning, powerful Seattle running back Marshawn Lynch scored from the three to tie it.

Brady found easy money with thirty-six seconds left in the half. He noticed linebacker K. J. Wright lined up one-on-one against Gronk. Wright was at a disadvantage, and even the Seattle sideline knew it. "They're going to eighty-seven," one of the players said, without a trace of panic. Brady lofted it high where only Gronk could get it, and the tight end showed how he really plays when he's healthy in a Super Bowl. Twenty-two-yard touchdown and 14–7 lead.

Sometimes classic games can be identified early, and that's what this was becoming. It is also true that sometimes classic games are a function of poor plays, and that was the unfortunate Super Bowl story of Patriots corner Kyle Arrington. He was having a bad Sunday on the big stage, and Seahawks quarterback Russell Wilson routinely looked his way when he needed a completion. He got one, and more, with eleven seconds left in the half. He hit Lockette with a twenty-three-yard completion, and Arrington made it worse by grabbing his face mask.

Clock stopped. More yards. Touchdown to Chris Matthews on a back-shoulder fade just before the half.

With the score tied at 14 and the third quarter beginning, Seattle receiver Jermaine Kearse had a scoop for his offensive coordinator, Darrell Bevell. "So, twenty-five got benched," he said of Arrington. "Twenty-one is in the game now."

He was talking about Malcolm Butler, a player that most hardcore football fans had never heard of. His football journey was so unusual that it hadn't always included football. He and Gronk were just one year apart, twenty-four and twenty-five, respectively. When Gronk was being drafted by the Patriots in 2010, Butler was working the drive-through at a Popeyes Chicken in Mississippi. He had been kicked out of Hinds Community College near Jackson, Mississippi, taken some classes an hour away at Alcorn State, and then traveled another two hundred miles to the University of West Alabama in a remote town called Livingston. The university's motto is "Do Something That Matters." Butler tried: He was undrafted, but the Patriots signed him in May 2014, and by August he had a football future and two nicknames. Players called him "Strap" due to his propensity for big plays and shutting people down in practice. Strap was sometimes called "Scrap" as well because of his willingness to scrap for the ball, his position on the field, his place on the roster. Doug Baldwin and Ricardo Lockette could definitely relate to that mentality.

In a brief training camp update called "What We Learned," a reporter for the *Portland Press Herald* in Maine singled out Strap/Scrap: "Malcolm Butler, an undrafted free-agent cornerback from NCAA Division II West Alabama, continues to make plays, a forced fumble and fumble recovery on the same play, and looks like he's going to stick."

The problem in the third quarter was that the Seahawks, with the best defense in football, had surged ahead. A key play was an interception by Seahawks linebacker Bobby Wagner, who had been crouching in the zone unnoticed by Brady. "Dumb throw," Brady said dejectedly as he explained his thinking to McDaniels. When

Baldwin, nicknamed "Angry Doug" by his teammates, scored on a pick play (the back judge shielded Revis), it was 24–14. Richard Sherman, who had trolled Brady two years earlier, found a camera and held up two fingers, then four, and then two hands for a touchdown. He was either saying that the score was on Revis, number 24, or that the Seahawks had 24 points.

In any case, things didn't look good. The Patriots went three plays and out on their next possession after the Seahawks touchdown, and with Seattle getting the ball and up by 10, a classic game had a chance to turn ugly. New England got a soon-to-be forgotten big play from Rob Ninkovich, an eight-yard sack of Russell Wilson, to stop a Seattle drive and return the ball to the offense and Brady.

Before the offense took the field, Belichick had been on the sideline, instructing. Brady was on the bench and Belichick was on one knee in front of him. "No negative plays," he reminded him. "If you gotta get rid of it, you gotta get rid of it. The chances of them playing three good plays on defense in a row; they don't look very good. You know, pass rush, everybody is running by you. They get misplaced in their zone, you know what I mean? Just no negative plays, and we'll keep it close."

After a nine-play drive that began with 12:10 left in the fourth quarter, Brady responded with a touchdown to Danny Amendola, and it was 24–21.

Seattle, strangely, got pass-happy. Leading by 3 with the ball and under eight minutes remaining, the Seahawks didn't try to grind it away with Lynch. They tried two passes and a run, and gave the ball back to Brady and the Patriots.

Ten plays and nearly five minutes later, Brady found Julian Edelman for a touchdown and 28–24 advantage. "That's a championship drive, Jules," he told him.

Seattle coach Pete Carroll, the man who had the distinction of succeeding Bill Parcells and preceding Bill Belichick as the Patriots head coach, was unconcerned. "Here we go. We've got two minutes to go," he said into his headset as he confidently walked the sideline. "We've got three timeouts. We need a touchdown to win. We've been doing this all year. Let's go do it again."

No one in the stadium or New England was relaxed. The Patriots had been here before, and these were the situations that had led to abbreviated nights of sleep and what-if debates over breakfast in the cafeteria. They had led the Giants by 4 here in 2008, roughly with the same amount of time in the game, and lost. They led the Giants again, in 2012, late in the game. Ahead by 2. And lost. Belichick always talked about doing your job, and part of that meant focusing on the present, not reliving yesteryear.

But it was hard. On the very first play of the drive, Wilson found—who else?—Lynch on a wheel route for thirty-one yards. One play, and nearly one-third of the field was taken. This was going to be yet another dramatic finish. The Patriots just didn't play breathe-easy Super Bowls.

After Malcolm Butler defended a pass to Kearse and defensive back Brandon Browner, a former Seahawk, did the same thing on an attempt to Chris Matthews, agita descended on the Patriots bench. Brady sat next to McDaniels and they both shook their heads, silently, as if they both knew they were in an impossible spot. Kearse was defended by Butler, and young Strap made a good play by getting his hands on the ball and tipping it. But Kearse continued to focus on it and made the reception on his back. Butler kept his eyes on the receiver, noticed that he still had the ball, and got up to tackle him at the five.

"He caught it! He caught it! He caught the ball!" Carroll exulted.

"Man," Brady said softly, his energy from a few minutes earlier gone. He had thrown for 328 yards and four touchdowns. He was well on his way to being the Super Bowl MVP, for the third time. He was going to match Joe Montana with his fourth Super Bowl win. None of that mattered now. "The D's gotta make a play," he said to McDaniels.

Lynch got the ball on the next play and barreled four yards to the one. There were smiles across the Seattle sideline, and Super Bowl parties in the Pacific Northwest were jubilant with the expected winning score. It wasn't just the Northwest. It was everybody but New England. They were the cheaters, the guys who were one yard away from remaining in the noose of Spygate and, now, Deflategate.

Palms were sweating. The crowd had a nervous buzz. Time seemed to be going faster than it was. "If I'm Bill Belichick, I've got to be calling timeout!" a raspy-voiced Boomer Esiason told his national radio audience. The clock went from fifty-seven seconds to fifty to forty-five. "I don't understand why he's not calling timeout!" The clock went all the way to twenty-six seconds. The Seahawks had called a timeout, surprised that Belichick hadn't done it first. His assistants had shouted into his headset, asking him if he wanted to pause here and discuss strategies, but he hadn't said anything. His eyes were fastened on the Seahawks and the activity on their sideline. They seemed to be in a bit of chaos.

He noticed that they were sending three receivers onto the field, so the Patriots were going to match the formation with their goal-line package, which included three corners. One of them was Strap. "Three corners, three corners. Malcolm, go!" yelled safeties coach Brian Flores.

Less than a year ago, he was unemployed. Now he was lined up in the Super Bowl, and he knew exactly what was coming. He had been beaten on this play in practice, and the coaches told him that he needed to do his job better and get over to the receiver faster. It was a pick play, and there was a two-step method to defending it: quick recognition and relying on a teammate. It was the formula that made the first three Super Bowl winners so beloved in New England. Those players studied, and they leaned on one another.

In this case, thirteen years after the Patriots' first Super Bowl win in New Orleans, Butler needed to know what the two receivers across from him and Browner wanted to do. Kearse planned to pick Butler, setting up a clear path for intended receiver Ricardo Lockette. The Seahawks had run the play three times during the season in the same situation, and they hadn't been stopped. Butler remembered this play from practice and so did Browner. The veteran, Browner, would jam Kearse and allow Butler to make a one-on-one football play with Lockette.

The Seahawks had a former first-round pick in the backfield in running back Lynch. They had a third-round pick at quarterback who could run in Wilson. But with one yard to decide the Super Bowl winner, this came down to two undrafted players from the South, Butler and Lockette. One of them, either Butler from Vicksburg, Mississippi, or Lockette from Albany, Georgia, was going to become his hometown's star of the night.

At the beginning of the season, in New England, the idea was that a new cornerback would help the Patriots win a Super Bowl. But Darrelle Revis was in a matchup on the other side of the field.

Just as expected, the play came. Butler was ready for it. He ran full speed and got to the spot the same time as Lockette, which was the receiver's first surprise. Lockette had been a track star in high school, and his raw speed at the scouting combine was the characteristic that made teams remember him. But Belichick always preferred football-playing speed over sprinting, and the instincts of Butler proved why that was so important. The second surprise for Lockette was that he was bumped off the play and lost sight of the ball. He fell to the ground, initially facing the Patriots bench, and the first person he identified was number 12, Brady, excitedly jumping and screaming. Then he turned to the other sideline, with all his teammates and coaches, and that was truly his ground-level view of what had just happened. Back at Butler's last school, West Alabama, the motto was in flashing lights; Butler had unquestionably done something that mattered.

"It's intercepted at the goal line!" Kevin Harlan declared on the radio. "It's intercepted by Malcolm Butler! Malcolm Butler has intercepted Russell Wilson... at the goal line!"

It was the play that won Super Bowl XLIX, with a nod to the previous three that the Patriots had already captured. They used to be known for players and plays like this. They knew all about low-drafted and undrafted players, starting with their quarterback. They knew about the power of collaboration, which is why they got a thrill from being introduced as a team and promoting football's least regarded, the kicker, as one of their heroes. They even knew about cornerbacks changing the course of Super Bowls with interceptions. Now there was a link, from Law to Butler.

"No matter what he does the rest of his career, he's got a memory that's going to extend beyond his own lifetime," Law says. "I thought that was a helluva play. He went in hard, he read it, he knew it. He was confident. For a young guy to have that type of confidence and go for it, I love it. Just that play right there is going to put him in the conversation with the greats. Forever. If he puts in a decent body of work over a period of time, that's going to define him. You never want one play to define you, but sometimes it's not your choice."

Butler was so overcome by the moment that he cried. He had a hard time speaking when teammate Chandler Jones looked at him, beaming, and said, "Hey, man. You just won us the Super Bowl."

Brady approached and said, "Malcolm! Are you kidding me? You're unbelievable, man." Brady was due a new truck for being the game's MVP, but he had already decided what driveway that vehicle would be parked in: Butler's. Because of tax codes, this was going to be a costly gift from Brady to Butler, even though the car was free. It didn't matter.

For a night, at least, this was better than the requested apology from the NFL. If the league ever did something like that, it would be forced and corporate. The displays breaking out on the field here were genuine. There was an "I love you" uttered at a rate of once every fifteen seconds. Actor Mark Wahlberg, a Boston native, hugged Brady and told him he was the best quarterback of all time. Julian Edelman told him the same thing, while the receiver told Belichick, "I'll do anything for you, Coach."

It was such a special night that even Marshall Faulk, a frequent Patriots critic and Spygate commentator, didn't mention it once. Instead, he sat on the NFL Network set and smiled and shook hands with Brady, three-time Super Bowl MVP. Brady complimented all the ex-players on the set, Faulk, Michael Irvin, and Deion Sanders. At the end of their nearly ten-minute conversation, Brady warmly put his right hand on Faulk's bald head and again gave him a compliment. He was aware of all the things Faulk had said over the years, but now those things were irrelevant.

The Patriots had indeed won since Spygate, so there was no need to think about that anymore. But Deflategate wasn't going away. The bill was due on yet another scandal. It was a scandal with consequences, and thinking about and protesting them was going to occupy most of spring and all of summer.

CHAPTER NINETEEN

THE NATION VERSUS PATRIOTS NATION

This little curve of the city, Boylston Street to Tremont Street to City Hall Plaza, has done something to every shivering soul standing here. It is February 3, 2015, New England's version of Super Tuesday, and some among the restless crowd are attending their first championship parade of the century. For others, it is their ninth.

Newbies and veterans alike hold up signs and phones into the twenty-two-degree air, hoping to get the attention of a Patriot and, with luck, maybe a short video. This ritual has changed them all and changed the city as well, and that's not easy to do in Boston. No matter where they stand along the parade route, they are within ten feet of some schoolteacher's lesson plan. How do you change the course of a city that helped change the course of history?

This is the land of once upon a time, with the country's oldest public park, its first botanical garden, first restaurant, oldest subway tunnel, aged churches where the first hallelujahs were shouted in the 1700s, and the place where Paul Revere signaled the first signs of trouble to the other patriots. "One if by land, two if by sea..."

And that's just the history on or near this special-occasion route.

Even with the scope limited to recent history, no one thought Bill Belichick and Tom Brady would be a historic duo the first time they rode on duck boats through these streets in February 2002. But that's what started it all, this new spirit in the old city. They are the ones who initiated this ever-flowing spring of multisport success.

Fifteen years ago, they arrived in a city that wanted to talk about sports scars, featuring a series of generational gut punches thrown by the Red Sox. They heard about second-place finishes and play-off droughts and old men, long gone and in some cases long dead, who were sold by the Sox and gave their best years to the Yankees. Or had too many men on the ice against the Canadiens. Or had more chances to win and still lost the get-rich-quick NBA lottery that had Tim Duncan as its prize. They heard all the stories that helped put the edge and anxiety of the New England sports fan into perspective. Then Belichick and Brady added their story, the one that almost always ended with New England winning, and hardened hearts began to melt.

It explains why Belichick, in an orange boat with his girlfriend Linda Holliday, can see a red, white, and blue sign in the crowd that reads BELICHICK FOR PRESIDENT, 2016. When Brady comes by, holding and kissing his son, Ben, many in the crowd hold up four fingers and begin to chant, "MVP." They're the ones who changed the standard for how local coaches and superstars are measured. Their first title was earned when they overcame steep odds and a talent gap that was perceived to be huge. In the eyes of New Englanders, it was also proof of what could be accomplished with the right amount of talent, grit, and want-to. It was the century's first championship, and appropriately so; it was all New England industriousness, spunk, and substance.

If the Patriots could stare down and beat a 14-point favorite like the Rams, then of course the Red Sox could overcome the biggest seven-game series deficit, 0-3, in baseball history and beat the Yankees in 2004. That was the same time when the Patriots were setting an NFL record with twenty-one consecutive wins. The message was loud and bold, and it was for all pro sports teams in the region: Get it done. The odds are irrelevant. Close the deal.

The Celtics caught on in 2008, taking control of the NBA Finals after they erased a 24-point deficit in game four. It was the biggest comeback victory in finals history. And if they could do that, why couldn't the Bruins feel confident three years later? They were down 0-2, at home, in their first series of the postseason and then won four out of the next five. In their last series of the play-offs, they went down 0-2 again. This time they did it against a Vancouver team that had scored the most goals in the league and given up the fewest. Game seven of the Stanley Cup Finals was in Vancouver. The Bruins won in a shutout.

All that winning can skew a region, internally and externally. It becomes a region of optimists, always hopeful, even if the Seattle Seahawks are a single yard away from keeping the championship count at eight. It becomes a region of fighters, too, unwilling to back down from anyone, any team, any league, no matter how well credentialed and deep pocketed. Optimistic fighters. That's who these people are in the cold, holding up defiant signs that read DEFLATE THIS and singing along, word for word, to the Beastie Boys. *You gotta fight... for your right... to party.*

The fight won't be necessary today. The memories of the game are still too fresh.

Next week will still require no wars. There will be trips to Disney World. Butler will learn how quickly life changes: a trip to the Grammys, where he chats with John Legend on the red carpet; a trip to an auto dealer in Norwood, Massachusetts, who hands him the keys to his red Chevy pickup gifted to him by Brady.

It was coming, though, a fight bloodier than the ones that New England's Rocky Marciano used to have in the 1950s (although, as almost anyone in the city could tell you, "The Rock" from Brockton never lost a fight). The heavyweight fight over air pressure looked more absurd the more serious it became.

It had been nearly a month since ESPN's respected football insider, Chris Mortensen, posted the following erroneous tweet: "NFL has found that 11 of the Patriots footballs used in Sunday's AFC title game were under-inflated by 2 lbs each, per league sources." There were entire shows on the network, whether news-based or opinion-driven, that were built around the premise that the cheatin' Patriots were using footballs that were as flat as their reporter suggested. Mortensen never corrected the tweet. When the Patriots made a simple request to the league to publicly correct the misinformation, they were rejected—an ominous sign.

Stacey James, the Patriots' media relations chief, wrote to Greg Aiello, the NFL's communications head, on February 17: "What is unconscionable to me is that the league holds data that could very well exonerate us from any wrongdoing and completely dismiss the rampant reports and allegations of nefarious actions, but the league refuses to provide the data. I cannot comprehend how withholding the range of PSIs measured in the game is beneficial to the NFL or the Patriots...Meanwhile, leaks continue to cause us irreparable harm. Imagine if you were in my position. I would love to know what you would be doing to get the league to help."

James had his e-mail forwarded to Jeff Pash, the league's executive vice president and, according to an NFL-generated press release, a coleader of the league's football investigation. Pash began communicating with Patriots attorney Robyn Glaser. If it wasn't obvious to the Patriots then that they were in trouble, it should have been. Glaser sent several e-mails, practically begging the league to at the very least release a statement saying that the often repeated "eleven out of twelve" story line was wildly inaccurate. The tone, from Glaser's side, was pleading.

Referencing an ESPN story in which Jim McNally was accused of personally handing illegal footballs to officials (which wasn't true), Glaser wrote to Pash, "Surely you have seen the ABUN-DANCE of stories and articles this new ESPN piece has prompted since last night. If not, do let me know so I can send you links. This ESPN piece, which by its own admission is supported by not one but 'FOUR sources familiar with the investigation' is yet the latest in League leaks (because the only others 'familiar' with this investigation are us, and we can assure you we are not talking to ESPN or anyone else). And, once again, the information is not only inaccurate, but completely inflammatory and profoundly damaging to our brand."

Pash's response to such pleading and warning, twenty-five minutes later, was laconic: "I want to acknowledge your note and Stacey's note to Greg. I have seen the ESPN story. I have no reason to think it came from our office but I certainly do not condone leaks which I do not [sic] serve anyone's interest."

They were having different conversations, at different levels of urgency, and that wasn't going to change. Remarkably, the Patriots didn't protest the biggest fundamental flaw in the investigation. On one hand, the league said Ted Wells was acting independently. On the other, the league said that Pash was the coleader of the investigation.

Wells, as a solo investigator, most certainly had the ability to be objective; Wells, working along with Pash, was tethered to the league agenda, no matter what his intentions were. As one of the top attorneys in the country, he could easily poke holes in and destroy a similar setup if, for example, it was used in an attempt to undermine one of his clients. But there were too many intersecting layers here. Wells and the members of his team, Lorin Reisner and Brad Karp, had worked with and defended the league in the past in, as they cited on the Paul, Weiss website, "several litigation matters."

For the Patriots, it felt like something big was going to happen. Wells had requested the cell phones of many people he wanted to interview. When he asked for Brady's and kicker Stephen Gostkowski's, each told him no. Wells countered to Brady and his representative, Don Yee, that he didn't need the phone, per se. What would suffice instead was any communication that was relevant to inflation or deflation of the ball. Brady and his representatives declined again. Wells didn't say anything at the time, but he believed Brady was making a crucial mistake.

Each week, at every corner, it seemed that the Patriots were in a brawl of some sort. The league hadn't announced its ruling on the Patriots' tampering charge against the Jets, but a contractual decision needed to be made on the principal involved.

The Patriots had enough cap room to pick up Darrelle Revis's sizable option, but it would change who they were as team-builders. They'd have to let three or four good players leave (which some fans supported) to hold on to one All-Pro player at those numbers. They declined his option and tried to make a deal that was more cap-friendly. But he got his ring, and now he was ready to be a Jet again. They gave him $39 million fully guaranteed in March.

There was foreboding in the region in April. Where was that report from Wells and Pash? What was it going to say? Were the Patriots going to be cleared? Or would the NFL find that McNally had actually made an unusual bathroom break: stop in, take a smidgen of air out of a bag of footballs, and then walk out, all in ninety seconds?

The latter scenario is what most people outside of New England believed. Some would support their argument by using that tweet from Mortensen, still uncorrected, that had reached its eighty-fourth consecutive day of posting on April 15. But if there was a day not to think about air pressure, it was that one. Early that morning, word began to spread that the jurors in the Aaron Hernandez murder case had reached a verdict. Even though the prosecution never produced a weapon or a motive, it put together such a compelling case that the defense, in closing arguments, admitted for the first time that Hernandez was at the scene of the crime on the June 2013 night that Odin Lloyd was murdered. The defense argued that Hernandez, then twenty-three, didn't know what to do after witnessing his two friends, who were to be tried separately, commit the horrific act.

At roughly 10:25 a.m. on the fifteenth, the jury agreed that they didn't believe that version of events. They convicted the former Patriots tight end of first-degree murder. His sentence was a formality: life in prison without parole. He'd spent almost two years in custody, continuing to walk into court with confidence and nonchalance. He often joked with his attorneys, his fiancée, and court officials. There were times when he even chuckled when prosecution witnesses were testifying against him. That was his consistent behavior from the day of his arraignment in June 2013 to the moment he was convicted.

As the verdict was read, his mother and his fiancée sobbed loudly as they hugged and rocked slowly back and forth. Hernandez shook his head, the first time that he displayed a sense of disbelief, and made eye contact with his fiancée and mother. "Be strong," he said to them. "Be strong."

Nothing that the Patriots experienced could compare to the

gravity of the Hernandez situation. Their issues were merely work-place grievances. But as trivial as they were when contrasted to the society at large, there was something bothersome about them. They were talking to an entity, their own league, that either wasn't listening to them or listened and rejected every idea that they had. The major issues that had to be resolved were the findings of the report, which had begun nearly one hundred days earlier, and the status of the tampering charge against the Jets.

Talking with the league was not enjoyable, though. The Patriots felt like a state abandoned by its own country. The NFL never said, *Hey, you're on your own.* It didn't have to for the feeling to be internalized.

At least, a week after the verdict, there was the respite of going to the White House. For some. Even that trip turned into a controversy when Brady elected not to go and gave no reason for missing the trip with his team. Was he angry? Busy? Making a political statement? It wasn't clear.

The team carried on without him and seemed to enjoy the trip to the capital. Some players went to visit the veterans at Walter Reed National Military Medical Center before hanging out with a bunch of their fans in the House and Senate. With Bill Belichick standing to his right and Robert Kraft to his left, President Obama couldn't resist letting the moment pass without mentioning the number one Patriots topic in America.

"I usually tell a bunch of jokes at these events, but with the Patriots in town I was afraid that eleven out of twelve of them would fall flat."

There were groans. Kraft and Belichick tried to force smiles, while a few of the players actually did laugh. Sore subject. Much more sore than anyone knew because this was the point Glaser was trying to make in those private e-mails to Pash. The inaccurate story would never be referred to as inaccurate anymore because it had existed so long on its own without being straightened out. The Patriots knew this all too well. It's why they still had to remind major outlets, such as ESPN, and reporters that, no, the Patriots never did tape a Rams walk-through in 2002. A *Boston Herald* article just said they did.

"All right, all right," the president said, "that whole story got blown a little bit out of proportion."

Puns all day long. Was this Wes Welker or Barack Obama?

Eventually, the president got to the substance, saying that "Belichick and Brady is the most successful player-coach tandem, perhaps, in NFL history." He even gave up the podium, creating a photo op for the ages: Belichick, in a suit and tie, behind a lectern that read SEAL OF THE PRESIDENT OF THE UNITED STATES.

Shortly after returning from Washington, the Patriots had to know that the league report was going to go harshly against them. This could no longer be considered paranoia or coincidence; every time members of the organization felt that they had a good case for something, the league either ignored them or shut them down. The NFL said nothing about the leaks. It said nothing about the incorrect PSI numbers. It didn't engage in constructive e-mails. And now, the league ruling on whether the Jets tampered was insulting and unprecedented. The NFL agreed that the Jets tampered. The penalty: $100,000. Roger Goodell had spent years droning on about the shield and the integrity of the game. Now he was saying that a divisional rival broke the rules, got the player it wanted all along, and the punishment was just one hundred grand. So why the moralizing about air pressure in the balls?

The previous two tampering cases, both on Goodell's watch,

had led to the offending teams losing fifth- and seventh-round picks as well as swapping draft positions, in the fifth and third rounds, respectively.

Just when the Patriots were ready to shake their fists at the injustice of that, it dropped. The date was May 6, 2015. It was Wells's report, all 243 pages of it. It had footnotes, it had a science section, it had a table of contents, and, most important, it had these phrases: "generally aware" and "more probable than not."

"For the reasons described in this Report, and after a comprehensive investigation, we have concluded that, in connection with the AFC Championship Game, it is more probable than not that New England Patriots personnel participated in violations of the Playing Rules and were involved in a deliberate effort to circumvent the rules," Wells and his team wrote. "In particular, we have concluded that it is more probable than not that Jim McNally (the Officials Locker Room attendant for the Patriots) and John Jastremski (an equipment assistant for the Patriots) participated in a deliberate effort to release air from Patriots game balls after the balls were examined by the referee. Based on the evidence, it also is our view that it is more probable than not that Tom Brady (the quarterback for the Patriots) was at least generally aware of the inappropriate activities of McNally and Jastremski involving the release of air from Patriots game balls."

The opinions were swift, and in some cases immediate. Hosts from both of Boston's full-time sports radio stations picked through the report and read chunks of it live on the air. ESPN went to live coverage and got takeaways from its analysts. CBS, NBC, CNN, Fox News, and NPR all had coverage. Twitter had Wells, the Patriots, Brady, and "more probable than not" all trending. It was a day that showed the power and weakness of the media. The power is that the news got out fast. The weakness is that no one had time to read it before being asked to comment on it. So there was some skimming and then incomplete concluding.

Still, some of the arguments were fascinating. The Patriots slammed the report as "incomprehensible." Don Yee, Brady's agent, said that Wells and the league went into the investigation with its mind made up and that "there was no fairness in the Wells investigation whatsoever" and that the report was "a significant and terrible disappointment." Wells, taking exception to the criticism of Yee and others about his work, held a conference call to address some of the point-by-point attacks.

"I think it is wrong to criticize my independence just because you disagree with my findings," he said. "I totally reject any suggestion that I was not independent or that the report was slanted in some way to reach a particular result."

He said Pash assisted as a facilitator and not much else in the process. That statement would be revisited and tested in several weeks. He also said that the Patriots cooperated with him except in one major area. He wanted another interview with "The Deflator," McNally, who called himself that in a text to Jastremski in May 2014. The Patriots countered that they had made him available four times to Wells, and a fifth interview was just excessive. For those who didn't read the report, the texts between McNally and Jastremski were all they needed to see. The dude called himself The Deflator. What else is there to say?

The report was so divisive that it split a football family. At ESPN, analyst Damien Woody discussed the findings with analyst Tedy Bruschi. Both former Patriots. They practiced together. Traveled together. Essentially lived with each other for four years and won a pair of Super Bowls together. Now they sat across from each other, on TV, and had a tense back-and-forth over The Deflator and Brady.

Woody: These guys handle the rock, handle the ball. So you mean to tell me that Tom Brady when it comes to these individuals working on the equipment staff, that he wouldn't know who these guys are?

Bruschi: This is what I believe. Tom Brady would not tell anyone to do anything illegal. That's what I believe.

Woody: And that's fine.

Both: We disagree.

Bruschi: You think Tom Brady would tell someone to do something illegal?

Woody: Yes!

Bruschi: That's fine. I do not believe that. I know Tom Brady. I know his integrity. I can vouch for him. I've spent a lot of time with him, all right? I vouch for this guy's integrity, up and down, as long as you want me to do it. He would not ever tell anyone to implicate themselves or do something illegally that would circumvent the rules of competitive play. That's not who he is. That's the person that I know. And that's what I believe.

Woody: It wouldn't be the first time that an athlete has been caught with his pants down in a situation like this. I respect Tom Brady just like you respect Tom Brady.

Bruschi: You don't respect him!

Woody: Why is that? I do!

Bruschi: You don't respect him. You're saying that he told these guys to break the rules.

Woody: Okay, but that's like the same thing as my kids in certain situations...They might tell me a story. That doesn't mean I have less respect for them.

Bruschi: Tom Brady had said that he did not tell them. In his press conference, post–AFC Championship Game, he said,

"I had no knowledge of the situation." In so many words. You don't believe him.

Woody: Right. I don't. You do.

Bruschi: A guy that you played with for years and won two Super Bowls with...and you don't know him?

Woody: I do know him. But that's okay, though.

Bruschi (his most animated now): Then you know him as someone who would say, who would tell someone, "Man, listen. Go break the rules. Deflate those balls after I'm done with them."

Woody: We're talking about a competitor.

Bruschi: Do you believe that?

Woody: We're talking about the ultimate competitor.

Bruschi: You really believe he would do that?

Woody: Why not? It happens...Everyone is always—

Bruschi: My former teammate, my friend Tom Brady, would not do that.

Woody: We're talking—playing in a league where everybody is trying to look for the competitive edge. I've tried to look for the competitive edge. Everyone is always looking for the competitive edge to stay on top. Do rules get broken sometimes? Of course they do!

The two of them had a host to moderate their discussion, but it was unnecessary. They not only represented themselves and their personal opinions; they staked flags for two of the most passionate camps that were arguing the details of this case nationally. Bruschi would be the overwhelming president of the New England states; Woody would have the rest of the country. Truly, it was The Nation versus Patriots Nation.

In New England, though, the borders got tighter. The walls were fortified. For or against? You had to declare, early in the conversation. They mobilized in person and online. They monitored and quickly identified friends and foes. For example, Damien Woody, former Patriot who attended Boston College, was now an enemy for his comments on Brady.

"I honestly felt like I was being excommunicated from the entire city of Boston," Woody says now. "Throughout the whole thing, I used common sense and the smell test. I have a tremendous amount of respect for Tom. I love him. He's the GOAT. Some people were like, 'Damien must be bitter' or 'It didn't end well with the Patriots.'

"Look, I never thought that this was anything big. I was blown away by how big this thing got. 'Defend the Wall!' and all this other stuff. It's not that serious. I felt the media was being irresponsible about it. Some of ESPN was irresponsible, too. I was asked a question about it and I gave an honest answer. I'm always willing to have a healthy conversation about it."

Real conversations were impossible to have once the league announced its penalties: the loss of a first-round pick in 2016, the loss of a fourth-round pick in 2017, a $1 million fine, and a four-game suspension for Brady. It was the biggest fine in league history. Wells said in his report that he found no fault with Robert Kraft, Belichick, or equipment manager Dave Schoenfeld. The penalty suggests the league believed otherwise. If the harshness was due to Spygate eight years earlier, the league is admitting that it is reprosecuting a violation that has already been paid for by the Patriots. Are they assumed to be guilty as long as Belichick is their coach and Kraft is their owner?

The weekend before heading to San Francisco for the league's spring meetings, Kraft talked with *Sports Illustrated*'s Peter King. The owner wouldn't characterize his relationship with Goodell. He wouldn't say whether he planned to sue the league. He wouldn't get into the much-debated text messages of Jim McNally and John Jastremski or why they were suspended if the Patriots did nothing wrong. But it was clear that he was angry and considering his options.

"I just get really worked up. To receive the harshest penalty in league history is just not fair. The anger and frustration with this process, to me, it wasn't fair. If we're giving all the power to the NFL and the office of the commissioner, this is something that can happen to all thirty-two teams. We need to have fair and balanced investigating and reporting. But in this report, every inference went against us...inferences from ambiguous, circumstantial evidence all went against us. That's the thing that really bothers me."

It sounded like Kraft was ready to fight when he went to the Bay Area. Many of the people in his hometown certainly were. They were the ones who offered to buy him drinks in New Orleans in 2002. They slapped him on the back down on Bourbon Street, called him Bobby, ecstatic that their owner was one of them. He had sat on those aluminum benches at old Foxboro Stadium like they had. He knew the distance they had traveled, as Patriots fans, to even have a franchise for which to cheer.

They didn't have to hear that conversation with King to know exactly how he felt. They got it.

So when he held a press conference saying that he would reluctantly accept the penalties...

When he said he wanted the rhetoric to stop, and that the Patriots were one of thirty-two in this collective...

He didn't sound like one of them anymore.

He sounded like one of *them*. As in the billionaires' club. No one from Kraft's old neighborhood, in Brookline, begrudged him for making money. They didn't care about that as much as they did roots. Had he forgotten about them and decided to protect his influence and committee connections in the league? That had to be it. He and his attorneys had been fighting with the league since January. It was now May, and one thing should have been clear to this most successful businessman: The league was not reasonable when it came to the Patriots.

There was no reason or relief from the league when Stacey James, the PR chief, asked for it. Robyn Glaser, the attorney, asked for help from the league and was ignored. Football operations asked for it, by way of the tampering charge against the Jets, and pretty much got that gesture, common in Massachusetts, that one receives after cutting someone off in traffic. The Wells Report itself, 243 pages long without a single critical comment about the league—which is nearly impossible from an "independent" document—didn't provide a reasonable view for the Patriots. Goodell took two draft picks and cash and returned a four-game suspension, based on text interpretation and air pressure. What on earth made Kraft think that the NFL was going to be reasonable now?

At home, he was being ripped up and down the radio dial, by Patriots supporters and haters alike. The supporters, the fighters, were shocked that the general didn't have the mind-set to wrestle. The detractors used the opportunity to point out that the retreat was an admission of guilt.

One man who didn't contribute much to the commentary was Tom Brady. It seemed as if it were ten years ago when he made that remark about being surprised by nothing in the league anymore. He said it in 2013 after losing receivers and watching other teammates traded in a blink. But that was just basic, ground-level NFL stuff.

Brady was nearly thirty-eight years old. Even after all his time spent in the public eye, the public didn't believe that what they were seeing and hearing was real. He liked to win, so he was going to compete against the Ivy League lawyers just like he would against some middle linebacker from a football factory.

The people who said he took a little off the top were calling him a liar. Those angry and disappointed that he just didn't "admit it" were saying they didn't believe him. Some were telling him to move on and accept his fate like Kraft did. That was not going to happen.

"Tom's integrity is one of the most important things to him," says Chris Eitzmann, one of Brady's first roommates with the Patriots. "He's always been that way."

The modern sports fan is used to athletes going the other way. They don't mention integrity all that much, nor do they give long press conferences about conscientiously staying within the lines. It's ironic that Kraft backed down in San Francisco, where Brady learned to win. The owner could say whatever he wanted, but he wasn't speaking for Tom Brady. Brady had won on the road before, in his day job, and now he was prepared to take the fight to his opponents. He'd go to their habitat, in Manhattan, whether conference room or, if necessary, courtroom.

The anticipation of and release of Wells's report had overshadowed nearly every significant football event in the spring and early summer. At least there was the championship celebration itself, a party at Kraft's house in June. It was one of the few times in the first six months of the year that players could relax and not hear about air pressure and suspensions. Brady and Gisele Bündchen were there, as was pop star Wiz Khalifa, and a video of the quarterback dancing went viral. The biggest party takeaway was the ring, each one loaded with 205 white diamonds.

A week after the party, it was time for business again. Tom Brady arrived at 345 Park Avenue in Manhattan, NFL headquarters, on Tuesday morning, June 23. The last time he saw Roger Goodell, Brady was receiving the Super Bowl MVP trophy, the third one of his career. He was smiling that day, wearing jeans and a cream-colored sweater. But today was about business. He wore a navy suit, white shirt, and dark tie. He arrived in a sedan, surrounded by lawyers armed with files and exhibits.

It was just before nine thirty a.m., and Brady was about to experience how conflict looks and sounds when it's unleashed at the corporate level. The two dozen people there, mostly lawyers, were adept at white-collar combat. This was officially Brady's appeals hearing, although the tension in the room didn't suggest a spirit of flexibility or negotiation. Both sides were entrenched, intent on pointing out the absurdities on the other side of the table.

The art of refusing to listen was perfectly displayed by Lorin Reisner. On this morning, Reisner was a double threat: He was one of the authors of the "independent" Wells Report, as well as the attorney who was doggedly trying to get Brady to incriminate himself on air pressure in footballs. Brady had gladly shared that he was angry with the size and hardness of the footballs in a 2014 win over the Jets. After that game, John Jastremski measured the footballs and found that they were grossly over the legal limit, at 16 PSI. Brady was livid. The officials hadn't been mindful. From that moment on, he asked the equipment staff to insist to the officials that they know the rules and inflate the ball to a proper level, at 12.5.

But Reisner didn't focus on the total news of that story. He wanted to talk about Brady's preference for 12.5, which is a legal number; he ignored the fact that a game ball was at 16, which was well past illegal.

"Now, you have said publically that you like footballs to be inflated to a level of 12.5 PSI, correct?" Reisner asked.

"I said that after the championship game," Brady replied.

"And so, how long have you known that 12.5 is your preferred level of inflation?"

"After the Jets game," Brady answered.

"And how did you come to learn that 12.5 is your preferred level of inflation?"

It was obvious that Reisner's questioning here was following his contributions to the Wells Report. He wasn't buying the explanations. Brady told Reisner that before Jastremski got to New England, the quarterback learned that the PSI had always been at 12.7 or 12.8. He didn't know that until the Jets fiasco. But Reisner didn't want to talk about the Jets fiasco.

"You say you 'just picked the number.' Did you pick that number for any particular reason?"

"Ball pressure has been so inconsequential," Brady answered. "I haven't even thought about that. I think at the end of the day, the only time I thought about it was after the Jet game, and then after this was brought up, after the championship game. It's never something that has been on my radar, registered. I never said 'PSI.' I don't think I even knew what that meant until after the championship game. It was never something that even crossed my mind."

Reisner's approach was the same. He backed up and sped forward again: "How did you come to pick 12.5 as the number?"

"We looked in the rulebook," Brady replied.

"How did you come to pick 12.5 as the number for your preferred pressure level for the footballs?"

One of the first statements of the day, from league attorney Daniel Nash, was that this was not a criminal or civil trial. Reisner seemed to think differently. Brady mentioned the Jets game again, the rulebook again. It didn't matter.

"Did you pick 12.5 because it was toward the lower end or the lower end of the permissible range?"

Brady told the lawyer that they were looking for consistency, and they found a number that they liked in the rulebook. It would stand to reason that he would pick 12.5 when the league had gone as high as 16. It didn't matter what he said, although his next answer could have and would have been plausible if it had been a different room. But not with this rhetoric. Not with the opponents, like Reisner, that Brady could see along with the ones he couldn't, owners and GMs around the league who supported everything Team Goodell was doing.

"Is it fair to say that you prefer the footballs inflated to a pressure level at the low end of the range?"

Brady repeated his story about how that Jets game changed his outlook. And then he gave his best answer yet: "Whenever I went to pick the game balls, I never once in fifteen years ever asked what the ball pressure was set at until after the Jet game. So whether it's 12.5 or 12.6 or 12.7 or 12.8 or 12.9 or 13, all the way up to the Colts game, I still think it's inconsequential to what the actual feel of a grip of a football would be. So the fact is, there could be a ball that's set at 12.5 that I could disapprove of, there could be a ball that's 13 that I could approve of. It all is depending on how the ball feels in my hand on that particular day. So I don't think my liking to a football could be a very psychological thing. I just want to know that there is consistency in what I'm playing with."

Brady's team had a smart game plan, and it was able to produce some stunning admissions under oath. Ted Wells, for example, after harping on his independence for weeks, acknowledged that NFL executive vice president Jeff Pash read drafts of the Wells Report before its release and even included comments. Wells said he wasn't sure of the specifics of those comments because they weren't provided directly to him. They were given to a colleague and, he presumed, the contributions involved "some kind of wordsmithing." He said that one of his colleagues also prepared a first draft before

Wells reviewed it, and that colleague was Reisner. Literally, "independence" became "interdependence" in a New York minute.

"Would your principal colleague on this case be Mr. Lorin Reisner, who is seated over there?" Brady's attorney Jeffrey Kessler asked Wells.

"Correct," Wells answered.

Kessler got Wells to acknowledge that he and Reisner were being paid by the NFL for the appeals hearing. And since Pash, a league employee, obviously was as well, it led Kessler to a logical conclusion.

"Just for the record, my observation that the statement that the Paul, Weiss firm is independent is clearly not correct. We now have testimony that they represented the NFL in this proceeding. They viewed the NFL as their client."

The most confusing and contradictory testimony of the day belonged to Troy Vincent, a former player and the league's executive vice president of football operations. He said he had never heard of the ideal gas law and that he wasn't aware that in cold weather, the inflation level of the football would drop. He admitted that he put his signature on two incorrect reports. One, by league employee David Gardi, said the Patriots had a ball measuring at 10.1 PSI. Another suggested that all the Colts' balls were in compliance, which they weren't. Vincent also said that the league didn't record the data of its football tests and that the two pressure gauges it used were inconsistent.

"Is it fair to say, Mr. Vincent, that there was a lot of confusion about what these numbers were, that Mr. Gardi didn't even know what the numbers were correctly at this time?" Kessler asked.

"Not at all," replied Vincent.

"You think it was very clear?"

"I think it was clear," Vincent answered.

Kessler was incredulous. Perhaps some of Vincent's colleagues were, too. "If it was so clear, do you have any explanation as to how he could have '10.1' written down as the figure and it was not one of the figures?"

"I can't speak for David," Vincent said.

At one point, Brady was asked why he spoke to John Jastremski so much in the days after the air-pressure story broke. He said that they were talking about the Super Bowl and, candidly, all the developments of the deflation story. It seemed that the league was expecting a more sinister, less plausible answer than the one Brady gave. It had been a long, hot summer day in the city, and after a few breaks, it finally ended at 8:27 p.m. That had been exactly eleven hours of football and science talk, but even after a half day of talking, there was no resolution.

Anyone who looked at the transcript would have walked away thinking that Brady, at the very least, had a good chance of getting his suspension reduced. But consistent with the way things had gone in the previous six months, there was a chasm between what should have been and what actually was. On Tuesday morning, July 28, ESPN personality Stephen A. Smith had some breaking news. His sources were telling him that the suspension would likely be upheld, in part, because Brady "destroyed his phone."

Finally, after not seeing the signs for months, Kraft understood what was going on. This was a nasty fight, and there wasn't enough respect for any type of compromise to be reached. Brady had told Wells in the spring that he never planned to turn over his phone. Wells eventually told him that the phone was not required, just electronic data within a narrow scope. He and his team eventually agreed to that, as well as providing information for every person with whom he had been in contact. That led to a public release of

Brady's e-mails, in which he referenced pool covers, new shoes, his charitable endeavors, and a dinner meeting with the owner of the Vancouver Canucks. He also gave the league contacts for every person with whom he had sent one of his nearly ten thousand text messages that the league wanted to see. All mundane stuff, with no references to PSI. And now Goodell was saying that the new information, the damaging information, was that Brady destroyed a phone that he never planned to give them in the first place?

Worse than that, the league continued to change the script. May's "generally aware" became "orchestrated and provided rewards" in July. In the beginning, Brady was the quarterback who likely knew that the guys were up to something. Now the league was saying that he was the mastermind and that, although there was no precedent for what they believed Brady had done, Goodell placed it in the realm of using and/or masking performance-enhancing drugs.

After the upheld suspension and clumsy analogy from the commissioner, Kraft did a reversal.

"I first and foremost need to apologize to our fans, because I truly believed what I did in May, given the actual evidence of the situation and the league's history on discipline matters, would make it much easier for the league to exonerate Tom Brady. Unfortunately, I was wrong. Tom Brady is a person of great integrity, and is a great ambassador of the game, both on and off the field. Yet for reasons that I cannot comprehend, there are those in the league office who are more determined to prove that they were right rather than admit any culpability of their own or take responsibility for the initiation of a process and ensuing investigation that was flawed.

"I have come to the conclusion that this was never about doing what was fair and just. Back in May, I had to make a difficult decision that I now regret. I tried to do what I thought was right; I chose not to take legal action. I wanted to return the focus to football."

For the Patriots and Brady, the only way they could get the focus to football was to go through the court system first. It was yet another challenge for Brady, in a career of football mountain climbing. When he was eighteen, the obstacle was the depth chart, where he was so far down that they couldn't sense his presence or hear his voice. A few years later it was being asked to share the space with Drew Henson. He left that Drew and was blocked by another one, Bledsoe. He'd been coasting freely since those days, in his midtwenties, winning everything in his path: fans, games, endorsements, trust.

He'd played with dozens of teammates who'd claimed to love the game so much that they'd play it without compensation. They'd do anything to get on the field. They could never imagine this, suing your league for the chance to play and remaining professional even when the commissioner lies about you and yet calls you the liar. Players couldn't relate. Maybe only one other guy could. Bill Belichick. A scandal had been placed at his feet eight years ago, and he continued to coach through it. He was called every negative name possible and he led a team to the doorstep of perfection.

Brady had his scandal now. This was being put on him, and not only was he being called a cheater; he was being called a liar. Daily. When he held press conferences, he answered questions of those who said he was dishonest. When he sat in that room with Goodell for half a day, the commissioner walked away and wrote that he wasn't credible.

A few days away from Brady's thirty-eighth birthday, he got a gift without even realizing it. He and the Players Association planned to take the NFL to court to fight Goodell's decision. They filed their suit in Minnesota, where the association had enjoyed historic success, going back to the days when players were granted unrestricted free agency for the first time. But it was a sign of the times that there was a sprint between the league and the union to see who could file first, and the NFL won that race. After Goodell's decision to uphold the four-game suspension, the league strategically filed in U.S. District Court for the Southern District of New York, because they felt a Manhattan court was more likely to uphold its ruling.

Since the league filed first, a U.S. District judge in Minnesota, Richard Kyle, ordered the union's case be transferred to New York. It was viewed as a loss for Brady in some corners, but Brady's lead attorney, Jeffrey Kessler, wasn't just spouting lawyer-speak when he said, "We are happy in any federal court, which, unlike the arbitration before Goodell, provides a neutral forum."

The judge was randomly selected, and the one who happened to get the case was Richard Berman. A lifelong New Yorker, Berman had many instances in his career where he had either ruled against the status quo or strongly urged contentious sides to settle their differences so he wouldn't have to do it for them. He was passionate about defending the powerless and marginalized, and had written extensively on child services and the protection of children.

He was equally critical and complimentary of pop-culture stars, once ruling in favor of singer Mariah Carey in one case and against actor Cameron Douglas, the son of Michael and grandson of Kirk, in another.

It was going to take all Berman's experience and skill as a peacemaker to strike a conciliatory tone between the union and the league. He asked both sides to "tone down the rhetoric" and attempt to find common ground. He would soon learn that they weren't interested. The day before the Patriots played a preseason game against the Packers, Brady and Goodell were in court all day. The judge met with both sides separately, trying to convince them to settle. He sensed no movement, so he announced that there were varying strengths to both arguments. But since both sides believed that theirs was the stronger, that approach didn't work, either.

It was less than a month from the beginning of the season and football fans were live-tweeting quotes from a federal judge. There was the merger of football and the law on a daily basis, which led to everyone being a member of the debate team. Every word and mannerism of Judge Berman was parsed. Court dates became just as important as, if not more important than, preseason games. Both sides, from the lawyers to the fans on the street, routinely convinced themselves that they had an advantage.

Kessler was a rock star; Kessler was overmatched. Brady was being railroaded; Brady must have done something because those underlings wouldn't lift a finger without his permission. The air came out of the football due to the ideal gas law; the air came out because The Deflator went into that bathroom with a needle and drew it out. The Patriots are great and other teams and fans are just jealous; the Patriots habitually cross the line, and other teams are sick of it. It was the dominant topic in New England, much more so than the Patriots themselves. They had won the Super Bowl six months earlier, but it didn't feel that way. Their fans never got that victory-lap summer, that carefree, toes-up-at-the-beach summer that most champions and their observers enjoy. They didn't know if they were going to unveil a Super Bowl banner on September 10, the night of the opener, or if that would be the evening that Brady's burden—that four-game suspension—would begin.

When Brady walked out of court at five thirty p.m. on August 12, he got a preview of what was to come, regardless of Berman's ruling. "Cheater, cheater..." he heard as he got into a car and was driven away. Patriots fans were with him every step of the way, for obvious reasons, but the nation wasn't following New England's summer reading schedule: twenty pages of Goodell's appeal rejection, 243 pages of the Wells Report, and 457 pages of the appeal hearing transcript. It was far from J. K. Rowling and Stephen King. Who wanted to spend a summer like this? Besides, the average football fan, whether in media or in the break room, wasn't using those documents to form an opinion. Most of them had their minds made up already.

On September 3, 2015, the day Judge Berman's decision came down, it was worth noting that Brady had accumulated eleven wins while playing in the state of New Jersey against the Jets and Giants. That was cool, but this was better: He was now 1-0 in Manhattan, essentially playing a road game against the NFL, the biggest, baddest, and richest giant in North American sports. He had taken the league to court and had his suspension vacated.

New England reacted as if a war had been won. Television and radio stations interrupted programming with flashes of BREAKING NEWS. Fingers couldn't move fast enough as tweets and retweets were being processed with Brady-themed expressions of joy. Gronk tweeted a picture of Brady celebrating a touchdown by riding on the back of the big tight end. He wrote, "Let's go! This season to be one heck of another ride. #PatsNation." Devin McCourty tweeted an applauding meme of NBA star Kevin Durant, who had delivered one of the most inspirational and emotional MVP speeches ever. The caption was Durant's money line, delivered to his mother, "You the real MVP." McCourty wrote, "Judge Berman U know what u are." Brady jerseys and Brady-slogan shirts (FREE BRADY, DEFLATE THIS, and GOODELL SUCKS) could be seen all over the region. An elementary school principal, Mark Springer, learned the news and shared it on the PA system; his teachers, preparing lesson plans and classrooms, reacted with shouts and high fives. The latter was fitting, because the old elementary school script had been turned on its head: The bully had requested a three o'clock meeting by the bike rack, and this time he was the one who walked away with the bloody nose.

For now, no one was worried about the appeal immediately filed by the NFL. Sure, it was going to be heard, but not until after the season. There were also the words of the nation out there, the one with forty-four states and a negative view of the Patriots. They argued that the win was one of procedure, not a declaration of innocence. Commentators in New York, and even a couple in Boston, got it in their heads that Berman was somehow starstruck by Brady, and that's why he ruled as he did.

Brady used his personal Facebook page to post a message that was celebratory and reflective.

The regular season starts tomorrow morning and I can't wait to fully commit my energy and emotion to focus on the challenges of the 2015 NFL season. I want to thank my family, my friends, all of the fans, past and current players and my teammates for the support they have given me throughout this challenging experience. I also want to thank Judge Berman and his staff for their efforts to resolve this matter over the past five weeks. I am very grateful. My thanks also to the union's legal team who has fought so hard right along with me.

While I am pleased to be eligible to play, I am sorry our league had to endure this. I don't think it has been good for our sport—to a large degree, we have all lost. I am also sorry to anyone whose feelings I may have hurt as I have tried to work to resolve this situation. I love the NFL. It is a privilege to be a member of the NFL community and I will always try to do my best in representing my team and the league in a way that would make all members of this community proud.

I look forward to the competition on the playing field and I hope the attention of NFL fans can return to where it belongs—on the many great players and coaches who work so hard every week, and sacrifice so much, to make this game great. Most importantly, I look forward to representing the New England Patriots on Thursday night in our season opener. I hope to make all of our fans proud this year...and beyond!

His words were wiser than he could have imagined when he wrote them. There were going to be many conversations like the one his father, Tom Sr., had with San Francisco radio host Chip Franklin. Reacting to the big news of the day, Franklin told his KGO audience that he'd rather have out-of-football Tim Tebow over "Tom Brady, who is a cheater—a cheater and a bad sport and a big freaking baby." He went on to say that Tebow is a winner and that Brady is a system quarterback who doesn't have the commanding presence of Tebow. He was interrupted by a phone call from the quarterback's namesake.

"You're being silly," the senior Brady said. When the host asked him whom he would rather have, Tebow or his son, he replied, "That's a stupid question. But more important than being stupid on that point is the prior point you just made about Tom Brady telling the ball boys to put a pin in the ball. You have no evidence...you are full of crap."

The elder Brady had a couple of things in his favor on this call. He was incensed, perfect for talk radio, and he understandably was well versed in the facts. While readership of the Wells Report was high in Boston, it certainly was not in San Francisco. Brady made a reference to the host's deficiency as he answered a question about why the quarterback disposed of his phone. "If you read the Wells Report, which you probably didn't, Wells said that Brady cooperated one hundred percent. The second thing that the Wells Report said was, 'We don't need your phone.' If you don't need somebody's phone, what the heck do you care what happens to the phone?"

The tense conversation lasted for just a few minutes, but it lasted long enough for some cutting and honest commentary from the senior Brady. When Franklin began to say that he was merely offering analysis based on the "facts" from the NFL, Brady interrupted, "Wait a sec, wait a sec. Is that the same facts that Chris Mortensen put out, that all the balls were underinflated by two pounds? It's all lies. It's all ESPN. It's all NFL propaganda. Don't you get it? The only person who has testified under oath in this is Tom Brady. We know that Goodell has lied. He lied in the Ray Rice case. He lied in this case. He lied in the Peterson case. How many times do you need to know that this guy is a flaming liar?"

The exchange was coming to a close, and Brady had one more piece of advice for the host: "If you're going to be on the radio, know the facts." The NFL, the most powerful sports brand on its continent, had the resources and the operatives to create its own facts. How many Franklins were out there on the radio, reciting the league's version of the Brady Chronicles, without a Tom Brady Sr. to edit and check them?

One week after Judge Berman's ruling, the Steelers were in Foxboro and Goodell was not. The 2014 championship banner was unfurled and the sellout crowd could finally let go after an entire offseason of holding its breath. At times they sarcastically chanted for the commissioner, who has a summer home in Maine. "Where is Roger?" they teased as they reveled in the return of Brady. Pittsburgh would have to be the first team to pay for the stressful offseason and the contentious NFL leadership. So much for Brady and the preoccupations of his training camp. He completed twenty-five of thirty-two passes for 288 yards and four touchdowns. He looked the same, and so did the Patriots. They won again, 28–21. Once again, they also had to defend themselves postgame.

Pittsburgh coach Mike Tomlin revealed in his press conference that at times his headset wasn't functional. When he expected to hear his coaches, he instead heard a familiar accent saying pro-Patriot things. Former Patriots quarterback Scott Zolak, who grew up twenty miles from Pittsburgh, was now a New England analyst on the Patriots' flagship radio station, WBZ-FM. The signals got crossed and Tomlin could hear the high-strung "Zo" and his Pittsburghese, talking about the prowess of Brady.

It was strange. Tomlin was asked postgame if his headset went out. "That's always the case," he answered. A reporter sought clarification and wanted to know if that was always the case at Gillette Stadium. "Yes," the coach replied. He was asked exactly what happened and he said, "We were listening to the Patriots' radio broadcast for the majority of the first half on our headsets." The implication was that the Patriots did this to them, although the league pointed out that it was in control of the headsets. The problem was due to an electrical issue, made worse by the weather.

Living as a perpetual suspect. That's what it meant to be a Patriot in 2015. Tomlin's complaint had a way of bringing everyone back to the street penalties of a scandal. The NFL's accounting department had already logged the $1 million air-pressure fine, and those 2016 and 2017 draft picks had evaporated into a computer program. Within weeks, Jim McNally and John Jastremski would be allowed to return to Foxboro and work for the team again, albeit with different job titles. But on the ground level, there was something folks were always trying to pin on you. There were always logic-defying tales from the underground, untold stories, conspiracies, plots.

It wasn't just Tomlin. ESPN and *Sports Illustrated* had both published stories about the illicit ways of the Patriots. They talked about videotaping, but also mentioned interns who were instructed to sweep trash cans and locker rooms for opponents' scouting reports and game plans. One story suggested that the Patriots offered warm sports drinks. Another one said that the stiffness and overzealousness of the air-pressure penalty was due to a leaguewide view that the Patriots had skated too easily with Spygate. For fans who tried to understand how a team could be so competitive year in and out, they'd believe anything. Why not? If the Patriots would take the time to train their cameras on other coaches…perhaps… possibly…maybe…

Just one game into the season, an unprompted Belichick used a conference call to defend his system, past, present, and near future. He had turned sixty-three in the spring, and his statement years earlier was that he wouldn't be coaching pro football well into his seventies. He was still at the top of his game, and so was Brady. The assumption a decade ago was that maybe burnout would get to the coach and age would slow down the quarterback. But those maladies weren't wearing on either of them. The innuendo and tragicomic investigations were burdensome.

"I just think overall it's kind of sad, really, to see some stories written that obviously have an agenda to them with misinformation and anonymous-type comments. Writing about warm drinks and trash cans, stuff like that, it's just, I think it's a sad commentary. It's gone to a pretty low level; it's sunk pretty deep."

Ten years ago, he wasn't always willing to look back. There was so much work to be done and a feeling that so much more could be accomplished. They had won three out of the previous four championships and all aspects of the organization were healthy. The quarterback was in his prime, the franchise vaults were lined with extra draft picks, and the same word could be used for the salary cap and the reputation of the Patriots: clean.

For the current Patriots, games just aren't questioned; plays, *legal plays*, are questioned. Belichick watched the Titans and Lions run offensive sets with unusual formations, to varying results. He and Josh McDaniels studied it, tweaked it to their needs, and brought it out for the play-off win over the Ravens. John Harbaugh claimed that no one in the league had done it before, although it happened twice already that season. The league apparently believed him and the rule was changed in the offseason.

Change is inevitable and necessary. Sometimes it is also messy and infuriating. On this day, Belichick doesn't mind looking back and thinking of some of those men who kept making those great plays, seemingly on demand. All of the guys who came in early to the meetings and took notes. The guys who refused to be idle during down moments in practice. There were so many great professionals, too many to name.

"This organization has won a lot of games, but particularly in reference to the great teams from '01, '03, '04, back in there, and all the great players that played on those teams, to take away from what those guys accomplished, what those teams accomplished, how good they were, how many great players we had, how well they played in big games, how they consistently showed up and made big plays, game-winning plays, it's just not right. I'm not going to get into a back-and-forth on it, but that's how I feel about it."

A lot of those guys are still applying the lessons that they learned from one another and Belichick, bringing their football concepts to the mainstream American workforce. In Indianapolis, former linebacker Rosevelt Colvin runs a UPS store. He hears himself being Patriot-like when he manages people and makes hiring decisions. His typical interview questions make it clear what he's looking for:

Do you have transportation? Does your voice mail work? Are you a drama person? If you wake up at nine and the store opens at nine, what's the first thing you do? If you take a shower, we open thirty minutes late; come right in and we're only ten minutes behind.

All over the country, Ty Law is running Launch, his trampoline-experience business, like an NFL team. When he played, he noticed that fans didn't just like football. They liked the pre- and postgame traditions, the smell of burgers and chicken during tailgates, Frisbees and cornhole in the parking lot three hours before kickoff. He designed Launch the same way. "It ain't just the jumping," he says. "You've got to have a certain energy, a certain experience. The jumping is just a by-product." After many battles with Belichick over contracts, Law is the economist now. He and Magic Johnson sat down for hours discussing business principles. Now Law frequently goes to his phone for the app that provides up-to-the-second financial reports from his ten Launch locations in Massachusetts, Florida, Connecticut, and North Carolina.

Tedy Bruschi, Roman Phifer, Matt Cassel, and many others still keep in touch with a free-flowing and often irreverent group text. They can all comment on the familiar Patriot on TV, Bruschi. They probably have no idea how much preparation he puts into work with his new team, at ESPN. He has multiple TVs in his home office and spends half of the week watching and taking notes on every game in the league. He's mastered the ESPN video system and sometimes helps new production assistants efficiently find film. He e-mails producers with segment ideas, complete with captions and graphics they can use.

Being a Patriot means that the lessons are always in you, even when you've been gone for a decade. Phifer still views the notebooks he kept and continues to be amazed by their depth and efficiency. A dozen years out of football, he still uses Belichick phrasing. "Bill always told us, 'Know your personnel,'" he says. "You have to know when and why a change-of-pace running back is out there. What's this tight end like to do? Know your personnel. I use it in everything. I can be talking to a friend of mine who's complaining about a relationship. 'Hey man, you've got to know your personnel...'"

If this season has a mission statement, Belichick has unintentionally defined it with his tribute to all the players who have provided a foundation for the 2015 Patriots. Every game is a defense of the system, today's and yesterday's. Every completed pass proof that Brady does it naturally.

Brady marched through the schedule, throwing touchdown passes and settling scores. There were those 28 points against the Steelers, followed by forty against the Bills, and 51 against the Jaguars. In an instant, 3-0. A squeezing of the Cowboys left them with 6 points and the Patriots with 30. The Colts, who started the air madness, were next in Indianapolis. Local bakeries had cakes with deflated football designs. There were re-creations of that night in Foxboro, when a conference championship game became an afterthought.

Many predicted that the Patriots would roll the Colts as they usually did. The Patriots did win, but there was nothing usual about it. The highlight of the night was a sloppily executed special-teams play in which the Colts tried to surprise the Patriots on fourth-and-three. If John Harbaugh wanted to see an illegal formation, this is what he was looking for: The Colts had nine players near the sideline and two, Colt Anderson and Griff Whalen, on the line of scrimmage. Whalen, a 195-pound receiver, was the center. Anderson, a 195-pound defensive back, was the quarterback. Several Patriots stood over the unprotected pair, almost daring them to run a play with no linemen and no chance to go anywhere. In one of the more bizarre decisions in NFL history, they did.

"What in the world?" Al Michaels wondered aloud to an NBC TV audience and his broadcast partner, Cris Collinsworth. "You tell me."

The play led to a flag and penalty description from referee Tony Corrente that may have been a first as well: "Illegal formation. The whole right side of the line was not on the line of scrimmage…"

Tom Brady's Revenge Tour was what some people called it. At home, New York, Miami, and Washington were taken care of. On the road, as time expired, Stephen Gostkowski made a field goal to beat the Giants by a point. The Bills, now coached by Rex Ryan, were beaten for the second time in the season, this time 20–13. The Revenge Tour had played ten dates and been perfect on them all. But this had begun as an odd year and now was carrying over to a disturbing season.

The Patriots were in Denver, which was without Peyton Manning. The annual Brady-Manning game was replaced by Brady–Brock Osweiler. Manning was on the sideline, unable to play due to both injuries and ineffectiveness. He still saw more of the field than most, and brought high-definition vision to things that defensive coordinators tried to camouflage. You weren't going to fool Peyton. The problem for him was that his brain was his only remaining superior football asset. His arm strength was gone. Some throws couldn't be made. There was real talk that he would be forced to retire at the end of the year.

Brady had other issues. His players were falling all around him, on offense and defense. The Patriots entered the Broncos game without Julian Edelman, Danny Amendola, and linebacker Jamie Collins. During the game another linebacker, Dont'a Hightower, left with an injury and, after a high Brady pass to the right side, it appeared that there was yet another serious injury. To Gronk. Brady clasped his own helmet when he saw Gronk writhing on the field. This was the Rx Revenge Tour: injuries popping up to cut the season short.

The game in Denver was lost, and so was the one the following week against the Eagles.

It's humbling to observe how the world works, how a career can be celebrated, for the most part, with no critics or enemies around for miles and miles. And then, overnight, you're a cheater. You're a liar. The critics are at the front door, actually there, standing beside news trucks and behind cameras. They wield microphones, wanting to know what *you* know and when you knew it. They realize that they don't have the legal power to arrest you, but their portrayals can imprison you for a long time, possibly forever.

As the Patriots were wrapping up their thirteenth division title with Belichick and Brady, Manning was being questioned about an Al Jazeera America report that suggested he was using an NFL-banned substance, human growth hormone, to extend his career. He called the story "garbage" and never backed down from that position. Most people in the media believed him, and said so. Most people in the media didn't believe Brady, and continued to say that also.

Brady had heard his coach talk about distractions and uninformed opinions hundreds of times over the years. He'd heard the message presented to different audiences: a veteran and hungry Patriots team, looking to win its first title; an experienced, championship group trying to maintain its edge; a team in transition trying not to be overwhelmed by the dominance of past teams (Belichick had taken down some of the Super Bowl pictures in the building because he wanted his players to focus on the present).

What exactly they were now was hard to say. They had a recent championship and they had youth. They had health as well because the injury to Gronk wasn't nearly as serious as it had appeared. They had the deferred scandal, the one that Brady would likely have to fight again in the spring. That would be in Manhattan as well, in the U.S. Court of Appeals for the Second Circuit. They also had a current scandal, a mini one by comparison.

Defensive end Chandler Jones, six days before a divisional play-off game with Kansas City, walked to a Foxboro police station and asked for help. It was a cold January morning in New England, yet the six-foot-five Jones was shirtless as he wandered toward the police station at 7:45 a.m. He wasn't arrested but instead was taken to a local hospital for treatment. It was later reported that he had experimented with synthetic marijuana, much more dangerous than cannabis, and composed of psychoactive chemicals. Jones briefly chatted with the media leading up to the Chiefs game, vaguely apologizing for a stupid mistake.

What was this team? No one knew. The record said 12-4, the number two seed in the play-offs. The offensive line and the focus said something else. No one paid attention to either one after the Kansas City game because Brady had helped mask it all. He made quick decisions in the pocket, wasn't sacked all day, and finished with over three hundred yards and a pair of touchdown passes. He and the Patriots were now ready for a couple of firsts and lasts. They were moving on to the conference championship game for the fifth consecutive season. That hadn't been done since the Raiders pulled it off, a few months after Brady was born. The Patriots' opponent for the conference title was the Broncos, led this time by Peyton Manning.

He was back, he was healthy, and he was realistic. This was going to be the last Brady-Manning game and he knew it. This wasn't going to be like the others. He was going to be charged with staying out of the way so his defense could carry him to the Super

Bowl. That had never been the story of a Brady-Manning game, ever. It played out that way precisely on this day, though.

It wasn't a day for offense, as both quarterbacks struggled to get conversions on third downs. It was worse for the Patriots because they were on the road, and the home crowd made it difficult for Brady to alter his communication with the offensive line. As a result, the Broncos had a good idea when the ball was going to be snapped, and they sped past flat-footed linemen and were on Brady in an instant. The seventeenth and final Brady-Manning game lacked the artistic flourishes that many of the sixteen before it had. In the end, the Patriots made it competitive, despite their untrustworthy line, but they lost 20–18.

At midfield, Belichick and Manning embraced. The quarterback leaned down and said in Belichick's left ear, "Hey, listen. This might be my last rodeo. So it sure has been a pleasure." The coach in the gray hooded sweatshirt hugged Manning and said, "You're a great competitor."

A full year had passed since the previous championship game, against the Colts, and the Patriots' offseason seemed to mirror the previous one, too. Last year, they waited to hear from Ted Wells. This year, they waited to hear from a three-judge panel that would determine if Brady's record in Manhattan would be pushed to an overwhelming 2-0 or a suspension-worthy 1-1.

In between the wait, there were changes. Chandler Jones, aside from his Sunday morning issue at the Foxboro police station, was entering a contract year. The Patriots decided to trade him to Arizona, in exchange for a second-round pick and guard Jonathan Cooper. They moved on from receiver Brandon LaFell and brought in Chris Hogan, from divisional rival Buffalo, and veteran Nate Washington. There was a complementary tight end swap, too:

Scott Chandler, who was disappointing, left and Martellus Bennett arrived via trade. Defensive end Chris Long, son of Hall of Fame lineman Howie Long, was signed as well.

The point in 2016 was the same as it was in 2015, and 2014, and 2013...all the way back to Belichick's first draft class when he told the skinny quarterback, Brady, to make sure the rookies knew what the hell they were supposed to be doing. This game is fast, baby. Sit around too long and the next trend, the next great talent, the next rule change, will make you suddenly irrelevant. Adapt or be consumed. That is true in all aspects of the game, whether it is the young men who play it, the older ones who coach it, or the lawyers and marketers and accountants who run it. Or, in some cases, such as Tom Brady versus the NFL, the jurists who officiate it.

On a solemn April morning in New England, seven months after Judge Berman's words had sparked a regional party, the news came from New York. Brady had lost this one. Two judges, Barrington Daniels Parker Jr. and Denny Chin, said that Roger Goodell had properly used his "broad discretion" as commissioner and had exercised fundamental fairness as stipulated by the Collective Bargaining Agreement. Another judge, Robert Katzmann, the chief, disagreed. The four-game suspension was back on. Those who weren't paying attention wondered what Brady would do next.

He is a New Englander now, no "honorary" required as a preface. The area claimed him after the first title, swore him in for life after the second or third, became sisters and brothers prepared to fight for his reputation after the fourth. They would never back down if he didn't, and if he chose to keep going, since he previously had no experience backing down, the games would continue.

One game had him in tailored suits and expensive watches that he endorsed, competing against men who went to school for this, guys who never lofted MVP trophies but instead have "JD" and

"Esq." after their names. If there'd been a path that allowed him to go all the way to victory in the Supreme Court, unlikely as that might have been, he'd have taken it. But even Tom Brady knows that you can't win 'em all.

The other game is the one that he and Belichick have been engrossed by, together, for sixteen years. They are the two anomalies in this system, all things around them spinning and changing as they remain the same. Two adaptable personalities, built for any era. They came into New England and stood behind other franchises and their personalities. They've seen dozens of them come and go, would-be coaching stars like Rick Pitino and actual ones like Doc Rivers and Claude Julien and Terry Francona. They've seen superstars drop in and exit, often amicably and sometimes angrily. They were here before Kevin Garnett and Ray Allen and after them. They were entertained by Manny Ramirez, Pedro Martinez, Curt Schilling, Nomar Garciaparra. All of them gone now, talking about the game or coaching it.

For Belichick, sometimes the offseason coaching moves are reminders of wisdom and youth. All in one hire. Way back when he took the job, in 2000, it wasn't unusual to see his sons in his office. The older one, Steve, was twelve then. He'd ask questions and Belichick would give him answers. Sometimes he'd just watch. Steve eventually went to Rutgers to play football and lacrosse. Then he became a Patriots coaching assistant, a low man in the apprentice program. Now, at twenty-nine, he'll be the safeties coach on his father's staff. Naturally, there will be a story about the son taking over the family business for his father, who is sixty-four. It's not likely, for many reasons, the best one being obsession. Still. Belichick loves the job, and everything that goes with it, far too much to just walk away.

Belichick has had the same job description and mostly the same office for sixteen years. In that time, he's seen eighteen different

Boston head coaches and managers. That's the side of "do your job" that is assumed and rarely spoken: Do that job superbly and quickly, because eventually there will be an owner, a player, a media posse, even a scandal or two, that will get you fired.

Belichick and Brady have won, at historic levels, and the system says that's not supposed to be. It is rich and big and tyrannical, this system. But it can be beaten with talent and smarts. And a willingness to fight.

ACKNOWLEDGMENTS

I've never been nor aspired to be a comedy writer, yet I managed to write the most hilarious column of my career sixteen years ago. Of course, it was totally unintentional.

It was January 4, 2000, and I had all the answers for the New England Patriots. They had fired their head coach, Pete Carroll, the day before, and they wanted to replace him with New York Jets assistant coach Bill Belichick. They were initially blocked by Bill Parcells, who had resigned at the end of the 1999 season, thus making Belichick contractually obligated to lead the Jets. I was raised in Akron, Ohio, about thirty miles south of Cleveland, and had worked there in the early 1990s when Belichick was the head coach of the Browns. I couldn't wait to tell my *Boston Globe* readers about Belichick, New York's disaster-in-waiting.

"Belichick is the number one football man for the New York Jets, an organization he will destroy if Parcells doesn't hold his hand—especially when it's time to draft players."

Unfortunately, that was merely the throat-clearing portion of the column. It got worse.

"[Robert Kraft] had intentions of giving Belichick coaching and personnel power; it would have left his organization looking like the ruins of Rome."

Full of confidence and insight, I raised the stakes. I went for the two-for-one, in which I swiftly dismissed not one but two future Super Bowl–winning head coaches in one neat paragraph.

"For now, I'll say that Pete Carroll is Bill Belichick, minus the association to Parcells. Both men are brilliant defensive coordinators. Both men probably should not be NFL head coaches, and that's not necessarily a demeaning thing."

I should have known better.

The theme of Belichick's story at the time, seeking redemption, is one that I've often found myself drawn to in sports and in life. As I reflect now, I'm humbled by God's grace and mercy and the situations in which I've been placed. Turnarounds can happen quickly; I'm certainly a witness to that. Here I am giving thanks for my fifth book, which is five more than I ever dreamed of writing. It's my third book with a connection to Belichick and team-building. I would have thought that *you* were the comedy writer if you'd told me that in 2000.

After I wrote that column on Belichick, I got a call from a guy who'd become a fast friend two years earlier. He worked in the Jets public relations department and, when we met in 1998, it was as if we'd known each other for a decade. His name was Berj Najarian. Unbeknownst to me, Najarian had become one of Belichick's go-to guys in New York. He was about to be a go-to guy in New England, too. "You were unfair in that column," Najarian said that day. "I think you and Bill should talk."

Belichick and I met for dinner near old Foxboro Stadium and went on for hours about a number of topics. I was struck most by his robust curiosity. He asked good and specific questions, for example, about preparing for a newscast and the dynamics of reporters doing live shots. I learned that he was as much of a student as he was a teacher. What he wasn't, at the time, was a Hall of Fame coach.

His 2000 Patriots weren't very good, and toward the end of the disappointing year, I asked if I could watch film with him. He was a couple of weeks away from a career record of 41-55. The record belied what I saw in that session; he had astonishing knowledge and attention to detail. Afterward, I told him that one day I'd like to write a book about the NFL that he experiences on a daily basis, the bustling Monday through Saturday operation that is cloistered from the public in Foxboro.

The next year, his workplace changed and so did the world around him. He and his backup quarterback, Tom Brady, became stars and champions. Talk about a turnaround. In the first ninety-six games of his career, Belichick was fourteen games below the break-even point. In the ninety-six games that followed, his teams went 72-24. I've been blessed to have seen the entirety of the Belichick-Brady partnership, many times with unprecedented access. Consider this book the third in a trilogy that also includes 2004's *Patriot Reign* and 2011's *War Room*.

To truly give proper thanks for how all of this came to be, I'd have to pen a memoir on gratitude. So many people over the years have prayed for and with me, poured knowledge into me, and been patient with me despite my mistakes. There are dozens of family members, friends, pastors, mentors, sources, associates, and even critics who have helped shape me into a better journalist and man.

I'm so thankful to have a literary family that I trust and respect. I'm not sure how that happened; my publisher and editor, Mauro DiPreta and Doug Grad, are both Jets fans. Seriously, thanks to both of them for their passion, smarts, and hunger to make everything better. The entire team at Hachette, including David Lamb, Ashley Yancey, Kristin Vorce Duran, and Carolyn Kurek, made sure that this project aimed high and stayed on course. My agent, Basil Kane, has been the kindest, steadiest, and most protective literary presence in my life for a dozen years. In those dozen years, Kane, DiPreta, and I have forged a bond that goes beyond the business of books. They both have the ability to tell me, at times, what I don't want to hear, yet they're still exceedingly constructive. It's reassuring to work with people when you know that friendship is at the foundation of the relationship.

As you might expect, there are numerous "characters" over the past sixteen years who have contributed to this book. I've never envisioned the Patriots' success as Belichick and Brady at the top and a crowd of players below. Rather, the coach and quarterback are bookends on a shelf, with innumerable personalities tucked between them. It's been an educational journey over the years to interview and observe those varied characters, whether they have risen, fallen, rebelled, or evolved. I'm thankful for all the conversations, even if all of them have not been pleasant (or received pleasantly once in print). Special thanks to Belichick, Brady, Ty Law, Tedy Bruschi, Richard Seymour, Roman Phifer, Willie McGinest, Troy Brown, Rosevelt Colvin, Matt Chatham, Damien Woody, Christian Fauria, Chris Eitzmann, Alge Crumpler, Deion Branch, Scott Zolak, Gil Santos, Lionel Vital, Adrian Klemm, Louis Riddick, Heath Evans, Robert Kraft, Jonathan Kraft, Dan Kraft, Scott Pioli, Thomas Dimitroff, Bob Quinn, Josh McDaniels, Nick Caserio, Berj Najarian, Stacey James, Ty Warren, Vince Wilfork, Ben Watson, Rodney Harrison, Jason Licht, Kyle O'Brien, Jay Muraco, Mike Woicik, Jim Whalen, Mike Vrabel, Ted Johnson, Adam Vinatieri, Nancy Maier, Anthony Pleasant, Romeo Crennel, Charlie Weis, Otis Smith, Jim Nagy, Kevin Faulk, Bobby Hamilton, Lawyer Milloy, Drew Bledsoe, Ivan Fears, Dante Scarnecchia, Brad Seely, Eric Mangini, Rob Ryan, John Van de Brook, Logan Mankins, David Patten, Joe Andruzzi, Jeff Davidson, Dallas Pioli, and, obviously, dozens upon dozens of others.

It's a tribute to the Patriots that they have carefully guarded inside information. It's a tribute to the men and women who have covered them that, despite the resistance, there has been some exceptional work submitted by beat reporters and football columnists over the years. My research was greatly helped by their contributions: Karen Guregian, Michael Felger, Kevin Mannix, Ian Rapoport, Gerry Callahan, George Kimball, Jim Baker, Albert Breer, John Tomase, Jeff Howe, Tom E. Curran, Mike Giardi, Ed Duckworth, Jim Donaldson, Shalise Manza Young, Mike Lowe, Christopher Price, Mike Reiss, Field Yates, Mike Rodak, Nick Cafardo, Michael Smith, Ron Borges, Dan Shaughnessy, Jackie MacMullan, Bob Ryan, Bill Griffith, Chad Finn, Jerome Solomon, Greg A. Bedard, Ben Volin, Michael Whitmer, Julian Benbow, Adam Kilgore, Jim McBride, Dan Ventura, Rich Thompson, Ron Hobson, Lenny Megliola, Mark Farinella. Michael Connelly's book *The President's Team* was a great resource for information on Steve Belichick. As many WEEI radio listeners learned, I was obsessed with transcripts from the Wells Report and Brady's suspension appeal hearing in New York. The voluminous record there was extremely helpful, as was the testimony from the Aaron Hernandez trial. NFL Films, with its 2011 documentary on Belichick and its recordings of specific Patriots games, was also resourceful.

Sometimes it's easy to miss excellence from the everyday workplace. Since 2005, I've been fortunate to work at WEEI in Boston. Four books have been completed since I've been there, and that couldn't happen without supportive management and colleagues. First and foremost, I want to thank the best quarterback I've ever worked with, Dale Arnold. There are many others, too: Jerry Thornton, Ben Kichen, Andy Massaua, Glenn Ordway, Lou Merloni, Joe Zarbano, Mike Adams, Mike Mutnansky, Kirk Minihane, John Dennis, Gerry Callahan, Phil Zachary, Kevin

Graham, Jason Wolfe, Julie Kahn, Weezie Kramer, and David Field. The archives at the station were full of nuggets from exclusive Belichick and Brady interviews in the past sixteen years, and transcripts from those are reflected here. Thanks, in particular, to Kichen, Massaua, and Zarbano for helping track down the sound.

There is no way I would have made it through this project without prayer. I thank God for His anointed ones, in Boston and across the country: Ray Hammond, Gloria White-Hammond, Robert Gray, Brandon Thomas Crowley, Alicia Johnson, John Borders, Howard-John Wesley, Lance Watson, Tony Evans, Jeremiah Wright, Otis Moss III, Wyatt Jackson, and many others who unknowingly helped guide my faith walk.

Finally, I'm overwhelmed by the unending love and patience shown by my wife, Oni, and our three children. I thought Basil Kane was joking a few years ago when he quipped, "With three kids, you'll just have to learn to write with the kids bouncing on your lap and draped around your neck." Well, that actually happened a few times. Most of the time, though, everyone understood that a closed office door meant that Daddy was unavailable. They gave me some great and necessary moments of levity, though, with my five-year-old son, Beckham, once asking, "What are you writing, the Bible? Are you done yet?"

Beckham is a voracious reader in his own right, and when the book was finished, he had a question about the next one. "Can it be a children's book?" Sixteen years ago, I would have said no way. Now, well, I won't rule out anything.

INDEX

#27.— 9/22/16

WITHDRAWN